*Revolution and Tradition
in Tientsin, 1949-1952*

KENNETH G. LIEBERTHAL

Revolution and Tradition
in Tientsin, 1949-1952

STANFORD UNIVERSITY PRESS
STANFORD, CALIFORNIA
1980

Stanford University Press
Stanford, California

© *1980 by the Board of Trustees of the*
Leland Stanford Junior University

Printed in the United States of America
ISBN 0-8047-1044-9
LC 79-64215

\ ۰

To my sons, KEITH *and* JEFF

Acknowledgments

I benefited from the assistance of many individuals and institutions in preparing this volume. A. Doak Barnett, Zbigniew Brzezinski, Andrew Nathan, Michel Oksenberg, Ezra Vogel, and C. Martin Wilbur commented on the manuscript either in its original dissertation form or in subsequent revisions. Essential research and writing support came from the Joint Committee on Contemporary China of the American Council of Learned Societies and the Social Science Research Council, the Ford Foundation (via its Foreign Area Fellowship Program), Swarthmore College, and Harvard's East Asian Research Center (now called the John King Fairbank Center for East Asian Research). The Universities Service Centre in Hong Kong; the China Association in London; the Hoover Institution; the East Asian Research Center at Harvard; and the East Asian Institute at Columbia University hosted me during various phases of my work and put their extensive facilities at my disposal. Yeung Sai-cheung provided outstanding research assistance, and Heath B. Chamberlain generously shared his data on Tientsin's personnel changes. I am enormously grateful for the advice, encouragement, and support I received from all these sources.

I unfortunately cannot thank by name another group whose contribution proved fundamental to making this project possible—the almost three-score former residents of Tientsin who shared their wisdom about the city with me. The case study in Chapter 7 of a particular chemical firm during the Five Anti campaign makes explicit the value of this interviewing. In a more subtle but no less significant way, the perspectives voiced by people who lived in Tientsin shaped the questions I asked of the documentary sources in all the other chapters in this volume.

I also want to thank the *China Quarterly* for permission to use some material that I originally published in an article entitled "The Post-Liberation Suppression of Secret Societies in Tientsin" (*China Quarterly*, 54: 242–66; April–June 1973).

Finally, Jane Lieberthal has earned far more than the usual encomium due a patient and understanding wife. She conducted a portion of the original research for this volume in Chinese and French sources, typed one of the early drafts of the manuscript, made numerous valuable editorial and substantive suggestions, and provided the encouragement that made me complete the effort of turning a Ph.D. dissertation into a book. This volume, in short, would not have appeared without the help she gave at every stage. The fact that even Jane would have written a very different book from this, however, highlights the importance of explicitly absolving everyone named above from any responsibility for the deficiencies that remain in final text.

K.G.L.

Contents

Abbreviations

ACPRC	All Circles People's Representatives Conference
AIC	Austerity Investigation Committee
CCC	Tientsin Construction Workers' Cooperative Construction Company
CCP	Chinese Communist Party
CPG	Chinese People's Government
FIC	Federation of Industry and Commerce
GAC	Government Administrative Council
IKT	I Kuan Tao society
KMT	Kuomintang
LCCC	Labor-Capital Consultative Conference
MCC	Tientsin Military Affairs Control Commission
MPG	Tientsin Municipal People's Government
PLA	People's Liberation Army
PRC	People's Republic of China

Revolution and Tradition
in Tientsin, 1949-1952

CHAPTER 1 *Introduction*

The major cleavage in the People's Republic of China (PRC) remains the enormous gulf between the country's 150,000,000 urban dwellers and its 800,000,000 peasants. The cities, and especially the major metropolises, are the advanced wedge recently directed to drive the country toward modernization over the coming decades. But even the cities pulse with the tensions generated by the continuing attempts of revolutionary forces—both political and economic—to erode the strength of deeply rooted traditional attitudes and methods. These are tensions, moreover, that are affected by the economic structure of each city and its particular history over the past century, as well as by the actions and policies of the Communist leaders. The organizational capabilities of the Communists have remained decidedly finite (propaganda during the height of political mobilization campaigns notwithstanding). One of the most vexing problems for the Chinese Communist leaders has been to decide how much they should rely on traditional socioeconomic units and practices to accomplish tasks that would swamp the political organizations if the state tried to take them over. For these and other reasons, traditional perspectives have not vanished since 1949, and for many years to come urban China will strike a complex and shifting balance between modern and traditional elements. This volume's analysis of Tientsin during 1949–52 examines China's second-largest city during a period when the problem of defining the relationship of revolution to tradition was particularly acute, and thus it affords an opportunity to understand the underlying dynamics of a process that is still at work, although perhaps more subtly, today.

The central concern of this volume is to understand the interaction of economic development, organizational control, and mass mobilization in shaping the political consciousness of China's city dwellers. To examine this issue, the book traces the Chinese Communist Party's (CCP) use of ideologically inspired mass mobilization and of organizational development and control in Tientsin during 1949–52. It does so in terms of three key elements: the political and economic ramifications of China's refined and intricate system of personal relations (*kuan-hsi*); the very different characteristics of workers in the modern and traditional sectors of Tientsin's economy; and the inherent trade-offs that accompany a strategy of organizing "from the top down" (that is, where an organizational structure is imposed from above rather than emerging as a result of the actions of its constituents). Because the materials available for this period are particularly rich and include the accounts of many direct participants as well as a relatively informative set of pre- and post-1949 documentary sources, they permit a more intimate glimpse of the processes of change in urban China than is possible for later years.

Tientsin's Place in the Chinese Revolution

By 1949 all Chinese Communist Party (CCP) leaders had accepted the proposition that while only a peasant revolution could bring the Party to power, only an urban industrial revolution could lay the basis for an independent socialist society. With the capture of Tientsin on January 15, 1949, therefore, the Communists shifted the focus of the revolution from the countryside to the city.

The first of the former treaty ports to come under Communist control, Tientsin was well suited to introduce the CCP to the cities. This North China metropolis embodied nearly all the diverse elements that had shaped the country's urban development over the previous century. First, Tientsin was an old city that had served as a southern gateway to the capital (Peking) ever since Ming times and had thrived even before then. It had an ancient and deeply rooted urban social structure that distinguished it from a city like Shanghai, which had grown almost from scratch as a treaty port during the nineteenth century. At the same time, because of its proximity to the national capital, Tientsin's role as a political center had not been commensurate with its military and commercial importance. The city's age and its long association with the capital gave it a decidedly conservative political cast that did not change during more than three decades of warlord, Kuomintang (KMT), and Japanese rule between the collapse of the Ch'ing Dynasty in 1911 and the arrival of the Communist revolution in 1949.

Second, Tientsin in 1949 was a bifurcated society. The city had become a treaty port as a result of the Anglo-French war with China in 1858–60. Under Western impetus, it gradually developed a modern economic structure that centered in the concession areas of the great powers—England, France, Japan, and Russia. Situated at the northern terminus of the grand canal, Tientsin had for centuries been a major artery for the shipment of foods from central China to Peking and other northern points. As a treaty port, it also became the major entrepôt for trade between foreign countries and all of North and Northwest China. A modern banking system developed, along with relatively modern factories that produced textiles and other products. Chambers of Commerce emerged both in the Chinese-administered portions of the city and within the various foreign concessions. Still, this modern economic structure did not displace the older society and economy on which it had been built. Rather, the two dimensions of Tientsin existed side by side, partially complementing and partially oblivious of each other. These two different economic systems shaped the city's social and political contours in such a way that the Chinese Communists were faced with two quite distinct societies when they sought to establish their control over and weave anew the fabric of the city. When the CCP fully realized the implications of this bifurcation of Tientsin's society, it radically altered its strategy for consolidating its position in the city and carrying out the urban revolution.

Third, as a port city that had experienced rapid growth during

the twentieth century, Tientsin had developed within its boundaries two types of organization that wielded important influence
over significant segments of the city's adult population. These
were the urban secret societies, which drew their membership
mainly from among people engaged in transport work, and the
various fatalistic quasi-religious societies, which recruited their
followers primarily from among the people involved in the more
traditional segment of Tientsin's economy. Together, these two
types of social organization encompassed some 40 percent of Tientsin's adult population. Both were relatively rational responses to the conditions of urban life in China during the first
half of the twentieth century, but both were incompatible with
the revolutionary transformation of Tientsin's society under the
Chinese Communists.

Finally, Tientsin had fully experienced China's humiliation at
the hands of foreign powers during the last century. The city
was sacked by the British and French in 1860 and again by the
international expedition sent in to suppress the Boxer Rebellion
in 1900. Tientsin students rallied to the May Fourth Movement
directed against both Japan and the Western betrayal of Chinese
interests at the conclusion of World War I. The Japanese nevertheless steadily increased their influence over Tientsin during
the ensuing years, until in 1935 they forced the Nationalists to
accept an agreement that prohibited the stationing of Nationalist
forces in the Peking-Tientsin region. Again, Tientsin's students
joined in rebellion, this time in a protest dubbed the December
Ninth Movement. While this movement may have increased
political pressure on Chiang Kai-shek to turn his attention from
suppressing the Communists to expelling the Japanese, it did
not prevent Japan from launching a full-scale attack on China
south of the Great Wall in 1937—an attack that left Tientsin in
Japan's grip from 1937 to 1945.

Although these experiences, combined with the presence of
foreign concession areas, made nationalism a strong sentiment
among Tientsin's population, nationalism and radical social reform were very different issues in pre-1949 China. The Chinese
Communists wove these issues together and argued that China

could protect its national identity only through radical social revolution combined with rapid industrial development. The citizens of Tientsin, however, had lived near the center of conservative political power all of their lives. Most were politically apathetic, even though they harbored anti-foreign sentiments and were susceptible to nationalist appeals. The Communists could bolster their support in Tientsin through their strong identification with Chinese nationalism, but they had to work hard to mold a constituency for the social reform they envisaged. Even with regard to the issue of nationalism, moreover, the CCP found that many of Tientsin's citizens, being situated in North China near Manchuria, resented both the Japanese and the Soviets while having a somewhat less jaundiced view of the United States. And the PRC's close alliance with the USSR during the 1950's weakened the Communists' nationalistic appeal to the city's populace, and especially to its intellectuals.

Thus, Tientsin presented the Chinese Communists with all the problems of China's recent urban development. The Communists also had to sculpt their policy within the city with one eye constantly fixed on the needs of the revolution beyond the confines of this municipality. Tientsin came under Communist control at the beginning of the year that saw the People's Liberation Army sweep across the Mainland and drive the Kuomintang to Taiwan. For most of this year, Tientsin was called upon to support the rapidly escalating Communist effort elsewhere, and the city had to contribute funds, goods and cadres to this larger crusade. It also had to set an example of urban rule that would decrease resistance to a Communist takeover in the great cities of Central and South China during the spring and fall. In 1950 the CCP completed its sweep across the Chinese mainland, but during the latter part of the year the Korean War imposed new demands on this North China industrial and commercial center. In these and other ways, the revolution in Tientsin had a complex symbiotic relationship with the larger national revolution.

The Communists were not interested in simply imposing control over the city. They were determined to carry out a revolu-

tionary transformation of Tientsin, and their previous experience in the countryside had fully convinced them of the need to
sink roots deep into the social structure in order to transform
that structure from its very foundations. The demands of the
movement on a national level did not dictate that the CCP sacrifice revolution in Tientsin for the sake of control and exploitation of local resources, but required rather that the Party devise
means to make these different demands compatible with each
other. A major part of the following chapters analyzes how the
CCP in Tientsin accomplished this extraordinarily difficult task.

The Revolution in Tientsin

In examining the CCP's first four years in Tientsin, this book
focuses on the measures taken by the revolutionary leaders to
penetrate, gain leverage over, and transform the major socioeconomic units of Tientsin. Revolution is a process, not an
event. When the Communits captured Tientsin, they took control of a governmental apparatus that itself had barely penetrated the society it ruled. During the next three years, the CCP
made a gradual effort to accumulate both the knowledge and
the organizational and physical resources that would be necessary to effect a fundamental transformation of Tientsin's society. This process required a highly selective and differentiated
strategy, one that fully respected the CCP's shortage of loyal
and skilled cadres, that gave sufficient priority to economic
reconstruction, and that recognized the division of Tientsin's
economy into modern and traditional sectors, with the attendant substantial differences in social and political perspectives
among the populace.

Naturally, this range of constraints and demands forced the
Communists to make difficult choices between seemingly irre-
concilable alternatives. How, for example, could the Party convince capitalists to reinvest their money in Tientsin while ap-
pealing to the workers to join the proletarian revolution? How
could the new leaders attack the secret societies in 1949–50 and
the quasi-religious societies in 1951 without frightening other

key groups into at least passive opposition? Such problems forced the CCP to make numerous adjustments to three dimensions of its strategy: the range of its targets at any given time; the speed with which it tried to effect major changes; and the intensity, or depth, of the transformation it carried out in the various segments of the city's society.

When the CCP entered Tientsin, the new leaders tried a strategy that proved to be too ambitious in all three of these dimensions. The Party, in brief, had started a revolution that it could not control and from which it would not benefit. Consequently, Peking intervened in April–May 1949 and dispatched Liu Shao-ch'i to investigate the situation and devise an appropriate set of strategies.

Liu worked out a more refined policy that greatly reduced the scope of the CCP's efforts and provided for a more moderate pacing of the Party's engagement of Tientsin society. His goal remained that of fundamental revolutionary change in the city, but it was change that *would at all times be guided by, and serve the interests of, the Chinese Communist Party.*

Liu's strategy altered the balance between the forces of spontaneity and those of organization in the CCP's approach to the revolutionary transformation of China's cities. It required major changes in the Communists' political apparatus, for Liu believed that only a more centralized and disciplined political organization could carry out the relatively patient and complex revolution that he advocated. Liu's strategy worked extremely well in Tientsin, and reconciled to a remarkable degree the demands for stability and production with the goals of socioeconomic revolution. However, it also contained elements that would themselves become highly controversial as the Communist revolution neared the end of its first decade in power. This controversy has persisted and formed one of the central topics of political debate in China during the last decade and more. The conclusion to this volume, therefore, places the story of the early years in Tientsin within the context of the PRC's subsequent history.

Liu Shao-ch'i's strategy of rather carefully controlled revolution "from the top down" required that the Communists in Tientsin *demobilize* many sectors of the population that had been stimulated to make political demands during the harsh winter of 1948–49. The new strategy quite literally brought the revolution to different sectors of the population at different times. And because *kuan-hsi* defined people's level of social awareness, those not in a targeted sector of the populace remained remarkably ignorant of the CCP's policies. Thus, to understand the contours of the revolution as it unfolded in Tientsin after Liu Shao-ch'i's visit, it is necessary to delineate the growth of Communist-sponsored organizations (such as the trade unions) and the precise dimensions of their involvement in Communist-sponsored campaigns and programs. This analysis reveals that only with the Three Anti and Five Anti campaigns in early 1952 did the Chinese Communists in Tientsin establish themselves as a truly revolutionary force for the majority of the city's population. With these campaigns, the CCP in Tientsin completed a giant step forward in the transition from military conquest to socioeconomic revolution.

Although political campaigns were the most dramatic moments in the Communists' attempt to penetrate and transform Tientsin's society, they were invariably built on a carefully laid infrastructure that had been prepared before. Most political campaigns amount, in fact, to an *intensification of processes already under way* that break through previous barriers, change some of the rules of the game, and permit a new system to be established on a "higher" stage than the previous one. Far more research on Chinese politics must be done to place the campaigns of subsequent years more clearly in their political and organizational contexts.

This study also shows how the Chinese media tended to make campaigns seem both more abrupt in their inception and more widespread in their impact than was actually the case. Most political campaigns focused on relatively specific targets and left large sectors of the population virtually untouched. Indeed, to the degree that a campaign actually included the governing bureaucracy among its targets and therefore disrupted the ability of the political authorities to function effectively, it temporarily *decreased* the exposure of certain segments of the populace to new and different ideas. In this sense, as analyzed in the Conclusion, even some of the most dramatic political campaigns—such as the Cultural Revolution—have been experienced by many people as a time of lessened government interference in their lives. These observations, and the story of the revolution in Tientsin presented in the following chapters, argue for a more carefully differentiated sector-by-sector approach to studying political change in Chinese society over the past 30 years.

CHAPTER 2

The Old Order

The January 1949 capture of Tientsin, followed shortly by the fall of Peking and the other major cities of North and East China, immediately thrust China's major metropolises into center stage in both the short- and the long-term development of the Chinese revolution. Party Chairman Mao Tse-tung stressed this fundamental change in his March 5, 1949, speech to a gathering of the approximately 50 highest-ranking members of the Chinese Communist Party:

From 1927 to the present the center of gravity of our work has been in the villages, using the villages in order to surround the cities and then taking the cities. The period for this method of work has now ended. The period of "from the city to the village" and of the city leading the village has now begun. The center of gravity of the Party's work has shifted from the village to the city. . . . We must do our utmost to learn how to administer and build the cities. In the cities we must learn how to wage political, economic and cultural struggles against the imperialists, the Kuomintang and the bourgeoisie. . . . If we do not pay attention to these problems, if we do not learn how to wage these struggles against them and win victories in the struggles, we shall be unable to maintain our political power, we shall be unable to stand on our feet, we shall fail.[1]

Mao correctly stressed the need to *learn* in this speech, since many of the lessons of political organization and action so painfully acquired in two decades in China's hinterland would prove ineffective and even counterproductive in the radically different milieu of the major cities. China's treaty ports had developed as the beachheads of imperialist penetration of China, sometimes on the basis of a preexisting Chinese city, as in Tientsin, and sometimes on the basis of an area that had previously supported little human habitation, as in Shanghai.[2] Physically, most treaty ports were collages of European and Oriental architecture hung on the Chinese landscape, a result of various foreign powers having gained sole control over their own "concession areas" within the boundaries of each metropolis. Thus, England, France, Germany, Italy, Belgium, Austria-Hungary, Russia, the United States, and Japan had each at one time held "concessional" territory in Tientsin, and all but the United States had developed their sections using their own national architecture.[3] The "old" Chinese city with its narrow alleys and low huts also remained, a reminder of the foundation on which the pink stadium of the Italian sector and the monumental bank buildings of the British area had been erected.

For the Communists in 1949, however, the division of the city into concession areas as symbolized by its architectural diversity no longer posed a serious problem. The German, Italian, Austro-Hungarian, and Russian governments had lost control over their concessions in Tientsin at the conclusion of World War I, and World War II in turn had spelled the doom of the remaining British, French, Belgian, and Japanese concessions in the city (the Americans had sold their concession area to the British in the late nineteenth century).[4] In Tientsin, rather, the obstacles standing between the Chinese Communists and achievement of their revolutionary goals were rooted far deeper than the mere presence of a range of foreign powers and went to the very heart of the socioeconomic physiology of the city.

There were both physical and psychological aspects to these problems. Physically, aside from its division into separate concessional territories, Tientsin was distinctly divided into modern and traditional enterprises, with the size of a firm frequently reflecting its degree of modernity. The larger, newer enterprises employed hundreds of workers, utilized machine production, often took advantage of the developing modern banking system, and played a central role in the trade between foreign countries and all of North China. The smaller firms typically employed less than a dozen workers, utilized only the crudest type of machinery, rarely relied on the banking system for credit or capital, and played at best an ancillary role (by doing "putting-out" work for the larger firms) in China's interregional and overseas trade. Although these two segments of the economy did interact to the benefit of both, Tientsin had an essentially bifurcated economy in which each half was characterized by fundamentally different financial, commercial, production and social relationships.

This economic cleavage largely structured psychological boundaries in Tientsin. Employers and employees in the modern sector had radically different life experiences from their counterparts in the traditional firms, and these experiences shaped their perceptions in politically significant ways. In addition to these two groups, a third must also be distinguished in the economy of the port city of Tientsin—the dock workers and freight haulers who made up the city's vital transportation sector.

The Traditional Sector

Far more than half of Tientsin's workers found employment in the tens of thousands of minuscule handicraft and commercial firms that made up the traditional sector of the city's economy.[5] In 1949, for instance, the city contained some 25,000 commercial shops with an average of six employees per firm.[6] Such large numbers alone rendered the administrative task confronting any government that sought to penetrate these tiny units forbidding. The *parochialism* of the people in this segment of Tientsin's economy, however, proved to be an even greater obstacle to the effective expansion of revolutionary power into the traditional sector of the city's economy.

From the early 1920's through the 1940's, peasant migration provided the major source of workers for all sizes of enterprises in Tientsin.[7] But there is some evidence, based on surveys of Tientsin's large-scale cotton mills and smaller firms in the carpet and hosiery industries of the late 1920's and early 1930's, that the modern sector of the economy quickly began drawing its workers from the increasing pool of second-generation city dwellers, while most first-generation workers concentrated more in smaller enterprises and shops.[8]

Workers who entered Tientsin as adults carried their rural values into the city with them.[9] These values frequently included deference to the owners of wealth and property, trust in those from the same village or *hsiang* (administrative grouping of several villages), suspicion of "outsiders," and faith in the efficacy of personal relations rather than formal contractual obligations.[10] The work environment of the new city dweller, however, exercised a major influence on his attitudes during subsequent years.

A great many peasants who found work in the traditional sector of the economy had entered the city in the first place with the assistance of a fellow villager who had contacts in the city. Once in Tientsin, the peasant relied on personal connections, most likely another friend from his village or a relative, to land a job. Almost all of the enterprises in Tientsin's traditional sector required personal introductions before they hired new employees. The importance of personal introductions made the traditional *t'ung-hsiang* (same locale) ties particularly important and in all probability reinforced these ties in the urban milieu.[11] They also provide dramatic evidence of the traditional sector's continuing faith in personal relationships as the only reliable basis for mutual trust.

Both wealthy and poor peasants came into the city. The more well-to-do migrant, usually the son of a rich peasant or landlord, brought some capital into town and set up a very small commercial or handicrafts establishment. His poorer counterpart typically arrived in the city penniless and sought only to remove himself as a financial burden on his family, especially during the slack seasons in agriculture. His employer in a small firm in the city, therefore, might well be the same type of person to whom he had deferred in his village.

Life in the typical small firm in Tientsin was not pleasant. Extremely long hours (in some trades averaging 15–16 hours per day), lack of sanitary facilities, poor ventilation, inadequate heating, and high disease rates pressed down on the workers. Their one day off each month had to be spent at the barber and attending to other necessities. To make matters worse, they usually ate and slept in the room where they labored, a discomfort often shared by the owner and his family. In these close quarters, tensions ran high, especially since the peasant immigrant had previously been accustomed to seasonal labor under the open sky. Politically and socially, nevertheless, the small firm formed a cocoon that shielded the peasant almost completely from contact with other city people. Moreover, the system of personal introductions typically ensured that even the majority of his co-workers came from the immigrant's own village or *hsiang*. Through these means, basic peasant values persisted among those working in the small firms in the traditional sector of Tientsin's economy.[12]

One example of such persistence was the great popularity of millenarian quasi-religious societies that reflected many immigrants' fatalistic response to their urban milieu. These societies in Tientsin drew their membership overwhelmingly from newly immigrated women and from workers in the traditional sector. They often assumed exotic names, such as the Way of Basic Unity (I Kuan Tao), the Dragon China Association (Lung Hua Hui), the Way of Former Heaven (Hsien-t'ien Tao), and the Nine Senses Sect (Chiu Kuan Tao). The I Kuan Tao was the most prominent of these societies, and as late as 1951 counted one out of every five adults among its members.[13]

The IKT promised future redemption for the suffering and good deeds of one's present life. Not surprisingly, therefore, the society experienced rapid growth during times of special hardship in Tientsin, as when the Japanese imposed a harsh occupation regime on the city during World War II. In such times of stress, the society claimed that its rituals permitted the faithful to reach the end of their difficulties and misfortunes, surmount the consequences of natural calamities, perfect themselves, and achieve salvation in a future life. That the society combined the traditional morality of Confucianism with Taoist rituals and Buddhist sutras probably enhanced its appeal to untutored peasant immigrants.[14]

The IKT offered the additional lure of magic. Instead of prayer and meditation, its rituals emphasized prostrations, incense burning, revelations through mediums, and other spiritual practices.[15] These, it was claimed, could cure illnesses, make a barren woman fertile, and work other such miracles. In return for performing these services, the IKT clerical hierarchy, organized around "altars" in various parts of the city, solicited numerous contributions from the believers.

Communist organizers in the rural areas during the 1920's had found that the greatest obstacle to mobilizing the peasants was their "millenial attitudes that rationalized their passive acceptance of a miserable life,"* thus rendering ineffective any political propaganda aimed at organizing them to change the system. These same attitudes, expressed in the popularity of the quasi-religious societies, remained strong among the new immigrant women and workers in the traditional sector.

The hiring practice of insisting on a personal introduction illustrates another fundamental facet of life in urban Tientsin—that the importance of *kuan-hsi* was undiminished as one moved from the countryside into the city. To the Chinese, a clearly structured system of rights and obligations based on personal relationships provided a far more solid basis for trust than any piece of paper or legal obligation. The most important personal relationships for city life were those based on common place of origin, school, teacher, or year of passing the official examination (these were abolished in 1905), or a blood relationship. Other ties, such as sharing the same surname or having worked in the same office, could also confer rights and obligations in certain circumstances. Indeed, an enterprising person could follow a conscious strategy of developing *kuan-hsi* with people important for his career through, for instance, a well-chosen marriage, proper entertaining, correct schooling, and so forth.[16] As discussed later, through *kuan-hsi* one could evade taxes, receive

---

*P'eng P'ai, the great organizer of peasants in the 1920's, found this to be a very common response among China's poor peasants. See Richard Solomon, "On Activism and Activists: Marxist Conceptions of Motivation and Political Role Linking State to Society," *China Quarterly,* 39: 84–85 (July–Sept. 1969).

special favors from the government or colleagues, and in a wide range of ways improve one's fortunes.

A poor peasant immigrant into Tientsin confronted the overwhelming fact that he lacked *kuan-hsi* with people of power and influence and furthermore that he did not have the means at his disposal to develop these relations. His social net extended from his native village almost directly into a very limited number of workshops and stores in the traditional sector of the economy, and it was only these that could provide him with some protection and sustenance in a bewildering urban environment. He might also turn in desperation to his *t'ung-hsiang hui* (a club of people from the same native place) for assistance, but even this would most likely at best produce a loan and an introduction to a job in the traditional sector of the economy.

The system of *kuan-hsi* ensured that even in the city people retained a clear distinction between "outsiders" and an "in" group. This distinction prevented effective cooperation among, for instance, workers in different handicraft workshops who shared similar needs but were enmeshed in different nets of *kuan-hsi*. It also created a filter that removed most of the potential forcefulness from political promises and programs offered by those who ruled the city. The prudent strategy for a peasant who had a very limited circle of "connections" was to avoid all involvement with "outsiders" in the city and take care not to destroy the *kuan-hsi* that provided him with his only haven. His *kuan-hsi* determined and defined an individual's social identity, the circle of people to whom he had obligations and who, in turn, were indebted to him.

The Modern Sector

As of 1949, approximately 40,500 workers in Tientsin's industrial sector labored in factories that averaged 375 workers per firm (in contrast to 80,000 industrial workers in handicrafts shops averaging seven employees apiece).[17] In the commercial sector, only a minuscule percentage of the 150,000 employees worked in firms of over 50 employees.[18] All of these workers in the larger modern firms had to contend with an environment that battered their inclinations to rely on *kuan-hsi.*

Many of these workers found their jobs though the system of personal introductions mentioned above. Indeed, the first Tientsin employment bureau was established only in 1946 and enjoyed very limited success because it had great difficulty locating employers who would accept people without personal introductions.[19] Some workers, however, experienced a considerably less personal ritual in finding employment. The Yu Yuan cotton mill, for instance, hired its casual coolie labor on a day-to-day basis by dispatching one of its staff members to the front gate with a batch of numbered sticks to throw out to the waiting crowd. Whoever caught a stick had a job for the day.[20]

Regardless of how they found their work, the people employed in the larger enterprises lived very different lives from their brethren in the handicraft shops and small stores. They enjoyed almost no job security, they frequently labored in workshops where they knew nobody else, and almost all, of course, were subjected to the discipline of machine production.

Coming constantly into contact with people with whom they shared no *kuan-hsi,* these workers had to survive in an environment where the "rules of the game" as they had learned them in the village did not apply. They had to become tolerant of people who spoke with peculiar accents. They were exposed to new and strange ideas simply through their range of daily contacts with co-workers. For them, the closed and structured environment of the village had given way to the more open, impersonal, and fluid dynamics of the large factory. This, in turn, changed many of their perspectives, as shown, for instance, by the incidence of thievery within the firms. One contemporary Chinese analyst observed in Tientsin that "traditionally, the Chinese laborer who works for an employer for the time being regards himself as a member of the household. Just as Chinese servants are known as very rarely stealing from their employers, so also in the small shops apprentices and laborers are too much still under the influence of the traditional attitude as to place their selfish interest in opposition to that of their master in such a flagrant way. In large factories, however, one hears constant complaints about the thievery of the workers."[21]

It is somewhat surprising, given the influences at work on the employees of large firms in the modern sector, that Tientsin never developed a history of substantial labor unrest. Indeed, even during the relatively freewheeling days between 1918 and 1926, Tientsin lagged behind Shanghai, Canton, Wusih, Hsüchou, Peking, Fengtien, and Swatow in the number of strikes recorded by the municipal government.[22] For instance, while Shanghai cotton mills reported 181 strikes from 1925 to 1929, Tientsin could boast only six.[23] There is a range of possible explanations for this relative absence of worker militancy in Tientsin—the city's proximity to Peking with its concentration of troops, the almost constant labor surplus that made it easy to recruit strikebreakers, the relatively large number of women and children employed in the textile mills,[24] and (as a number of former residents of the city have commented) the greater docility of the North China worker, who considered himself more cultured than his counterpart farther south.

As of 1949, then, the workers in Tientsin's modern sector could not look back on a tradition of battles fought and won. But they were also no longer cut of the same cloth as those employed in the traditional sector. Their work experiences had begun to expand their horizons beyond their own networks of *kuan-hsi* and thus made them potentially more receptive to political spokesmen with whom they shared no personal ties. The fact, moreover, that these workers were concentrated in approximately 150 enterprises would greatly simplify the purely administrative problems of penetrating their places of work.

Not all of Tientsin's modern firms were privately or corporately owned. After World War II, many were the stepchildren of the KMT political apparatus, having been nationalized by government fiat and sustained by public funds and favorable marketing arrangements created by the system of government licensing (for instance, for exports and imports).[25] A number of the larger firms, however, were run by capitalists who would

continue to play a pivotal economic role during the years immediately following the Communist victory in Tientsin.

Many of Tientsin's capitalists certainly appear more modern
than the workers and owners in the traditional sector of the
economy. They engaged in large-scale business endeavors that
often involved supply and marketing arrangements stretching
across North China and the Pacific Ocean. They sponsored
some civic activities, especially charitable works of various
kinds. They had contact to varying degrees with the municipal
government bureaucracy and cultivated political relationships.
And most of them had on their staffs some people who had
received a Western education and could speak a foreign language, even if the entrepreneurs themselves could not do so.[26]

The capitalists of medium and large firms also organized themselves into trade associations and a municipal Chinese Chamber
of Commerce.* Many of the trade associations established ap-
prenticeship rules for the trade concerned, set standards of
weight and quality where appropriate,[27] settled disputes between members of the association,[28] and represented the interests of their members to the Chamber of Commerce and,
through it, to the municipal government. On the surface, the
capitalists in Tientsin's modern sector recognized their real common interests and to promote them, organized along lines having little to do with *kuan-hsi*.

Interviews reveal, however, that these appearances are highly
misleading. The capitalists continued to adhere to the system of
kuan-hsi almost as faithfully as the workers in the traditional sector of the economy. This is not surprising, since the capitalists,
especially, had the resources to make this system work very
much to their benefit. Thus, for instance, many businessmen
did not write contracts even for large-scale transactions, but relied on doing business only through those to whom they were
personally connected. They utilized verbal agreements (con-

*There were also British, American, Russian, and French Chambers of Com-
merce in Tientsin in the late 1940's. The minutes of the meetings of the British
Chamber of Commerce for 1946–52 are available in the archives of the China Association in London.

veyed by the Chinese term *i yen wei ting*—literally, settled by one word) instead of written contracts because the latter inevitably contained loopholes and opportunities for cheating. The only *reliable* way of accomplishing something was to base the transaction on *kuan-hsi*. This extended even to the financial arena, where as late as 1950 less than 10 percent of Tientsin's firms had ever had any type of relationship with a banking institution.[29] The capitalists preferred to rely on fellow natives from their own province or on others with whom they shared a personal connection in order to secure the capital they required.

Even the trade associations and the Chamber of Commerce worked very differently from what outward appearances might suggest. These organizations had grown out of the earlier craft guilds[30] and originally did serve the needs of their membership, especially in seeking tax abatement from the government. However, as the KMT became more firmly established in Tientsin (especially after World War II), these organizations became the handmaidens of the government rather than its adversaries. Indeed, a system developed wherein the municipal government simply gave the Chamber of Commerce a tax figure and the Chamber then divided this responsibility among the trade associations, which in turn distributed it among their member firms.[31] By the postwar years, the government itself largely determined who would lead each trade association, and the person it selected could be counted on to remain compliant. Real tax relief for a firm depended on its owner or manager establishing some direct *kuan-hsi* with an appropriate government official and using that personal connection for the benefit of the firm. Since many large firms did in fact employ people with such connections, the tax burden tended to fall disproportionately on the smaller firms in the modern sector.[32]

Corruption in business practices provides another indicator of the continuing importance of the concept of *kuan-hsi* among the capitalists. Both interviews and press reports confirm that practices such as adulterating goods, short-weighting, kickbacks, and misrepresentation, to say nothing of keeping two sets of account books for tax purposes, were almost universal among the modern Chinese firms. These practices found acceptance because the system of *kuan-hsi* imposed a moral obligation to treat fairly and have concern for *only* those with whom one had some personal connection. One simply did not have such an obligation toward anyone else, and not to take appropriate measures to maximize profits was considered unfair to the network of people who in some way depended on one. Nepotism was one way in which the system of *kuan-hsi* clearly did serious harm to the functioning and profitability of modern enterprises, and the few hard facts available suggest that attitudes toward nepotism were accordingly mixed among the entrepreneurs.[33]

The administrative staff members of the modern firms would play a key role in subsequent Communist attempts to penetrate and restructure these organizations. These people are extremely difficult to characterize as a group, however, for some had attained their positions by merit and others by nepotism. A modern firm might well employ in ostensibly similar positions a person who had received a technical education abroad and a functionally illiterate distant relative of the owner or manager. Given the importance of "connections" for transacting business at all levels of Chinese society, moreover, it made good economic sense to place people on the payroll simply because their particular nets of social relations could prove important in protecting the firm from government taxation, in facilitating procurement of goods, or in making marketing arrangements. Thus, the administrative staffs of large enterprises often included peculiar mixtures of highly competent managers and technical specialists, almost totally incompetent hangers-on, and people of substantial social standing.[34]

In sum, the modern sector of Tientsin's economy harbored some 40,000–50,000 workers who had to varying degrees modified their traditional views of human relations as a result of their experiences in large-scale factory production. The owners and managers of these enterprises, however, like their counterparts in the small firms of the traditional sector, had retained a basic faith in the importance and propriety of *kuan-hsi* as a way of ordering all relationships. The staff members who occupied the positions between the factory floor and the front office hailed from almost comically diverse backgrounds and not surprisingly brimmed with internal tensions and cleavages.

The Transport Workers

Tientsin ranked second only to Shanghai as a commercial and industrial complex in China of the late 1940's. It functioned as the entrepôt for the sea trade between all foreign countries and Northwest, North, and Northeast China and as the juncture for North–South trade within the country. Its famous carpet industry utilized wool from as far away as Tibet, while its textile mills processed the cotton grown in Shantung and other nearby provinces. Commerce was the lifeblood of Tientsin, and the transport industry of the city formed the arteries through which that blood flowed. The ability of the nearly 30,000 Tientsin transport workers—the dock laborers and freight haulers—to constrict those arteries thus became a crucial fact of economic life for this great port city. Significantly, the people who worked in Tientsin's transport industry differed in social background from those who labored in the large and small enterprises, and were, moreover, organized into what many viewed as the most powerful associations in the city—the secret societies. They thus demand separate analysis from those who toiled indoors.

Transport of goods in Tientsin required crossing numerous unseen but important boundaries. These were the borders of the 227 "turfs" into which the city was divided, in each of which a particular coolie association monopolized all transport activities.[35] The coolie associations maintained these monopolies through threats and thuggery against businessmen, bribes and favors for the authorities, and guile accompanied by occasional savagery in thwarting the avarice of predatory neighboring coolie associations.[36]

The coolie associations themselves were grounded in the underlying secret society network. The associations' leaders were almost without exception secret-society heads of greater or lesser stature, and they typically hired only other members of the

same secret society—usually the Green Gang (Ch'ing-pang).*
Most secret-society leaders, moreover, preferred to hire coolies
who had joined the society under their personal tutelage, for
this established a "teacher-student" relationship that both parties valued as the closest form of secret-society bond. Most
coolie associations in Tientsin, therefore, were coterminous with
"teacher-student" groups in the secret societies.

Put differently, the coolie associations functioned as front organizations for secret-society leaders to control the Tientsin
transport industry. The associations provided a convenient organizational structure through which to manage transport.
Within the coolie associations themselves, the coolie bosses
handled the management aspects of the business and the workers performed the physical labor.[37] This organizational form in
turn undoubtedly permitted business to be carried on with
greater dispatch than the more amorphous and flexible secret-
society relationships would have allowed. The secret societies
(through the coolie associations) thus set the price structure in
transport, provided the necessary labor, and guaranteed the
safe shipment of goods.

Analysis of life in the lower depths of Tientsin society makes
the renowned tenacity of the secret societies' hold over their
members understandable. Typically, the potential dock or freight
worker in Tientsin came from a very poor urban background.†
For him, life in the city approached the Hobbesian world of a
war of all against all, since the municipal government's power
did not reach down far enough to protect people in his social
stratum. Living in this relatively anarchic environment, the po-

---

*A coolie association often had more than one boss, organized into a hierar-
chy with one person clearly recognized as exercising overall command. The
number of bosses per association in Tientsin varied from 45 at a maximum (for a
coolie association encompassing 275 workers) to one at a minimum (for an association of six workers). For an explanation of the hierarchy of coolie bosses, see
An Li-fu, *Tien-chin pan-yun kung-jen kung-tso pao-kao* (Tientsin, 1950), p. 3. Regarding membership in the Ch'ing-pang, see *PKKKTT*, pp. 6, 16; *JM*, 11.v.50, p.
2; and *CP*, 20.vi.50, p. 2, 24.vi.50, p. 2.

†Investigation of a random sample in 1949 showed that only about 20% of the
freight workers, 34% of the dock workers, and 19% of the railroad cargo workers had lived in the countryside before beginning work in the transport industry
in Tientsin. *PKKKTT*, p. 44.

tential secret-society member encountered violence as a way of life. On the margin of subsistence, with no recourse to police protection and unable to sustain missing more than a few days' work, he fully understood the aphorism that "might makes right." He had to establish *kuan-hsi* with the strongest power in his area in order to survive.

The secret society's value in this context lay in its ability to offer a potential member *security*. To gain this security, recruits might have to turn over as much as 80 percent of their earnings to the secret-society leaders. Ironically, some members occasionally had to risk their lives in rumbles with people from other turfs.[38] In exchange for these obvious disadvantages of secret-society membership, the recruit won job security on the docks or in freight hauling. He also became the holder of a crude form of insurance policy, since the society pledged to look after the family of a member injured or killed during a rumble with another turf. In family-centered China, where the inability to provide for one's offspring was one of the greatest curses of poverty, this peculiar type of insurance was considered an important benefit of secret-society membership.[39] Additionally, a *pang-hui* member in time of desperate need could legitimately turn to his brethren in the society for assistance; indeed, *pang-hui* itself means help association. To a degree, therefore, secret societies relieved a coolie of anxiety over the consequences of an accident or illness.

Secret-society membership also conveyed status, which in the lower reaches of China's urban society matched a person's ability to defend his interests.[40] Participating in a *pang* meant that a person had dependable allies against non-*pang* adversaries, thereby enhancing his status in his locale.

In sum, the *pang-hui* provided its rank and file with some of the *kuan-hsi* so important to Chinese urban society. Indeed, the structure and functioning of the Green Gang in many ways resembled, at least in theory, that of an extended family.[41] Because the Green Gang existed in almost all of China's major port cities, the poor secret-society member recently arrived in a city could quickly establish the connections that would permit him to find a job, housing, and a relatively safe haven in a hostile environment. The importance of these advantages to the geographically mobile coolie who lacked other ways of establishing webs of personal relationships can hardly be exaggerated.

Thus, the *pang-hui* provided their members in the transport industry not only with jobs, but also with some insurance, status, protection, and a sense of belonging. In most vital respects, then, the secret societies both defined and structured the world in which the transport coolie lived. Not surprisingly, a former Tientsin dock worker could describe the city's geography only in terms of the various turf boundaries when he was interviewed many years later in Hong Kong. The ability of the secret societies to provide security in an anarchic environment formed the linchpin of this system. Any political movement that sought to displace these organizations would have to take account of this central fact.

The people in the traditional, modern, and transport sectors of Tientsin's economy were not, of course, the only characters who would play a part in the drama that unfolded in the city after 1949. The intelligentsia, former members of the KMT, and the civil servants also merit brief attention.

Nearby Peking always overshadowed Tientsin in the cultural realm, but Tientsin nevertheless boasted some of the best middle schools and universities in the country at the time of the Communist takeover. Tientsin students had participated in the major anti-imperialist movements that erupted in Chinese society during the previous decades, from the May Fourth Movement of 1919, to the December Ninth Movement of 1935, through the anti-Japanese struggle of World War II. By 1949 the Communist underground had successfully wooed these students through patriotic appeals and had developed them into a major reservoir of support for the Party when it achieved power. Many of their professors, however, continued to mix their patriotism with western liberalism and found themselves less wholeheartedly committed to a Maoist solution for China.

Because of the vagaries of Tientsin's recent political history, Kuomintang leaders who ruled the city in 1945–48 posed almost no problem for the CCP when it entered Tientsin in early 1949. The KMT's forced exile to Southwest China during World War II had made its leaders distrust and resent those who remained behind in the Japanese-occupied areas. Consequently, the political elite of postwar Tientsin consisted mostly of outsiders— KMT political stalwarts who had joined the party in the south and become the carpetbaggers of China in the wake of the Japanese defeat in 1945. Most of these southerners fled Tientsin in the waning days of Nationalist rule in the city, and thus the Communists did not encounter an entrenched political elite when they entered the city.[42]

The majority of the city's civil servants did not flee with the departing KMT leaders, and during the initial takeover period they had to provide the skills and information necessary to make the city function. However, 40 years of almost continuous conservative rule in Tientsin, from the downfall of the Ch'ing Dynasty to the establishment of the People's Republic, had left its mark on these civil servants. It had given Tientsin a decidedly conservative political cast that distinguished it from Shanghai, Wuhan, Canton, and other cities that the Communists would conquer. Thus, within the civil service as elsewhere, the CCP would have to contend with the legacy of a modern political history in which no proponents of a radical political program had been able to hold a position of power or influence in the city.

Through a process detailed in the following chapter, the Communists decided in 1949 that the economic system would have to provide the springboard for the Party's efforts to transform all of Tientsin society. The entrepreneurs and workers in the economic system composed the overwhelming majority of the employed adult population. They produced the goods on which the standard of living in the city would depend and, because of Tientsin's pivotal role in the national commercial system, their active cooperation would be critical to the Communists' rehabilitation efforts far beyond the city's boundaries.

What were the lines of cleavage among the businessmen and workers in Tientsin? As we have seen, these people could be divided according to their work in the traditional, modern, or transport sectors of the economy. The above analysis, however, suggests the existence of a far more intricate pattern of social divisions. Workers in the traditional sector typically could not look beyond the horizons of their own small shops, where they were surrounded by co-provincials and cut off both psychologically and physically from the rest of urban society. Their counterparts in the modern sector experienced the city in a more open way and formed a potentially more cohesive group. Still, the traditional notions of *kuan-hsi* shaped and constrained fundamental perspectives of the capitalists in the modern sector, so that webs of personal connections defined their real social boundaries. Transport workers, too, were confined to highly discrete units, alienated from society at large, and cut off from each other by the turf system and the secret-society structure that girded it.

In a prosaic sense, Tientsin existed as a great metropolis. Economic interdependence and geographic proximity defined a political unit that had to be treated as a single entity. However, the high percentage of first-generation city dwellers and the tenacity of traditional modes of thought meant that few of the inhabitants perceived the city as a whole. Tientsin in fact resembled a multi-cellular organism: it required complex forms of cooperation in order to function, but at the same time permitted cell walls to screen out all but the bare essentials that each minuscule part required from the whole. The individual parts by their very number, moreover, presented insuperable obstacles to any agent that sought to penetrate and transform everyone without first dismantling many of the boundaries separating them. How to accomplish this task without paralyzing and debilitating the organism itself became the critical dilemma that faced the Chinese Communist Party on the morrow of its victory in Tientsin in January 1949.

CHAPTER 3 *Strategies*

On January 15, 1949, the People's Liberation Army stormed and occupied Tientsin, bringing to an end the agony that had tormented the city for months. Although the victorious Communists inherited an urban plant that had suffered little physical damage from battle, they now possessed a city laid prostrate by the ravages of almost uncontrolled inflation and exhausted by the depredations of a marauding and demoralized KMT army. The situation was made worse by shortages of goods resulting from the two-month seige of the city, by the tension of anticipating house-to-house fighting, and by fear of the behavior of the revolutionary forces once they captured the city.

The deterioration of the economic and social fabric of Tientsin had in fact begun in 1947, assumed serious proportions by early 1948, and become catastrophic in the months preceding the Communist takeover. Two viruses had undermined the health of the city—the civil war between the KMT and the Communists, and corruption and malfeasance within the KMT itself.[1]

The civil war attacked the economic heart of the trading city of Tientsin, progressively cutting off the sources of supply for its industry and exports and constricting the markets for its imports. Adding insult to injury, this conflict also brought a rising tide of refugees into the city, greatly aggravating unemployment, welfare, and public order problems.[2] In this time of stress and shortages, hoarding, speculation, and corruption abounded, and many of the KMT municipal leaders and their colleagues seized the opportunity to feather their nests.[3] Pressed by corruption and civil war, Tientsin's economy spun out of control. The cost-of-living index for Tientsin workers increased 1,550 percent during 1947,[4] but the events of 1948, which boosted the cost of living 3,700 percent during January–August alone, caused residents of the city to look back on the previous year as a period of relative price stability. In August 1948, the government carried out a national currency reform, designed to put the *yuan* back on a solid footing.[5] Inflation in terms of the new currency, however, soared 2,090 percent during September–December, making money essentially useless as a medium of exchange in Tientsin. Former residents remember the collapse of the currency as the most demoralizing aspect of this extraordinarily dismal period.[6]

The Communists laid seige to Tientsin early in December 1948 as part of a coordinated plan to capture Peking, Tientsin, T'angshan, T'angku, Hsin Pao-an, and Changchiak'ou.[7] PLA general Lin Piao threw approximately 150,000 troops into the operations around Tientsin.[8] These faced some 90,000 Nationalist soldiers in the city and its environs,[9] along with 20,000 troops that had fled in defeat from the Communist armies in Manchuria to seek refuge in Tientsin.[10] As the noose tightened around Tientsin, the government conscripted large numbers of civilians to build fortifications in the streets, causing panic among the many who anticipated a house-to-house battle that would destroy the city and produce casualty figures in the tens of thousands. A declaration of martial law on November 22 had the effect of encouraging demoralized soldiers within the city to take greater liberties with civilians and their property.[11] Inhabitants responded by closing down their businesses and remaining indoors, nearly bringing the economy to a complete halt.[12] During the course of the two-month seige, sporadic fighting occurred around December 20 and from January 5 to January 8.[13] The final assault began on January 14 and achieved victory in 28 hours.[14]

While Tientsin was the largest and most sophisticated city yet to come under Communist control, the CCP had already gained some experience in urban takeover work during the previous two years.[15] Until late 1947, the CCP's policy toward the small cities it had captured was little more than rapid exploitation of the town's resources in anticipation of a successful KMT counterattack in the near future. As the fortunes of war changed in favor of the Communists, however, Party policy toward captured cities shifted toward rehabilitating the urban economies so that these prices of battle could quickly contribute to the national war effort.

Mao Tse-tung in late December 1947 signaled this shift to a more constructive urban policy and summed up the spirit of this new approach in four slogans: develop production; make the economy prosper; consider both the public and private sector; and benefit both labor and capital. Through the course of 1948, the upper levels of the Party and army leadership fleshed out the new policy administratively, so that by the end of the year this policy included the following concrete measures: to move troops out of a newly captured city immediately and to disarm the population; to confirm temporarily all civil servants and employees in the positions they had held prior to the Communist victory; to grant loans to entrepreneurs in the private sector to help them reestablish their businesses; to exert every effort to resume production as quickly as possible in the enterprises that had been nationalized (these were firms that the Communists had previously labeled as being owned by "bureaucratic capital"); to prohibit efforts at wage leveling; to restore rapidly the commercial relations between the city and the hinterland that had been severed by the civil war; and to send all refugees back to their places of origin.

The Communist leadership had difficulty persuading its local-level cadres to implement these policy measures during 1948. Peasant soldiers who had suffered so greatly in their years of fighting occasionally proved difficult to discipline when they entered cities and for the first time encountered urban amenities. More fundamentally, these rustics had carried out land reform and related measures in the countryside, where rewards for the revolutionary victory tended to be both immediate and tangible. They could not see that the more complex and subtle urban forms of interdependence required a more prolonged and indirect strategy of change. There were reports, for instance, of attempts by these peasant soldiers to divide up the machinery in factories and distribute it to workers in the urban equivalent of land reform, not understanding that in the rural areas this redistribution of property could aid production while in the cities it would produce only future unemployment and misery. This gap between urban policy formulation at the top and implementation at the lower levels continued to plague the Chinese Communist Party as it marched into Tientsin in January 1949.

While the capture of Tientsin on January 15 confronted the Communists with a wholly new level of urban administrative tasks, the Party could not pause to adapt previous practice to the new situations at the time. Peiping (renamed Peking on October 1, 1949) fell on January 30,[16] and the civil war continued to be waged full tilt throughout the remainder of the year. In 11 months, from January to November 1949, the PLA advanced more than 2,000 miles from Mukden to Chengtu, averaging over six miles per day. They breached the Yangtze on April 20, captured Nanking three days later, seized Hankow on May 3, liberated Shanghai on May 27, took Canton on October 16, and were in control of both Chungking and Chengtu by late November.[17] On October 1, while the Nationalists still governed large areas of Central–South and Southwest China, the People's Republic of China was founded in Peking. Events in Tientsin during 1949 marched to the drumbeat of this national arena.

Initial Tasks and Problems

The Communists quickly tried to bring Tientsin out of its stupor. They immediately published decrees naming the personnel on the Tientsin Military Affairs Control Commission (MCC), the Tientsin Municipal People's Government (MPG), and the Tientsin Emergency Headquarters, and placed Tientsin under martial law.[18] The CCP also rapidly removed the most obvious signs of the chaos that had preceded liberation—the scattered soldiers, refugees from other areas, homeless persons from the suburbs, and so forth. Within several days, all of the thousands of street barricades and fortifications erected by the KMT had come down. By the end of the first week, the streets were clear of battle-related debris, all the dead were buried, and over 28,000 former KMT soldiers were registered and put under control. The city's trains resumed operations on the second day, and bus service was restored on the third. The Communists registered the over 22,000 students and landlords who had fled to Tientsin from the Northeast and sent them back to their native areas. They sent an additional 5,700 students and teachers from North China back to the countryside. The government also distributed food to the several hundred thousand people who had been made homeless by Ch'en Chang-chieh's policy of destroying homes in Tientsin's suburbs to establish a clear line of fire for the city's defenders; and it gave small loans both to these people and to many of the thousands of Tientsin's unemployed.[19] All of these measures were completed within two weeks.

Taking over political organs, KMT-run economic enterprises, and public institutions such as schools and hospitals consumed a major part of the victors' energies during the initial weeks. To accomplish this task, the Tientsin MCC established a "takeover department," which in turn dispatched military representatives and civilian work teams to all of the 663 affected units. The 700 trade union cadres who worked under the Tientsin Division of the North China Federation of Trade Unions participated in these teams. In the factories, the work teams quickly audited assets, set priorities for immediate attention, and assigned responsibility for various types of work. Establishing order and restoring production in the factories took first priority, and therefore the Communists permitted (indeed encouraged) everyone to retain the positions they had held prior to the city's liberation.[20]

But as these initial tasks yielded to longer term policy initiatives, the Communists found themselves hampered by severe constraints, especially by shortages of funds and qualified cadres. Their problems were compounded by the march of events occurring well beyond the boundaries of the city. In their struggle to enhance their positions so they could shift from short-term palliatives to complex programs of economic reconstruction and social transformation, Tientsin's leaders had to fo-

cus much of their attention during 1949 on finances, cadre recruitment, and inflation.

When the CCP entered Tientsin, it inherited a bankrupt city.
The Communists wanted to raise the tax revenue necessary to
support the Party's ambitious plans, but they found themselves
constrained by the deplorable state of the city's economy and by
their own desire to appear more equitable and responsible than
the KMT. They finally adopted a rather traditional approach
that was especially well suited to their lack of information about
the financial situation in the city: they announced very heavy tax
levies and then bargained with the various business groups in
order to determine how much each would have to pay. This bargaining frequently resulted in a diminution of the government's
demand for funds.* At the same time, the MPG during 1949 collected taxes for both the latter half of 1948 and for all of 1949,
disregarding the fact that the KMT had already taxed the people
heavily for the former period. Even using the above measures,
the amount of money they could collect through taxes remained
limited by the very low level of production in Tientsin's economy at the time.† In addition, the municipal authorities had to
turn over a large percentage of the revenues they did raise to
help the civil war effort farther south.

An interim report on municipal finances covering January–
July 1949 disclosed that the government had already produced
revenues of 171.3 million *chin*‡ of millet, of which half had been
spent in the city and half had been given to higher authorities
for use elsewhere. The same report predicted that revenues for
August–December 1949 would be at least 320 million *chin*, of

---

*For instance, from early September, when the tax authorities first announced
the industry and commerce tax for January–June 1949, to late October, when the
tax was paid, the amount demanded decreased by over 7 percent. See the China
Association Archives report dated Oct. 31, 1949, which contains an outstanding
description of the bargaining process involved.

†At least 79 percent of the proposed tax revenue in the first 1950 municipal
government budget consisted of items such as an industry and commerce tax, a
commodity tax, and an income tax; their size would be directly affected by the
state of the economy. *CP*, 16.ii.50, p. 4.

‡A *chin* is a catty. This measure is employed because it provides a stable base
for comparative evaluation over the years 1949–53, a period during which inflationary surges made *yuan* (Chinese dollar) comparisons meaningless.

which the city would retain only some 40 percent to spend on local affairs. This increase in the percentage of revenue given to the war effort was to be made possible through both an economy drive in Tientsin and the growth of the revenue base for August–December.[21]

In practice, the Tientsin MPG managed to collect more than it had anticipated for the second half of 1949 but was permitted to keep less. Actual municipal government revenues for this period amounted to 406.5 million *chin* (27 percent more than anticipated), of which the MPG was allowed to keep only 22 percent, or 88.2 million *chin*. This amounted to 49.7 million *chin* (or 31 percent) less than the *minimum* that the authorities in early September had anticipated would be available to them for municipal expenditures for this six-month period.[22] The total 1949 municipal tax revenues of 577.8 million *chin* in any event amounted to a very small financial base. By way of comparison, during 1950, with the city's economy largely recovered, tax revenues totaled 1.5 billion *chin* of millet—an increase of 270 percent since 1949.[23]

Heavy administrative overhead expenses also drained the MPG's resources during 1949. For the January–July period, 45 percent of the government's expenditures in the city went to salaries and other administrative expenses, a figure that the authorities hoped to reduce substantially during the latter half of the year.[24] In fact, however, administrative costs for the last five months of 1949 climbed to 50 percent of municipal expenditures, thus limiting non-administrative outlays during August–December to an average monthly increase in absolute terms of less than 10 percent over the preceding six months.* For all of 1949, then, the Tientsin government had to turn over 70 percent of its tax revenues to the higher authorities for use elsewhere and spend fully 48 percent of the remainder to meet purely administrative expenses.

The shortage of skilled and loyal cadres proved a more severe

---

*CP, 16.ii.50, p. 4. Moreover, in 1949 all expenditures for public security work were listed under headings other than "administrative expenses," a practice that changed in 1950. A substantial proportion of these public security expenses were for administrative expenses such as salaries.

handicap than the dearth of funds during 1949, for cadre work placed the Communist leaders on the horns of a dilemma. Put simply, they brought at least 9,500 politically loyal cadres into the city during the course of 1949,[25] but many of these lacked necessary technical skills; at the same time, many of the 12,391 more technically proficient cadres who had been recruited within the city as of the end of 1949 were politically impure.* A significant amount of conflict, moreover, marred the relationship between these two groups.[26]

The municipal Communist leaders had a great deal of trouble with their "old cadres"—i.e., those who had joined the Communist cause in the rural areas and come to the city after liberation. These cadres were not accustomed to an urban environment, adjusted very slowly to the urban working day, and experienced great difficulty in grasping, for example, the discipline essential to factory work.[27]

The cadres retained from the KMT's administration in Tientsin and those who were newly recruited posed different kinds of problems. Many of them disparaged the old cadres' rustic ways and lack of understanding of the urban environment. Some new recruits quickly grew haughty when appointed to good positions, and most proved too individualistic for the Communists' liking. In short, the contrasting backgrounds, work styles, and attitudes of the old cadres and their newly recruited counterparts quickly produced a good deal of resentment between these two groups.[28] This tension in turn impaired their ability to work together and implement policies effectively.

The limited skills of the old cadres necessitated rapid recruitment of new personnel in Tientsin. An important part of this recruitment process centered on the schools, which had yielded a total of 1,292 middle-school and university students for cadre

*CP, 16.ii.50, p. 4, 1.ii.51, p. 5. The term cadre referred to any type of leadership position and was quite vague. The figures in this paragraph refer only to cadres who were "separated from production" (*t'o ch'an kan-pu*) and include all such cadres in the various MPG bureaus, divisions, committees, institutes, ward offices, public security branch bureaus and precinct stations, public security troops, and the various mass organizations. H. Franz Schurmann provides a brief overview of the evolution of the term cadre in *Ideology and Organization in Communist China*, rev. and enlarged ed. (Berkeley, Calif., 1971), pp. 162–67.

work by the end of 1949. Some of these students joined the Southbound Work Team to assist the takeover work in the cities below the Yangtze,[29] while others underwent crash courses at the Revolutionary University and the Chinese University before taking cadre positions in government offices and mass organizations in Tientsin and elsewhere.[30]

Another dimension of the recruitment effort focused on finding persons who could assume leadership roles on the shop floors in the factories, on the docks, and in the neighborhoods. The Communists believed in selecting these people from among those already at work in these occupations during 1949, for they recognized the importance of winning over leaders who understood the local situation and were able to communicate effectively with the local people. The selection process amounted to identifying workers who displayed enthusiasm and leadership skills in carrying out the CCP's initial policies, giving these "activists" responsibility for carrying out some tasks, and, after a short time, putting them through one or another training class, usually lasting no more than a week. All of these steps in 1949 were of necessity hurriedly and somewhat haphazardly implemented; this often resulted in the establishment of very imperfect organizational hierarchies that would have to be purified through subsequent "consolidation" campaigns.

The need for skilled cadres also forced Tientsin's leaders to retain and rely on many people who held significant municipal positions before 1949. At first, the Party could do little more than arrange for these holdovers to study the CCP's policies. One group posed a particularly vexing problem, the personnel in the former Nationalist government's police force. The Communists immediately put them through a training school to teach them how the new municipal authorities expected them to behave. Of the 11,800 municipal police remaining from before liberation, the Communists temporarily retained over 8,000.[31] However, an undisclosed number of these incumbents were dismissed in October 1949 following the order by a Central Public Security Conference to accelerate reform of police personnel and to tighten up the ranks of the public security bureau.[32] New recruitment to the police ranks also proceeded apace.*

Training of retained cadres outside the public security system went along in a slower and less-organized fashion. For example, one former civil servant in the MPG asserted that the people in his office had on their own initiative begun political study in early 1949 to learn about the policies of the new administration. The Communists at that time were urging everyone in the city to "study," and the government workers did not want to appear to be lagging behind. Initially they simply convened meetings of the office staff to discuss the policies of the new government as nearly as they could determine them. Soon, however, outside cadres began attending the meetings, and the program of study assumed a more regular form. Participants began to read some basic materials on Marxism-Leninism and recent articles and speeches (such as Mao Tse-tung's treatise *On New Democracy*). They also discussed Tientsin's particular problems and how to improve the work of their own office. They occasionally participated in plenary meetings of civil servants from a number of offices, and outside officials sometimes addressed these larger gatherings. Over time, therefore, the system of study in the municipal government offices became more organized and formal.

The Party and the Youth League tried to boost the Communists' cadre resources by fleshing out their internal organizational structures and recruiting new members. There are no reliable figures available for Party growth during 1949. The Youth League, however, began organizing in Tientsin in March, and within a year it had a local membership of 21,625.[33] During the same period, both the Party and the League established units in the various government organs, in each district, and in many of the schools and economic enterprises.[34] Indeed, throughout 1949, the Tientsin Party and League evidently directed their efforts more at building up their organizational resources than at

*For example, in early 1950 the authorities expected to have 800 new recruits participate in the public security school that year. *CP*, 16.ii.50, p. 4.

playing a leading role in guiding the work of other people in various organs, enterprises, and schools.

Few aspects of the final period of Nationalist rule in Tientsin had been as demoralizing as the rampant inflation. The victorious Communist leaders, therefore, tried mightily to bring inflation under control, but their best efforts were repeatedly tripped up by events beyond the borders of the municipality. Three inflationary surges rocked the Tientsin economy during 1949. In April and May, a food shortage created by a spring drought in Hopei sent grain prices skyrocketing, and this engendered a correspondingly steep decline of people's confidence in the value of the Communists' currency. The authorities tried to dampen inflationary pressures at this point with an emergency program of large-scale grain imports from the Northeast. No sooner had they gained control over this situation, however, than events south of the Yangtze threw the economy into another inflationary spiral. The capture of Shanghai and the surrounding territory in May 1949 had made the Communists responsible for a huge area that was suffering from acute economic breakdown with inflation completely out of control. Whereas in Tientsin the Communists had controlled the surrounding countryside for a substantial period of time and could thus use the nearby rural resources to alleviate the most pressing problems in the city, in the area below the Yangtze they did not have the power to mobilize the countryside quickly to support the city. The Shanghai authorities, therefore, appealed to Tientsin for help—a request that the Tientsin leadership honored even at the cost of increasing inflation in their own city during July and August.[35] In mid-October, the city again found itself caught in the grip of inflationary pressures not of its own making as the Central People's Government printed too much money to meet the continuing demands of the civil war. A plague in the Northwest that reduced food supplies to Tientsin also aggravated the city's monetary problems, and thus again the Tientsin government had to make emergency grain purchases from the Northeast. Not surprisingly, profiteering grain merchants exacerbated the situation.[36] As a result of all those

TABLE 1. *Tientsin Monthly Rates of Increases in Workers' Cost-of-Living Index, January– December 1949*

Month	Rate of increase[a] (percent)	Explanatory circumstances
February	19	
March	18	
April	33	
May	100	Hopei drought
June	−4	
July	42	Aid to Shanghai; Hopei floods
August	169	
September	−2	
October	14	
November	275	Overprinting of currency; Northwest plague
December	−5	

SOURCE: Calculated from figures available in *T'ien-chin kung-jen*, pp. 17–18.

[a]Calculated as the percentage increase from the third week of the previous month to the third week of the current month, except that the May figure is calculated from the third week of April to the *second* week of May.

factors, the workers' cost of living in Tientsin jumped by 5,440 percent between mid-January and late December.[37] Table 1 gives the monthly rate of increase in the workers' cost-of-living index for each month of 1949.

Thus, budget problems, inflationary pressures, a shortage of skilled cadres, and harsh demands made on Tientsin's leaders by Peking combined to buffet the victors in Tientsin as they struggled to consolidate their control over the city, to rehabilitate its economy, and to begin fashioning a social revolution. Throughout this period, moreover, the leaders battled to restore the reservoir of good will that in more normal times submerged conflicts of interest under a general desire to maintain social harmony. "Benefit both labor and capital," "consider both the public and private sectors," and "make the economy prosper" proved inherently contradictory slogans in resource-scarce and war-weary Tientsin. Should workers' demands for the three

months of pay that most had missed be honored against employers' arguments that doing so would spur inflation and re-
tard the process of resuming production?[38] Which sectors of the
economy should receive financial aid from the government's
limited coffers—the nationalized firms, the large private enterprises, or the small workshops? How could the new government raise productivity if the workers felt that their legitimate
grievances remained unresolved? If the government supported
these demands, how could it hope to convince the capitalists
that they, too, had a future worth striving for in the new society?[39] Slogans provided little guidance, and the situation in Tientsin soon forced the Communist leadership to make hard
choices concerning priorities for meeting the legitimate claims of
various sectors of the populace. These priorities, in turn, embodied fundamental strategic choices concerning the scope,
speed, and intensity of the revolutionary transformation of
Tientsin.

Setting Priorities

In April–May 1949, the CCP Central Committee dispatched
Liu Shao-ch'i, who ranked second only to Mao Tse-tung in the
Party hierarchy, to Tientsin on a fact-finding mission that would
produce a detailed set of policy recommendations. Liu accomplished three major tasks during his three-week stay in Tientsin:
he met with and allayed the fears of some important non-Communist figures in the city; he specified the strategy and tactics
that the municipal administration should subsequently follow in
the city; and he ordered critical administrative changes that
would enable the municipal government to exercise tighter control over the revolutionary organization nominally subordinate
to it.

The MPG from the start had focused its efforts on increasing
production in Tientsin, both to win favor among the populace
through restoring their standard of living and to meet the inces-
sant demands from the national Party leadership for material
support for the PLA in its continuing drive toward the South.

Communist cadres on the streets and in enterprises, however, repeatedly sabotaged this policy by exciting the workers to demand better pay and benefits. The Party had imported a three-level administrative system into the city that hamstrung municipal leaders trying to cope with local insubordination. Under this system, the MPG issued general decrees, collected taxes, managed several of the largest nationalized enterprises, and arbitrated disputes that could not be resolved at lower levels. Each of Tientsin's 11 ward governments simply mediated labor disputes that the street governments could not handle satisfactorily (presumably, the street-government cadres themselves judged whether their solutions were satisfactory). It was the numerous five-man street governments that shouldered the major burden under this decentralized system, for they assumed responsibility for adjudicating labor disputes, organizing trade unions and other mass organizations, and communicating the government's policies to the populace. This system had been devised in the rural areas, where the Party had achieved good results by allowing substantial operational flexibility at the village level—the rough equivalent of the street in the urban administrative hierarchy.[40] It proved ill-suited to the city, however, because the more complex urban environment made the street level inappropriate for dealing with the many issues that transcended single neighborhoods, and the unsophisticated street-level personnel, moreover, did not understand the nuances of the urban policy devised by their superiors.

Indeed, the street-level cadres not only urged the workers to fight for their interests, but also encouraged students to confront their professors and poor people to demand immediate social justice. These cadres thus sought to carry out a revolutionary strategy of extraordinary intensity, scope, and speed. In the nationalized enterprises they allied with the workers against the management,[41] in the privately managed firms with the workers against the owners, in the universities with the students against the faculty and administration, and in the residential areas with the poor against their more well-to-do neighbors. They sought to exacerbate these latent conflicts of interest and to mobilize people to look to the political arena for solutions to their problems. They proved willing, moreover, to spread themselves extremely thin in this effort, evidently believing that it was more important to foster class struggle than to concentrate on creating the type of organizational presence that would permit the Communists to guide, control, and utilize that struggle in a purposeful way.

The municipal leaders recognized that this revolutionary policy would inevitably maximize demands on the Communist movement at a time when they lacked a sufficient pool of politically and technically competent persons to satisfy these claims. The result could only be frustration producing future alienation or apathy. Yet the leadership watched helplessly while the economy deteriorated and tensions in the city rose.

Liu Shao-ch'i entered this situation on April 18. He quickly declared that the street-level cadres' leftist deviation harmed the revolution not only in Tientsin but, by retarding economic recovery, elsewhere as well. Within three weeks, Liu worked out an extraordinary range of corrective policy proposals that would define the Party's basic strategy in Tientsin and all other major Chinese cities through the early 1950's.*

Mao Tse-tung on March 5 had declared in a key speech that set the tasks for the next stage of the Communist revolution: "Only when production in cities is restored and developed, when consumer cities are transformed into producer cities, can the people's political power be consolidated. Other work in the

---

*Many of these proposals are contained in two speeches by Liu, the first of which he delivered on May 5 in Tientsin to a North China Staff and Workers' Representative Conference, and the second on May 19 to a cadre conference, possibly in Peking. The texts of both speeches became available only during the Cultural Revolution and are reprinted in *Liu Shao-ch'i wen-t'i tzu-liao chuan-chi* (Taipei, 1970), pp. 200–207 and 207–20, respectively. An analysis of Liu's policy prescriptions in Tientsin made solely on the basis of contemporary public documentation provides independent evidence attesting to the accuracy of these Cultural Revolution texts. For this analysis, see Kenneth Lieberthal, "Mao Versus Liu? Policy Towards Industry and Commerce, 1946–1949," *China Quarterly*, 47 (July–Sept. 1971), pp. 513–17. These policy prescriptions, as far as they can be discovered by this analysis, were identical to the suggestions contained in the texts of the two speeches that became available during the Cultural Revolution. Liu stayed in Tientsin from April 18 to May 7, 1949.

cities, for example, in Party organization, in organs of political power, in trade unions and other people's organizations, in culture and education, in the elimination of counterrevolutionaries, in news agencies, newspapers and broadcasting stations—all this work revolves around and serves the central task, production and construction."[42] It fell to Liu Shao-ch'i to translate Mao's order of priorities into concrete policy proposals.

Liu did so by insisting that the Party greatly narrow the scope of the revolution in Tientsin. He determined that the CCP lacked the manpower to establish a strong presence in the traditional sector of the economy and among people in the residential areas. To attempt to penetrate these sectors, he argued, would dangerously deplete the Party's resources within the higher priority modern economic sector, the educational sphere, and the civil service. He recommended a reallocation of the movement's cadres that would concentrate the Party's efforts on the more cosmopolitan portion of the city's population, where the CCP's nationalistic propaganda might strike a more responsive chord, and its organizational efforts might yield faster results.[43]

Liu in effect demanded that the Party in Tientsin *demobilize* major segments of the population, for he regarded political mobilization that could not be controlled and guided from above as harmful.* Even within the modern firms and the educational institutions, he recognized the overriding short-term need to win the cooperation of the people who virtually monopolized the city's scarce administrative and entrepreneurial skills—the capitalists, the administrative personnel in the nationalized enterprises, and the faculty and staff in the schools. Accordingly, he argued for the formation of labor-capital, worker-staff, and student-faculty "alliances" and stipulated that all subsequent "struggle" must take as its object the "strengthening" of such alliances.[44]

Patriotism could dissolve the antagonisms that had flared be-

---

*For instance, Liu asserted that "with respect to the street organizations of the Youth League and the Party, it is not the more the better but the fewer the better." *Liu Shao-ch'i wen-t'i*, p. 219.

tween these groups, Liu argued, because in China's current situation the class interests of almost all urban groups meshed easily with the national interest and the revolution. The workers in the modern firms had become the "masters" of society and had thereby assumed a special responsibility to devote their efforts to increasing output. The capitalists, like the Communists, desired an economically robust and independent China, and this common goal could provide the basis for long-term cooperation between them. Both students and teachers recognized the country's critical shortage of skilled personnel and could be united around a program designed to maximize the contribution the schools could make toward filling this need. A platform of governmental reform and service to the people, moreover, could be used to win cooperation from the civil servants. Liu's prescriptions, therefore, focused on ways to bring all key groups in Tientsin's society into at least a temporary alliance with each other and the Communists. Concomitantly, he called for a temporary "benign neglect" of nonessential segments of the populace, and recommended that the Party carefully limit and control all future efforts to mobilize people by cultivating inter-group hatred.

Liu Shao-ch'i coupled the above recommendations with a detailed proposal for administrative reform that would concentrate executive power in the hands of responsible municipal leaders and undercut the more radical basic level cadres. In Tientsin's three-tiered government system, Liu called upon the municipal level to assume control of virtually all aspects of policy-making and implementation. He reduced the ward level to an administrative appendage of the municipal government, stripping it of independent executive power, and abolished the street governments altogether. The Public Security (police) bureaucracy would be appropriately strengthened at the ward and street levels to assume many of the public order and administrative functions that the governments at these levels had previously shouldered. Because the government's interaction with Tientsin society was greatly reduced under Liu's new strategy, the concentration of power at the municipal level would not unduly overload the decision-making system at that point, especially since Liu ordered the assignment of the ablest cadres to the municipal departments. The government and Party could subsequently renew their organs at the ward and street levels when human resources allowed and expanding interaction with the society demanded it.[45]

It is one thing to call for antagonistic groups to form alliances and make arrangements that both parties accept, and quite another to translate this policy prescription into workable terms. During his stay in Tientsin, Liu Shao-ch'i did not shy away from discussing the specifics of his program for the various sectors of the society. He recommended that the Communists organize the city's key groups (employees, capitalists, students, teachers, and civil servants) into mass organizations, which could then serve as intermediaries between the revolutionary leaders and these critical non-Communist groups.[46] He also proposed a two fold "from the top down" organizational strategy, directing initial efforts toward the largest units, where the Communists had the most favorable proportion of cadres, and organizing each unit "from above" (i.e., by administrative action), establishing closer ties with its membership only as time went on.[47] This strategy assigned the mass organizations a central role in future policy implementation, so much so that their development provides a reasonably accurate measure of the Communists' progress in penetrating the various spheres of Tientsin's society during the next few years. Liu's strategy stressed the importance of the economy and also established an order of priorities for economic organization. It directed the CCP to organize first the nationalized enterprises (which tended to be the largest in the city), to turn later to the modern firms in the private sector, and to encompass last the units in the traditional sector. Liu directed that organizational work in the economy assume priority over that in other spheres.

Liu hoped to prevent the flight of Tientsin capital to South China (still in Nationalist hands at the time of his visit) and Hong Kong and to enlist the help of industrialists and businessmen in rehabilitating the city's devastated economy. To accom-

plish these goals, the second-ranking leader of the Chinese
Communist movement had to persuade the Tientsin bourgeoi-
sie that they had a future worth contemplating in the New
China.

Liu's overture to Tientsin's bourgeoisie had three themes. He
argued that the nationalized sector of the economy would be allowed to expand only very gradually, thereby posing no immediate threat to the economic interests of the private sector.[48] He
assured the capitalists in a series of face-to-face meetings that
the government would not arbitrarily limit the profits they could
make.[49] And finally, he spelled out a complicated plan for handling disputes over wages and working conditions that would
assure reasonable settlements of these conflicts from the point of
view of the employers.

Liu's case for restraining the expansion of the public sector of
the economy focused on the Communists' limited ability to
manage economic enterprises efficiently. Vigorous efforts to
bring more firms into the public sector, Liu contended, would
cause capitalists to seek their fortunes elsewhere, thus producing a self-generating process by which increasing numbers of
privately run businesses would move, by default, into the public
domain. This would so quickly and severely overtax the managerial resources of the government that it would bring about a
general economic collapse, with high unemployment, adverse
political effects, and other undesirable repercussions.[50] Thus,
while affirming that the public sector would grow in the future,
Liu stressed that this growth would be gradual, and that the private sector would continue to provide substantial rewards to entrepreneurs for a long time to come.

Liu maintained that the Communists' only restriction on profits would be to stipulate that all "unreasonable" profits be in-
vested in the Tientsin economy.[51] The credibility of his personal
assurances on this issue may have been enhanced by the fact
that Wang Kuang-mei, whom he had married the previous year,
came from a prominent Tientsin family that still had extensive
business interests in the city at the time of his visit.

The CCP's attitude toward labor disputes was the thorniest issue in Liu's courting of Tientsin's capitalists, and he proposed both stopgap and long-term solutions to this problem. For the short term, he directed the municipal government to organize a Labor Bureau that would arbitrate such disputes. A rather detailed set of principles, to be developed through a long and complex consultative process involving representatives of all concerned parties (including the government), would provide the basic guidelines for these arbitration decisions.[52] His long-term solution was to create a mechanism for negotiating collective contracts by entire trades.

Specifically, Liu sought to gain control over the labor situation by developing centralized, city-wide organizations susceptible to Communist control that would themselves negotiate new labor-capital contracts in the various trades. The first step entailed organizing labor unions by entire trades, taking each factory as the basic unit. The capitalists had traditionally organized by trade into trade associations, and Liu's plan sought to gradually restructure these so as to make them more amenable to CCP influence. As soon as practicable, the Communists would create a municipal Federation of Trade Unions and a Federation of Industry and Commerce to connect the city's political leadership with the trade unions and associations.

Having created centralized, city-wide capitalist associations and labor unions organized by trade, Liu's plan called for these organizations to negotiate a collective contract to regulate wage scales and other labor conditions. If no agreement could be reached, the municipal government's Labor Bureau would step in to arbitrate, and if arbitration failed the parties could as a last resort file suit in the People's Court. In such cases, the judicial decision would be binding.[53]

In this way, Liu's plan reduced the role of the more radical cadres in the factories to virtual insignificance in the actual labor negiotiations. Still, the plan clearly provided for the municipal government to exercise substantial leverage, albeit in somewhat indirect fashion, in settling these vital issues. Why should Tientsin's bourgeoisie place their trust in a proposal that encouraged a Communist government to play a decisive role in determining the working conditions within their firms?

A partial answer may lie in the fact that Liu's plan promised temporary relief from the deteriorating situation many business-men faced in late April 1949. Any proposal that took power away from the hotheads who had no knowledge of economics, but who nevertheless felt competent to raise and negotiate de-mands on behalf of the workers, had to be better than no change at all. However, Liu worked hard in Tientsin to persuade the capitalists that his proposals offered a more meaningful reprieve than this. He hoped, after all, to encourage businessmen and industrialists to keep their capital in Tientsin and invest it in plant expansion. While repeating the slogan "benefit to both labor and capital," Liu publicly asserted that a "leftist" deviation had occurred in Tientsin, and that the time had come to redress the wrongs. He affirmed the owners' right to dismiss workers, admitted that a workday longer than eight hours remained per-missible, stressed the obligation of workers to obey labor discip-line, and stipulated that the workers' real wages remain at or even return to the level that prevailed during the last three months of 1948. It was these specifics, later embodied in the written guidelines adopted by the municipal government, that most strongly induced the Tientsin bourgeoisie to join in the effort to revive and strengthen the city's economy.[54]

Labor-management relations within the nationalized enter-prises posed a particularly vexing problem for the Communists in Tientsin. Marxist ideology defines both workers and adminis-trators as proletarians because both work for wage labor, and it takes as an article of faith that no major clash of interests can mar the relationship between them. In Tientsin, however, the administration in these nationalized enterprises included people with managerial, technical, and financial experience that the Communists desperately needed, but it surrounded these peo-ple with others who had been appointed for purely political or personal reasons. Many workers, moreover, could well remember incidents that marked the administrative personnel as something other than class brethren. Indeed, pre-1949 newspapers had reported attempts—some successful—by groups of workers to murder their foremen while they traveled to and from the factories.[55]

Liu Shao-ch'i proposed a tripartite program to reduce these tensions within the public enterprises. He advocated criticism and self-criticism sessions among the staff members and between the staff and workers. In so doing, he evidently counted on these sessions to facilitate identification of the political appointees. The experience of mutual criticism would also lay the groundwork for the second step of his plan, institutionalizing future worker-staff discussion about major management decisions. Thirdly, Liu authorized the municipal government to fire all incompetent staff members and implement wide-ranging structural reforms to improve production.[56]

These directives attacked several problems. Identifying and dismissing the many administrators who had been hired on the basis of their personal connections reduced administrative overhead and at the same time weakened lingering KMT influence in the nationalized enterprises. Organizing criticism and self-criticism and providing for continuing consultation with representatives of the workers facilitated progress toward reducing the "we–they" feeling of the workers toward management. Implementing structural reforms increased incentives to maximize output. Most importantly, perhaps, the new trade unions in these firms assumed responsibility for organizing criticism and self-criticism sessions, represented the workers in ongoing consultations with the management, and recommended structural reforms. These tasks in turn enabled the nascent trade union organizations to identify promising workers and recruit them into their ranks, to become familiar with the wage structure and production process in the factory, and to take on relatively central and constructive roles in the ongoing operations of the firms. The need to woo the capitalists temporarily prevented Liu from proposing similar measures in the private enterprises. This program in the nationalized industries, however, would later provide a model for the expansion of Communist power into the firms in the private sector, too.

Liu Shao-ch'i combined the above recommendations with repeated appeals to the workers in both the public and the private sector to recognize the stake they had in a healthy and robust Tientsin economy. With high unemployment and continuing inflation, Liu argued, unreasonable wage demands and low productivity could only increase the misery of the workers' lot. Long-term improvement in their material situation would require short-term discipline and sacrifice. For the near future, the proletarians should rejoice in their increased prestige under a workers' state and trust that the Party would manage the revolution in their interests.[57]

Liu Shao-ch'i's proposals shaped the contours of the Communists' penetration of Tientsin society during the years that followed. His program, as noted above, directed the movement's resources primarily toward the economy and within that sphere initially toward the largest firms in the modern sector. It postulated that the future direction of penetration would be from the larger firms to the smaller, from the modern sector to the more traditional. By rejecting political mobilization that could not be controlled from above, Liu intended to postpone until the fairly distant future the Communists' agitation efforts among the majority of the population.

A clear political and economic calculus guided these policy recommendations. For the time being, it would be impossible to revolutionize the city and maintain production, and the needs of the movement nationwide demanded that the economic side of the equation assume priority. Liu therefore sought to wed economic recovery to the development of the Party's resources (human, informational, financial) so that gradually the Communists would acquire the leverage to carry out massive changes in the city without simultaneously doing irreparable damage to the urban economy. He accomplished this task by making the Party itself the guarantor of economic growth, thereby giving the CCP

and its auxiliary organizations a major legitimate (to the capitalists) role to play in Tientsin's economy.

Liu's plan required that the Communists for the time being
enlist the cooperation of those with needed entrepreneurial and
technical talent and financial resources, and his program made
the concessions necessary to accomplish this task.[58] At the same
time, he skillfully linked these concessions to provisions that
would subsequently increase the CCP's power over the entrepreneurs. "Excessive" profits had to be reinvested in Tientsin
and could not be retained in the form of liquid capital. Settlement of labor disputes on reasonable terms required giving the
Communist municipal authorities an important role in the negotiations and allowing these same authorities to organize the
workers in the private sector into collective bargaining agents
(unions) by factory and trade. Information needed to referee labor-capital negotiations would inevitably yield data that could
subsequently be used to effect a relatively peaceful takeover of
the private firms. The Communists at some future point could
likewise use the trade unions they had organized to destroy the
private sector rather than to increase the profits of capitalists
through wage restraint and labor discipline.

Liu's central premise that under the proper set of guidelines
the capitalists' desire for profits could prove completely compatible with the nationalist goals of the Communist revolution thus
laid the groundwork for cooperation with Tientsin's bourgeoisie
and provided the rationale for the government's gradual penetration of the private sector. His emphasis on the task of expanding the economy could—and would—also provide the jus-
tification for subsequent government initiatives to break the
secret societies and secure control over the economically vital
transport industry.[59]

Liu's program took implicit account of the sociological differences between workers in Tientsin's modern and traditional
firms. By concentrating the Party's organizational efforts on the
largest modern enterprises, he directed the major thrust of the
government's program toward the sector of the proletariat most

likely to be responsive to the class appeals of the Communists, thereby maximizing the chances for the rapid growth of the Party and trade union apparatuses. The fact that in the large modern firms the organizers could muster audiences of scores or hundreds rather than the five to ten individuals they could address at one time in a traditional firm also argued in favor of focusing the initial efforts on the modern factories. Liu Shao-ch'i's proposed strategy, therefore, seemed the one most likely to achieve rapid organizational success, given the sociological and structural composition of Tientsin's working force. Moreover, the development of the movement's organizational resources would in turn fairly accurately determine the boundaries of the Communists' ability to penetrate and remold the urban society. Within the constraints of his own precepts, therefore, Liu's strategy promised to expand the Communists' ability to "revolutionize" Tientsin as rapidly as possible.

The Chinese Communist leadership in Tientsin devoted over two years to erecting an edifice of revolutionary power in the city according to the plans mapped out by Liu Shao-ch'i in April–May of 1949. In a sense, however, it was a peculiar undertaking, for the architect had instructed that his masterpiece be built "from the top down," with the foundation laid only after the scaffolding had been bolted together. Even more exasperating, the support for this edifice was weak and shifting, the characteristics of the building materials little understood, and the availability of resources uncertain. Little wonder, then, that the problem of establishing a firm and united foundation for a Communist society remained.

CHAPTER 4

Suppressing Counterrevolution

The Chinese Communists in Tientsin had to carry out Liu Shao-ch'i's policies in a society in which many people simply accepted the new government without a real commitment to it, and many others actively opposed it. The Party sought to win the active cooperation of the former group in the short run and their hearts over the longer term. The latter group, however, posed an immediate threat to the CCP's program and thus demanded a more aggressive approach. No possibility existed for a successful KMT comeback in Tientsin after the city's capture on January 15. The Nationalists had just lost 500,000 of their best troops in the disastrous Huai-Hai campaign centered on Hsüchou that concluded on January 10. Another half million or more Nationalist forces were lost during the capture of Tientsin and Peiping. By the end of January 1949, therefore, there remained no Nationalist military forces that could threaten the CCP's hold over Tientsin. In the immediate post-liberation context, the major threats to the municipal authorities came instead from KMT agents and scattered diehard Nationalist soldiers who might engage in sabotage and assassination, and upon entering the city the Communist troops took immediate measures to minimize the danger from these sources. These measures are contained in a decree published by the Peiping-Tientsin Garrison Headquarters on January 15. It reads:

1. The army safeguards the lives and property of all the people. We hope each will put his own job in order and will strictly obey all laws, decrees, and regulations published by the People's Government, the Peiping and Tientsin Military Affairs Control Committee, and the

Emergency Headquarters. Do not blindly believe rumours, and do not frighten each other by spreading rumours.

2. The Kuomintang, San-ch'ing t'uan and all other anti-Communist, anti-people organizations must immediately announce their dissolution and cease all of their activities. The personnel of these organizations must, according to regulations of the People's Government and the Peiping-Tientsin MCC, register, hand over all documents of identification, and turn in all radio broadcasting equipment and weapons. All who remain in hiding and do not report or who secretly plot activities will, once they have been discovered and apprehended, receive serious punishment.

3. All scattered remnant enemy officers and soldiers must immediately turn themselves in and hand over their weapons to the nearest PLA troops. Our troops will receive them and treat them leniently. If these people cause trouble or make disturbances, they will be punished severely.

4. All destructive activities such as wrecking factories, warehouses, public buildings, and communications equipment and robbing, stealing, setting fires, secretly harming people, and starting rumours is strictly prohibited, and violators will be severely punished.

5. No person may harbour criminals and secret destructive elements who have carried out activities against our troops. No one may privately conceal weapons, ammunition, broadcasting equipment, or military articles. Violators will be handled according to the law.[1]

During the following weeks the municipal authorities issued detailed regulations specifying the means of compliance with the strictures listed above.[2] These regulations, however, were stopgap measures aimed primarily at securing the city militarily. They soon had to give way to a more gradual and systematic approach to the problem of potential counterrevolution.

What was a counterrevolutionary? According to the CCP, it was anyone irreconcilably opposed to an important Chinese Communist policy. However, the lack of reliable cadres and the difficult economic tasks ahead encouraged the municipal authorities to minimize the number of people designated as "counterrevolutionary" at any given time. In addition, as mentioned earlier, the Party hoped to reduce potential civilian opposition and the flight of capital abroad in the areas yet to be liberated. Thus, for the moment at least, the Communists wished to appear lenient and reasonable in their treatment of people who, while not sympathizing with the CCP, did not take action to oppose it.

This set of concerns produced a policy that focused on anti-revolutionary *organizations* rather than anti-Communist individuals. This policy in turn reflected an assumption that people posed an immediate threat only when organized, for without organization individual efforts were too dissipated to constitute a serious problem.[3] The CCP's specific tactics varied according to the type of target organization, but the Party's main objective was always to break up the organization and disintegrate its hierarchy.

This "organizational" perspective may reflect the fact that Marx, Lenin, and Mao each in turn increasingly stressed organization and voluntarism.[4] Not surprisingly, there was a similar progression in their thinking about counterrevolution. Marx pictured counterrevolution in terms of classes that could be overthrown only when the fundamental conditions of society were ripe for such a qualitative change. In this situation, planned and organized political actions could at best play a facilitating role. Lenin also tied counterrevolution to class conditions but felt that well-organized political actions could play a major role in hastening the demise of counterrevolutionary forces.[5] Mao, with his highly political concept of feudalism and semi-colonialism, largely cut the tie between economic classes and counterrevolution. His overwhelming emphasis on organization and on voluntarism enabled him to identify counterrevolutionary forces primarily in terms of organizations whose leaders opposed the CCP's outlook. To remove the danger, then, Mao's immediate imperative was to destroy the counterrevolutionary's source of strength, that is, his *organization*.

In applying Mao's policies, the Communist leadership in Tientsin at first branded very few capitalists as counterrevolutionaries. Rather, they directed their fire primarily at organizations such as the quasi-religious societies and secret societies, which in the cities drew most of their members from the lower classes. The leaders of these groups were frequently poor men who had gained power by their wits and who bore only the most remote resemblance to either capitalists or landlords.

The need to gain information, the desire to destroy organizations without penalizing their members, and the limited resources available for these operations produced certain similarities in the CCP's approach to all counterrevolutionary organizations. Generally, the Party tried to divide the leadership of these organizations by adopting a policy in which "the most wicked ones must be dealt with, those who were forced to participate will not be tried, and those who earn merit will be rewarded."[6] Secret denunciations and selective violence marked every one of these operations. Usually, the organization was first declared illegal and its highest leaders ordered to register with the CCP authorities. This registration requirement had the tactical virtue of making criminals of all leaders who failed to comply. Simultaneously, official pronouncements explicitly divided this leadership into categories, so that a person's treatment depended on the category in which he was placed.

The authorities coupled the above announcements with inducements to elicit public and secret denunciations. Open denunciations invariably took place at meetings and rallies and were designed to give people in the audience the courage to stand up and make their own accusations. The more insidious secret denunciations encouraged betrayal of superiors by subordinates and also created an atmosphere of uncertainty for leaders who had no way of knowing whether or not they had been secretly attacked. A good record of denunciation, in turn, marked a person as an activist and brightened his prospects for future advancement.

Selective violence usually took the form of arrest and public execution of several top leaders in a counterrevolutionary organization. Violence performed the important function of showing wavering members that the Communists meant business. The authorities frequently combined this tactic with publicity about the lenient treatment given to those who had cooperated with the government.

As a final step, the authorities told the general membership of a counterrevolutionary organization about the heinous crimes that it was accused of having committed. This propaganda effort was often designed simply to communicate to the members that their organization had been banned and to elicit some type of pledge of future non-participation in its activities. Unless the outlawed organization served some vital need of its members, no more immediate effort vis-à-vis the members was required.

This was the CCP's general strategy to break up the organizations that came under its fire. Nevertheless, the particular strengths and weaknesses of some organizations required modifications to this basic approach, as the suppression of two major groups of organizations deemed counterrevolutionary during 1949—the Kuomintang and its related bodies, and the secret societies—illustrate.

The Kuomintang, the Blue Shirts,[7] the Three People's Principles Youth League, and their related organizations were the groups most clearly compromised after Tientsin's liberation by their association with the former regime. Because many of the highest members of the KMT civil and military structure had fled the city, the Communists arrested only 30 to 40 heads of the local party, government, and military apparatus as war criminals.[8] The process of dismembering the remaining KMT-affiliated organizations began immediately. The knowledge that just prior to liberation Tientsin's three major spy organizations—the KMT Communication Bureau (Tang-t'ung chü), the Nationalist Defense Department's State Secrets Bureau (Pao-mi chü), and the Defense Department's Second Office—had dispersed 2,600–2,700 special agents throughout the city increased the urgency of this task. In addition, approximately 20,000 KMT and Three People's Principles Youth League members remained in the city, along with an undetermined number of other KMT and League members and special agents who had earlier fled to Tientsin from other cities (primarily from Mukden, Ch'ang-ch'un, Tsinan, and Tangshan) and then found themselves trapped.[9]

On January 15, 1949, the Communists' Peiping-Tientsin Garrison Command issued the above-noted demand that "the KMT, San-ch'ing t'uan, and all other anti-Communist, anti-people organizations" must announce the liquidation of their organizations, stop all activities, register, and hand over their membership cards, telegraphs, and weapons. A follow-up document issued on February 23 specified the means by which this admonition should be carried out.* This "implementing" document stated that personnel above a certain level (varying with each organizational hierarchy) had to register within 20 days at the government organs stipulated therein. Each person, when registering, was to bring his ID card, turn in his KMT membership card, insignias, badges, weapons, codes, files, documents, property, lists of members, and holdings, explain the organizational relationships of the body, and tell all that he knew about his organization and its personnel. If the person reported quickly and admonished others to do the same, voluntarily denounced "reactionary" organizations about which he had information, and made other "special contributions" to the investigative work accompanying registration, he would be treated very leniently, left alone, or rewarded. If, however, he failed to comply in any or all of these respects, he would be liable for severe punishment.

The participants in these particular organizations were well aware of the vulnerability of their positions after liberation. Some chose to go into hiding and engage in anti-Communist activity; others tried to remain inconspicuous, hoping that their past affiliations could be kept secret; and still others determined to make a clean breast of things in hopes of being able to achieve a satisfactory position in the new society.

At this time of considerable uncertainty for the members of counterrevolutionary organizations, Tientsin's leaders promised safety and rewards to those who cooperated and threatened retribution against all who remained obstinate. "Cooperation" required betraying everyone whom one knew in the organization. These measures in theory applied only to the hierarchy of the

---

Cheng-ts'e fa-ling hui-pien (Tientsin, n.d.), pp. 3–4, 15–20. The latter document is also reprinted in Liu Shao-ch'i et al., *Hsin min-chu-chu-i ch'eng-shih cheng-ts'e* (Hong Kong, 1949), pp. 56–62. The CCP frequently proclaimed general principles governing a particular problem and then at a future date specified the means by which these principles should be realized.

outlawed organizations and not to the mass membership. But subsequent figures on the number of organization members who registered indicate that more than upper-level leaders were induced to register.

The authorities immediately began "registering" KMT party and Youth League members and special agents. Relying on denunciations and their own investigations, they arrested both those who refused to come forward and those who, after making a "false" registration, allegedly utilized their new "legal" position to carry out anti-Communist activities. By the end of 1949, a total of 1,455 special agents and 13,166 members of "reactionary parties" had registered. In addition, the police reported having uncovered and broken up seven of the KMT Party Communications Bureau's district-level branch departments, 13 spy "teams," 16 teams of the State Secrets Bureau, a "technical squad" of the KMT Defense Department's Second Office, and eight other lesser known spy organizations. They arrested 306 people in connection with these activities. The major special agents apprehended were put under "collective control and training" while the lesser figures were simply placed under the "supervision" of the local public security precinct station and the masses. By late 1949, the Tientsin police could announce that the threat from KMT spies and saboteurs had been very greatly reduced.[10]

During the course of 1950, the Tientsin authorities arrested 429 more of "America's and Chiang's" spies.[11] These people were the principals in 73 of the 167 counterrevolutionary cases that the public security organs resolved that year. In addition, during the same period, "All of the KMT, San-ch'ing t'uan, and special agent elements who absolutely refused to register and who continued without repentence to carry out counterrevolutionary activities were arrested." This latter group amounted to 307 people.* From 1949 through 1950, however, the public rec-

*CP, 1.ii.51, pp. 4–6. The authorities announced the arrests of 1,081 "counterrevolutionary elements" between Jan. 1950 and Feb. 1951; 521 were incarcerated during the final four months of this period, when tension mounted over the Korean War.

ord reveals relatively few executions of those former leaders of "reactionary parties" or KMT spy networks.*

Thus, the Communists tried to divide the leaders of the KMT and its related organizations against themselves in order to gain the information necessary to undermine these structures. The CCP did not suppress every former participant, and evidently only the most "dangerous" people suffered arrest and possible execution. The public record does not suggest that any significant attempt was made to mobilize the rank-and-file members of these organizations.

The secret societies, in contrast, presented the Communists with a very much more complex problem when, several months into 1949, the CCP decided to suppress them. The *pang-hui* provided most of their members with a livelihood and in many ways defined their social and political horizons. Any attempt at suppression, therefore, required initiatives toward the rank-and-file members as a supplement to the basic strategy of sowing division among the leadership hierarchy.

In the long run, Communist rule would inevitably prove incompatible with the continued existence of secret societies in Tientsin. The secret societies thrived on the needs of people living beyond the reach of the government in the lowest strata of urban society; the Communist revolution sought to integrate these strata effectively into the polity. Members of the secret societies defined their environment in terms of the *pang-hui*; the Communist program called for "education" leading to a broader class and national basis of identification and awareness. The secret-society leaders, who had a strong hold over a large segment of Tientsin's proletariat, would increasingly recognize the threat posed to their position by the Communist regime and would act according to their interests; the Communists' definition of security included the eventual necessity of disbanding all organized anti-revolutionary groups. It was certain, then, that at some point the Communists would attempt to undermine the power of the secret societies in Tientsin. What changed this

*During 1950, a total of 89 such executions were announced. *TC*, 28.ii.51.

from a long-run problem to an immediate necessity in the spring of 1949, however, was a basic economic fact—the secret societies controlled Tientsin's transport industry at a time when Liu Shao-ch'i had pushed economic recovery to the top of the agenda of the municipal authorities. The CCP's solution was to attack and destroy Tientsin's secret societies and to try to win the 60,000 workers in the transport industry over to the Communist side.

Three major constraints shaped the strategy for eradicating the secret societies in the transport industry. The overriding goal of rapid economic recovery required that disruption of the city's transport be held to a minimum; the acute shortage of reliable cadres necessitated using recruits from *within* Tientsin's transport industry itself; and a dearth of information about some 227 "turfs" and over 3,000 coolie bosses dictated a strategy that would yield this information in the course of the attack on the *pang-hui*. [12] These constraints prevented the police from simply arresting identifiable secret society leaders, since without these men the transport industry could not run smoothly. Moreover, the new regime lacked the skilled manpower to replace those former leaders and believed that their arrest might well hinder the collection of information necessary to identify all of the former coolie bosses.

The CCP adopted a two-pronged strategy to cope with this problem. It launched a frontal attack against the coolie associations to break them up as functioning organizations; and it tried to satisfy the various needs that the secret societies had served in order to win workers over and use them in the fight against the secret-society bosses. Two bodies were organized to spearhead this dual attack: a "freight company" to replace the coolie associations and a "transport workers' trade union" to organize the workers and respond to their needs.

The new authorities in Tientsin took some time to decide on a policy toward the coolie associations. During the interlude from January to March 1949, a sense of doubt and confusion prevailed within the transport industry. [13] Some workers were so unhappy with the high percentage of their income taken by the coolie bosses that they advocated waging struggles "to settle accounts" against them. They were encouraged in this effort by some of the more radical cadres assigned to the transport industry. Some of the coolie bosses, fearing such struggles, fled to Shanghai, Canton, and other cities, but most remained behind and attempted to keep their workers docile through such tactics as spreading rumors about an imminent Communist collapse and lending money to the workers to help them meet Lunar New Year expenses. Worker unrest was heightened at this time because from January to March 1949 no ships had entered the Tientsin ports.

In March 1949, the Communist leaders initiated a more unified strategy against the secret societies by preparing to create their own Freight Company to handle transport affairs. First, they established so-called "service stations" in the various wards under the auspices of the Transport Affairs Office of the Municipal Public Utilities Bureau. After 18 of these "service stations" had been set up by June 1949, nine coordinating bodies ("offices") were organized as liaisons between the service stations and the municipal government. The first two service stations appeared in March in the Nos. 2 and 10 wards, and the ballyhoo accompanying their opening later characterized the establishment of each subsequent service station. The cadres organized the coolies into troops and marched them down the dock (or through the turf) in a parade. Interspersed throughout these troops, the Communists beat drums, struck gongs, waved pictures of Mao Tse-tung, and shouted "Overthrow the coolie bosses!" This whole exercise was intended, in the words of a contemporary CCP report to "ostentatiously display the workers' powers of intimidation."[14] In reality, it seemed better designed to convince the workers that they in fact possessed such power, and it indicates that the CCP recognized the pivotal role of the psychology of power in the lives of the transport workers. The government also gave the service stations some economic leverage by granting them the exclusive right to handle all foodstuffs.[15] By June 1949 all 18 service stations had been established and the Transport Affairs Office was revamped into the Freight Company.[16]

In June–July 1949, having gained some experience in transport work, the authorities stepped up their attack and tried to destroy the coolie associations themselves. They accomplished this goal through a combination of several policies. The Freight Company itself became far more aggressive in seeking control over the freight business in the city. No longer content to handle merely the foodstuffs, it challenged the coolie associations' right to handle any aspect of the transport business. At the same time, the authorities began to organize the Tientsin Municipal Transport Trade Union, which sought to enroll every transport worker as a member.* The policy adopted toward the coolie bosses conformed to the basic strategy used against the hierarchies of the KMT and related organizations. The less important and more reasonable coolie bosses were told that they could join the ranks of labor, while the "small minority" of important coolie bosses, whose evil deeds were "glaringly evident" and who "had clearly incurred the enmity of the workers," came under strong attack. This policy was first communicated to the relevant trade union cadres at a Municipal Transport Trade Union Cadres Conference on June 17, 1949.[17]

Following the cadres' conference on June 17, a Workers' Representative Conference was held June 25–28 and attended by 372 dock workers, freight haulers, railroad cargo handlers, pedicab drivers, and water and nightsoil carriers. The selection of representatives to the conference was somewhat marred by the fact that a number of workers had mistakenly believed that to be selected meant that one would be conscripted, sent south, stripped of his job, and so forth. Evidently the only ones who really tried (successfully, it turns out) to attend were the coolie bosses anxious to gain a toehold in the new organization.

In spite of this problem, the conference marked a fairly suc-

---

*Actually, separate trade unions were established for dock workers, freight haulers, railroad cargo handlers, pedicab and ricksha coolies, and water and nightsoil carriers. These diverse trade unions were then federated at the municipal level into the Transport Workers' Trade Union, which was in turn one of the units belonging to the Municipal Trade Union Council. Most relevant policy planning seems to have taken place at the level of the Transport Workers' Trade Union, although there were major differences in the problems that confronted some of its subordinate unions.

cessful beginning to the mobilization of workers in a transport trade union. Its goals were to tell the delegates about the trade union and to convince them that the workers as a body could be stronger than the coolie bosses. According to subsequent CCP assessment, the conference generally achieved these goals. The workers were reportedly very pleased that the new government thought enough of them to convene such a meeting, and they left the conference with high enthusiasm for establishing the trade union. The conference set up preparatory committees for each of the trades represented. It failed, however, to convince the representatives of the harmful effects of their narrowly particularistic secret-society mentality, largely because the Communist cadres monopolized the discussions and selected themselves to serve on the preparatory committees in order to gain a solid foothold in the new trade union. These cadres apparently feared that they themselves might otherwise be tapped to go south.[18]

The participants in the conference spent the first 10 days of July convening meetings of workers' representatives, workers, and activists, using these forums to explain the new trade union's nature, tasks, membership conditions, procedures, and rights of membership. This effort generally achieved good results. Workers in the transport trade were at the bottom of the social ladder, and they readily accepted their characterization as exploited underdogs and showed considerable enthusiasm for organizing the trade union. However, they were also very mobile and scattered, and communicating the message to them in a meaningful way presented great problems.

On July 10, recruitment to the trade union began. A strong propaganda thrust against the coolie bosses formed an integral part of this recruitment campaign. After some experimentation, the basic recommended method became to convene a meeting of transport workers in a given locale and explain to them the nature of the trade union and why membership would benefit them, then, directly after the meeting *and before the crowd had dispersed,* to invite the workers to apply to join the union.

By the end of July 1949, 20,222 transport workers (31 percent

TABLE 2. *Transport Trade Union Membership in Tientsin, July–November 1949*
(Percent of eligible workers in union)

Category of worker	July 30	Aug. 28	Sept. 30	Oct. 28	Nov.
Freight	25.0%	37.6%	45.4%	92.4%[a]	92.4%
Dock	28.4	47.2	n.a.	90.6	n.a.
Railroad	61.4	76.5	n.a.	95.5	n.a.
Pedicab	28.7	55.5	n.a.	63.3	n.a.
Nightsoil	38.1	44.8	n.a.	n.a.	n.a.
T'ang-ta	80.5	83.9	n.a.	96.8	n.a.
All workers	31.4%	49.6%	n.a.	n.a.	75.5%

SOURCE: For July 30, *PKKKTT,* p. 59. For Aug. 28, *ibid.,* p. 65. For Sept. 30, *ibid.,* p. 86. For Oct. 28, An Li-fu, p. 14. For November, *PKKKTT,* p. 105.

[a]This percentage is inexplicably based on a total figure of 11,824 freight workers. The earlier percentages for freight workers are based on a total figure of 25,000 eligible workers. If this larger base is used, the percentage figure for freight workers for October 1949 would be 44%. The 25,000 figure for the number of freight workers has been used in several sources (*PKKKTT,* pp. 52, 59, 65), while the 11,824 figure appears only in An Li-fu, p. 14. The three references to the 25,000 figure in *PKKKTT* were made by different authors at different times.

of the total number) had applied for membership in the union. (See Table 2.) The lower rate of development after July 1949 resulted from the following factors: most of the workers who regularly worked at a given place were already recruited, and the remaining workers were scattered about; the scattered workers had received less information about the trade union and were therefore less willing to join it; and finally the CCP's emphasis changed to consolidation, rather than expansion, of the trade union organization.

How did the transport workers view the trade union, and why did they join it? Mistaken ideas evidently ran rampant, and these in turn cast some doubt on the significance of the trade union membership figures recorded. Some workers believed that joining the trade union obligated them to pay high fees and do extra work; others felt that trade union membership guaranteed them a job and protected them against other people trying to take advantage of them; in the eyes of a few, registering a vehicle with the government *ipso facto* made the driver a trade union member; and many assumed that simply participating in one of the Freight Company's service stations meant that one had joined the trade union.[19] Thus, the members' understanding of the trade union was limited, at best.

The Municipal Public Security Bureau participated fully in the attack on the coolie associations. This was a prudent measure for the Communists to adopt because most workers believed that might made right. Public Security Bureau Chief Hsu Chienkuo set up a tripartite committee with the leaders of the Transport Trade Union and the Freight Company to coordinate strategy on a day-to-day basis. Public Security cadres made their presence felt by attending all meetings of the transport workers. Similarly, police accompanied the cadres from the pedicab and freight trade unions on rounds of inspection of the transport network. In this way, the transport workers were encouraged to identify the power of the Public Security Bureau with the authority of the Freight Company and the Transport Trade Union.

The Public Security Bureau combined this support for the Freight Company and Transport Trade Union with direct suppression of the coolie bosses. It convened meetings of the coolie bosses, at which Public Security officials explained government policy, declared past activities of the coolie bosses illegal, and warned the coolie bosses against carrying out any more unlawful actions. Following these meetings, in the words of a subsequent CCP report, the Public Security Bureau "used administrative power to bring the coolie bosses under control and severely attacked their activities." All of this, according to the official account, strengthened the "resolve" of the masses and undermined the "awe-inspiring reputation" of the coolie bosses. The authorities concluded that bringing the Public Security Bureau into visible play had been "the most important condition for doing well the work in transport."[20]

The coolie bosses, of course, did not give up without a fight, and the resources they could bring to bear, including intimate knowledge of local conditions, authority among the workers, an excellent network of "connections" throughout the city, and a great deal of past experience in dealing with intrusions from officials, assured that they would not be an easy match. In early July 1949, they launched a counterattack, which assumed a variety of forms. An important component consisted simply of flexing their muscles within the various turfs. One of the ways in which the workers had traditionally been chosen to participate in "rumbles" over turfs was by drawing lots, called "death lots." Those who drew the lots joined the "Dare to Die Corps" and formed the pool of those expected to fight to the death if necessary to protect the interests of the coolie association.[21] The coolie bosses now ordered the workers in the Dare to Die Corps to wreck the Freight Company and Trade Union organizational activities. These workers attacked the people who joined the new organizations, beat up and intimidated the cadres, and undertook sometimes bizarre and dramatic measures to break up meetings when they were convened—in at least one case even going so far as to lob several hand grenades into the meeting hall.

More subtle measures were also employed. The coolie associations launched a price war against the Freight Company. Coolie bosses took advantage of their connections with municipal civil servants held over from the pre-1949 period to distort information and confuse the government's plans from within. They even sent a delegation to Peking to initiate a formal lawsuit before the North China People's Government against the transport workers, alleging that the workers were illegally dividing up the property of the coolie bosses. All of these measures, however, seemed to achieve only limited success. The Freight Company joined in the price war and used its superior (municipal government) resources to undercut the coolie associations' transport rates. The Tientsin authorities got wind of the lawsuit and informed the North China People's Government of the "true" situation in the nick of time. Recruitment to the new organizations continued despite the intimidation by the agents of the coolie bosses. By the end of July, it was clear that the coolie associations were doomed.

A final strategy adopted by many of the coolie bosses, however, proved effective where their other tactics had failed. This last-ditch stratagem had the coolie bosses put on old clothes, eat simple food, and then demand to join the Trade Union as common workers. The real binding force among the transport workers was the secret-society tie, and not the organizational link of the coolie associations. If they could only remain on the local scene, then, the coolie bosses felt they would have a good chance of regaining their power under the guise of new organizational forms.[22] Nevertheless, this final tactic also bore mute testimony to the fact that the old coolie associations, as such, had lost their power.

Having demolished the coolie associations, the Communist cadres tried to develop and consolidate the Transport Trade Union and the Freight Company. This meant increasing union membership and enlarging the Freight Company's share of total transport work in the city. The relevant tasks consisted of changing the size of the basic units, recruiting new cadres from among the workers, and purifying the ranks of the organizations. Beyond these common tasks, each body engaged in some specialized activities. The Trade Union concentrated on questions of education and welfare, and the Freight Company dealt with price structure reform in the transport industry.

The Trade Union membership drive proceeded smoothly. By December, three-quarters of all transport workers belonged to the union; for the freight, dock, and railroad workers alone, the comparable figure reached over 90 percent.[23]

With no competition from the defunct coolie associations, it was a relatively simple matter for the Freight Company to develop to the point where it managed almost all of Tientsin's transport work. Consolidation, not expansion, soon formed the problem area for both the Freight Company and Transport Trade Union. Since the former coolie associations had clear territorial bases, moreover, both bodies considered changing the size of their basic units as a necessary and integral part of their efforts to strengthen themselves. This work proceeded in phases in the Trade Union but was telescoped into one campaign in the Freight Company.

Consolidation

The Trade Union began to establish "branches" and subordinate "teams" in August 1949, *taking care that each branch transcended the boundaries of the former turfs* (no information is available on the organizational basis of the teams). The largest of the new branch units had a membership of 350, the smallest 200.[24] The former coolie associations had varied in size from 275 to 9 members.[25] A committee of 9–11 people headed each of the new branches. Elections to these committees, with constituencies cutting across previous turf boundaries, were supposed to help break down the "turf mentality" of the coolies. These expectations about the elections, however, proved more a hope than a reality.[26]

Having set up the branches and teams, the Trade Union concentrated in September and October on providing training for the new cadres who were being recruited from among the ranks of the transport workers. It convened two training classes, the first from September 28 to October 13, and the second from October 7 to October 18. Some 200 people attended the first class, and 300 attended the second. All of the participants were either activists or members of the Trade Union branch committees, and they formed the backbone of the cadre force in the transport industry for the remainder of 1949.

Official reports on these two training classes, however, indicate that by late September the Trade Union was still largely a paper organization. Little contact occurred between the union and its members, and most workers had only a poor conception of the nature of the union. Even the activists and committee members attending the training classes had only hazy notions about the CCP. For instance, they generally did not know that the workers were supposed to be the leading element in the CCP, nor did they know about the Party's program. Their awareness of the difference between the CCP and the KMT was limited to a recognition that working conditions after liberation were slightly better than they had been before. The workers even remained unsure why the CCP had fought against the

KMT in the civil war. Within this context, the training classes made some headway. As one activist commented after the class: "Now it is clear. Formerly I could only mouth the words 'petit bourgeoisie,' but I could not elaborate any further. The way things were explained in this course was really pretty fine!" But not all of the participants emerged with a proper perspective. Some reported that "having been through the training class, my position in the trade union is consolidated! . . . This is like acquiring an insurance policy." Nevertheless, the cadres who conducted these training classes felt that the general results of the classes had been satisfactory, and that they now had a core of locally recruited workers who could effectively carry out a campaign to consolidate the new basic-level units of the trade union.[27]

The consolidation effort, which began in November, employed intensive criticism and self-criticism within the new basic-level units; put pressure on members to utilize their powers of election and recall to clean "bad elements" out of the lower ranks of the Trade Union hierarchy; and provided new union membership cards as an excuse for reviewing each person's credentials and weeding out the undesirables. Two basic principles of the campaign were local leadership, and "curing the illness to save the patient." The first was necessary because only local workers knew the specific situation well enough to carry out a thorough rectification of the ranks of the new union branches and teams. The second principle attested to the continuing shortage of skilled cadres among the transport workers and the attendant need to reform all of the former bosses who could be reformed in order to make use of their scarce skills. The union leaders hoped to rectify the basic levels of the Trade Union and to foster a sense of group identity (through shared experience in criticism and self-criticism) among the members of the new branches.[28]

The Freight Company tried to expand the size of its basic-level units and remove former coolie bosses from these units through a single campaign. The "democratic reorganization of crews,"* as the campaign was called, employed principles analogous to those of the Trade Union campaign. The Communists began this campaign by organizing activist workers into "evaluation teams."[29] These teams, a few of which were established in each city ward, carried out a systematic evaluation of the crews under their jurisdiction to determine what cliques and organizations existed, who held power in each, what sorts of corruption had occurred, and so forth. Each evaluation team consisted solely of workers from the given trade and area.

Once this initial investigation was completed, the evaluation team convened meetings in each crew to denounce secret-society leaders and persuade the workers to accept the changes in the size of the basic units that the evaluators themselves announced. To help build a new sense of group identity and to render even more meaningless the former turf boundaries, the Freight Company immediately began assigning workers to jobs on the basis of the new, larger units.

Thus, during August–December 1949, both the Transport Trade Union and the Freight Company adopted similar strategies that clearly recognized the important link between the geographical identity and the social and economic functions of the former coolie associations. In their specifics, these strategies also reflected both the CCP's continuing dearth of information on the leadership of the former coolie associations and its shortage of skilled cadres in the transport industry.

While supplanting the coolie associations as organizational units, the Trade Union and the Freight Company also sought to fulfill the various social functions that they had performed. The "education" program of the Trade Union began in August 1949. It had two main objectives: to introduce the concept of class relations and show how "reactionary," "feudal" organizations like the secret societies blurred class lines; and to foster among the transport workers a sense of self-esteem that would in turn increase their sense of honesty and integrity on the job. The first

*The "crew" was the term for the basic work unit in the transport industry.

of these objectives was particularly important, for it meant nothing less than raising the horizons of the transport workers beyond their self-enclosed universe at the bottom of Tientsin's society and making them think in terms of the larger community. To the extent that this effort was successful, it represented a fundamentally new level of social awareness among the city's secret-society members.

Because of the transport workers' low literacy rate* and their extraordinary geographic mobility, the Trade Union propagandists had to utilize every propaganda forum they could devise in order to reach them. They established study groups and newspaper reading groups; set up radio speakers and made special broadcasts; organized cultural and recreational activities (singing groups, *yang-ko* dance troupes); published a simple newspaper called the *Pan-yun kung-jen* (*Transport Worker*); encouraged blackboard newspapers; convened "classes" on street corners, at warehouse entrances, aboard ships, and in railroad stations; set up three-to-five-man mutual aid teams; and held meetings of "model" workers and teams. All this was conducted according to the principle of the "three un-fixes": no fixed time, no fixed place, and no fixed number of people.[30]

The Transport Trade Union also attempted to replace the economic security functions of the secret societies through welfare benefits and a rudimentary insurance program for former coolie association workers. The welfare program entailed organizing a wide range of cooperatives that would considerably reduce the workers' cost of living. These included cafeterias, small sanatoria, coal ball factories, soap factories, food markets, and schools for siblings and offspring. In addition, the Trade Union arranged for its members to have reduced prices for haircuts, baths, the cinema, and plays.

As a form of insurance, the Trade Union developed a mutual

*A chart of rates of literacy of Tientsin transport workers is presented in *PKKKTT,* p. 45. According to this chart, 64 percent of the freight haulers and 86 percent of the dock workers were totally illiterate, and an additional 19 percent of the freight haulers and 9 percent of the dock workers could recognize only a few characters.

assistance system that provided help in case of death or injury. The union also collected a small sum of money to assist with burial and medical expenses, and in addition contributed some of its own funds to these expenses.

In sum, during the last half of 1949 the Transport Trade Union tried to remove the psychological and physical props that had kept the transport workers dependent on the secret societies. It hoped that these initiatives, combined with the organizational measures discussed above, would deal a decisive blow to the secret societies' hold over their members and over the transport industry in Tientsin.

The purpose of the Freight Company was to enable the municipal government to take over the transport industry and keep this sector running smoothly even in the absence of the traditional coolie associations. As an important part of this effort, the Freight Company drastically reduced the rates for transporting various types of goods within the city. Previously, the coolie bosses had kept a percentage of the transport fees, sometimes 70 percent or more, and had frequently extorted additional sums from the various merchants for "protection" or "faster service." The Freight Company leaders reasoned that, since these sources of exploitation and corruption had now been abolished, it should be possible to lower transport rates substantially while still raising the level of take-home pay for the transport workers. The Freight Company itself took only 5 percent of the gross income to meet business expenses.

The Freight Company tried to standardize transport charges throughout the city on the basis of this lowered price structure. To maintain the integrity of the new unified price schedule the Company instituted a so-called three list system. This system required the merchant, the Freight Company, and the transport workers to sign each order before any money changed hands. The order itself had to specify clearly the quantity of goods, the shipping cost, addresses for pick-up and delivery, and the people through whose hands the goods should pass. By ensuring that at least the merchant and a Freight Company official knew and agreed upon the charge for any given transaction, the system provided safeguards for the unbiased implementation of the new, standardized rate structure.[31]

By the end of 1949, the Communists in Tientsin felt that they had effectively destroyed the hold of the secret societies over the transport industry. They had been flexible, dealing with the coolie bosses very much according to the basic model for counterrevolutionary organizations, while at the same time developing special programs to provide for the continued operation of the transport industry. With respect to the transport workers, they had taken seemingly effective measures to deal with job security, status considerations, fears about temporary disability, and the whole question of coercion in daily life. Although the need for the coolie bosses' continued active cooperation had forced the authorities to treat them leniently, reports filtering up the Trade Union and Freight Company hierarchies at the end of the year indicated that all was proceeding smoothly in the transport industry. Indeed, the authorities publicized Tientsin's work in this area as a model for cadres in other cities to follow.[32]

During the early months of 1950, however, scattered but disquieting signs began to appear indicating that something was amiss in the Tientsin transport industry. Some merchants complained that they were still being fleeced by the people handling the freight business.[33] A few of the CCP's cadres who held responsibility in this area did not seem to act with their customary aggressiveness. These hints prompted investigations, and by June the answer was clear: the secret societies had succeeded in taking over the local-level organs of both the Transport Trade Union and the Freight Company.

The response of the authorities was both swift and dramatic. Without prior warning, on June 19 seven of the most important leaders of the former coolie associations were arrested. Within several days, the newspapers announced the arrest of another 17 secret-society leaders, 10 of whom had served as coolie bosses, including Wang Chin-ts'ai, the reputed leader of the Ch'ing-pang in Tientsin.[34] At the same time, all former coolie bosses were ordered to register with the Municipal Public Security Bureau.[35] This registration undoubtedly required each coolie boss to disclose all he knew about the membership, history, finances, and general operations of the secret societies. The Public Security Bureau promised leniency to all who registered voluntarily and severe punishment for all who tried to avoid registration. Meanwhile, all transport workers in the city attended meetings at which they were mobilized to support the arrests and to denounce the hidden coolie bosses among their ranks.[36]

These actions reflected a concentrated campaign by the Tientsin authorities to root out the former coolie bosses from the transport industry. What had gone wrong with the strategy pursued from 1949 to early 1950? Hsu Chien-kuo outlined the answer in a radio broadcast of June 23. Hsu made three major points: first, that the former coolie bosses had used their secret society ties with the workers to circumvent the authorities' efforts; second, that all merchants and other citizens should report any continued secret-society activity they encountered; and third, that the Public Security Bureau would henceforth give effective protection to anyone who cooperated in providing information about the continued functioning of the secret societies.[37]

In retrospect, it is not difficult to see the weaknesses of the CCP's approach to the Tientsin transport industry. The authorities' shortage of cadres, combined with their belief that major changes required an intimate knowledge of the local area, dictated a reliance on activists from among the local workers to carry out the reorganization of the transport industry at the grassroots level. Whether in rectifying the ranks of the basic-level units, carrying out propaganda among the coolies, or enforcing the "three list" price system, it was the locally recruited activists staffing the lower levels of the Trade Union and the Freight Company who implemented policy. Upper levels knew the results of these policy initiatives almost solely from the reports made by lower-level activists. In addition, the authorities had made it clear that even when a coolie boss was identified, he would be permitted to continue to work in his former locale, the only change being that he would no longer hold a position of authority. This policy of breaking up the coolie associations and forcing the former coolie bosses to participate in manual labor proved to be a mistake, for it enabled the coolie bosses to remain in full view and to continue to use their secret-society connections to intimidate all workers who honestly sided with the government's policy. The fact that the former coolie bosses remained free even after the visible Public Security Bureau attack on them in June–July 1949 was sufficient to indicate to many workers that the power of the secret societies was still not something to dismiss lightly. Within this context, the *pang-hui* leaders in transport easily persuaded the workers to elect them to leadership positions in the basic-level units of the Trade Union and Freight Company. Having attained these positions, the *pang-hui* leaders were able to exercise considerable control over the information that higher levels received because they were themselves writing the reports that the higher-level authorities read.

The fundamental problem, then, was the municipal authorities' inability to penetrate the world of the transport worker with outside cadres and the consequent impossibility of monitoring the situation at the basic level over a period of time. To the average coolie, little had changed. After only a brief hiatus, the former coolie bosses again held the responsible positions. Beneath the new organizational boundaries, the old turf demarcations had reasserted themselves. The local policeman was the same man who had been on the beat before 1949, and he had long ago established a working relationship with the local secret-society leaders.[38] The small merchant had learned before 1949 that making a fuss over a grievance to higher levels of the government simply invited trouble, and nothing had happened since liberation to make him feel that anything had changed in this respect.[39] In a part of society where the first law of survival was that might made right, the CCP had failed to demonstrate the prudence of standing on the side of the new government in Tientsin.

After July 1950, the Tientsin press contains no concrete information on the campaign to suppress secret societies in the trans-

port industry.* During the Suppression of Counterrevolutionaries Campaign in the spring of 1951, the Communists publicly
executed a number of people whom they identified as former
coolie association heads and secret-society leaders.[40] It seems
reasonable to speculate that this campaign marked the last
phase of the CCP's efforts to eradicate the secret-society leadership in Tientsin, although the influence of the secret-society
mentality undoubtedly lingered on in the minds of many for a
long time.

Through the suppression of counterrevolutionary organizations the CCP secured its ability to rule in Tientsin during 1949–
50. The actions against the KMT and related organizations
greatly reduced the threat of anti-Communist armed attacks and
sabotage. The suppression of the secret societies gave the new
regime control over the city's transport industry and at the same
time broke up perhaps the strongest of the non-Communist
organized groups in the city. This repression had to be sharply
focused and handled somewhat gingerly, lest it undercut the
priority goals that Liu Shao-ch'i had specified. Indeed, the government's most important concern was to achieve these goals,
and it is to this effort that we now turn.

---

*The few subsequent articles on the transport system assumed that the secret
societies had been effectively suppressed but gave no indication of how this had
been accomplished. See, for instance, *CP*, 25.v.51, p. 2. Subsequent general reviews of the situation in the transport industry in other cities likewise cast little
light on this subject. See, for example, *Chung-kuo kung-jen*, 8 (Sept. 1950), pp.
66–67, and 10 (Nov. 1950), pp. 14–18.

CHAPTER 5 *Economic Measures*

The years 1950–51 witnessed a steady effort by Tientsin's Communist leaders to acquire resources that would increase their ability to control events in the city. Their program followed Liu Shao-ch'i's admonition that they concentrate first on the modern sector of Tientsin's society and then gradually penetrate the more traditional sphere. Although Liu had outlined this strategy in 1949, three major national events shaped the implementation of that strategy during 1950–51. These were the national unification of finances and the related "readjustment of industry and commerce" in the spring and summer of 1950; the Korean War, which began in June 1950 and drew China in as a combatant in late October of that year; and the Suppression of Counterrevolutionaries Campaign of the spring of 1951. Each of these events affected the options available to the Tientsin leaders during 1950 and 1951.

This chapter analyzes the first of these events and focuses, therefore, on the relatively prosaic topics of price indexes, economic contracts, organizational development, and the gradual accumulation of resources by the Communists. These dimensions of revolution are often slighted by scholars because they lack the drama and tensions usually associated with revolutionary change. In reality, however, the drastic political campaigns described in later chapters of this volume would unquestionably have failed without the foundation established by the economic measures discussed below. The processes analyzed are thus central to any understanding of the means by which the Chinese Communist Party transformed a military conquest into a social revolution in the city of Tientsin.

T A B L E 3. *Tientsin Municipal Tax Revenues, 1949–1951*

Category	1949	1950	1951
Expected tax revenues[a]	n.a.	780	2,311
Actual tax revenues[a]	578	1,568	2,750[b]
Increase of actual revenues over previous year *(percent)*	—	171.34%	75.41%
MPG tax revenues given to the center *(percent)*	69.89%	78%	ca.87%

SOURCES: *CP,* 16.ii.50, p. 4, 1.ii.51, p. 4, 28.ii.51, p. 2, 29.xii.51, p. 4.
[a] In million *chin* of millet.
[b] Calculated on the assumption that the tax revenues for October through December came in at the same rate as those for January through September.

The Communist government greatly strengthened its position in the city during 1950–51, as indicated by (among other things) its rapidly increasing tax collections. The improvement in Tientsin's economy accounted for a part of this growth in tax receipts, although the MPG's better tax collection machinery and its ability to make businessmen take tax demands more seriously were also important. Tax evasion had been almost universal in Tientsin at the time of liberation. Virtually every business large enough to be concerned about taxes kept two sets of books, and most firms viewed the government's tax laws simply as a statement of the authorities' opening bargaining position. Indeed, these attitudes and practices were so widespread that many foreign firms in Tientsin suffered excessive taxation during 1949 simply because the Communists would not believe that they did not also keep two sets of books.[1] Gradually, however, the government increased its ability to extract funds from the city's business community. In both 1950 and 1951, the MPG collected more tax revenue than it had anticipated at the beginning of the year, and more than it had collected the year before. Table 3 presents the details of the amounts anticipated and collected by the MPG. This table excludes items such as customs duties and the salt tax, which were collected directly by the central government,[2] income derived from the sale of bonds, and other types of solicited contributions that were not part of the regular tax system.[3] Table 3 reveals not only the increasing ability of the MPG to levy and collect taxes, but also the greater capacity of the national authorities to command the lion's share of Tientsin's tax revenues. This latter phenomenon reflected in part the regularization of bureaucratic procedures after the establishment of the national government in October 1949. As the bureaucracy at the Center became more settled, it was better able to impose demands on the local governments in various parts of the country. In addition, it is possible that Tientsin's proximity to Peking increased its vulnerability to these demands for funds.* The increased share of Tientsin's tax funds that went to the Central People's Government also reflects a major policy initiative taken by the CPG in the spring of 1950–the centralization of finance for the entire country.

On March 3, 1950, the Government Administrative Council issued a set of regulations that required all local governments to hand over their revenues directly to the CPG and spend themselves only what the CPG allotted them.† These regulations also contained stringent provisions to hold down the amount of cash in circulation by requiring that government, military, and mass organizations deposit all but a small amount of their petty cash in the People's Bank. By promulgating these regulations, Peking wished to give the CPG greater control over income and expenditures, to ensure that the CPG be able to support the front line in the ongoing civil war, and to reduce inflationary pressures by directly withdrawing cash from circulation and by undercutting the local governments' power to spend money.[4] Tientsin had suffered from rampant inflation during January–March 1950, with the MPG's price index based on 42 major commodities jumping 100 percent during these three months.[5] The unification of finances doused the inflationary fires, but almost immediately posed a new problem for the municipal leaders—how to

---

*This, however, is speculation. One could also argue that Tientsin's proximity to Peking enabled it to present and defend its interests more effectively. The empirical evidence to test these hypotheses is lacking.

†However, local governments were permitted to supplement the amount allotted to them by the CPG by imposing surtaxes, special levies, and so forth. But they could do this only after they had met their CPG tax obligation.

cope with the sharp recession that this dramatic policy initiative from Peking produced.

Why did the national unification of finances throw Tientsin into a recession? Immediately after liberation, the trade channels from Tientsin to the surrounding rural areas had been opened up for the first time in over a year. Because these rural areas had been starved for manufactured items, a robust demand for such goods quickly developed, and many of Tientsin's businesses rapidly expanded. During the following months, however, a spring drought and summer floods in North China caused major losses to the fall harvest, and as a consequence, peasant purchasing power declined more rapidly than expected. By the winter of 1949–50 it had become clear that many Tientsin businesses were overproducing. To this situation the CPG's finance measures introduced the problem of a liquidity crisis, which caused declining investment, decreasing demand, and plummeting prices. The fall of prices in turn made hoarding materials, previously a profitable activity in the inflation-prone Tientsin economy, a losing proposition, with the result that many businessmen quickly dumped their hoarded goods on the market in an attempt to cut their losses. This flooding of the market depressed prices further, so that the overall price index in Tientsin fell by almost 25 percent during April–May alone. These falling prices cut into profits and made it very difficult for many enterprises to repay loans taken out earlier at the high interest rates appropriate to an inflationary economy. A major recession resulted, with numerous businesses closing and many people thrown out of work. This crisis peaked in late May and did not end completely until August–September.[6]

The spring recession in Tientsin hit the private sector hardest. The publicly-run enterprises continued to have sufficient investment capital and were not burdened with debts based on high interest rates. While their sales and profits temporarily fell off, they had the resources of the government available to tide them over the difficult period. In the private sector, however, the recession undermined many firms, and in some cases entire trades. The Communist authorities took full advantage of this situation to increase the leverage of the public sector over the various private firms through a program called "readjusting industry and commerce," which began in May 1950.[7]

Before the government developed an integrated approach to the burgeoning crisis in the economy, the Tientsin leadership had assisted some of the firms in the private sector that were deemed important for the national economy by asking the relevant trade unions to persuade workers to make concessions. These concessions included voluntary leaves of absence during which the workers returned to their villages in the countryside and agreements to work longer hours at less pay. The MPG official position at this time stated that the current difficulties were an unavoidable reflection of the transition from an inflationary and war-torn economy to a healthy economy, and that the private industrialists and merchants should not shoulder the blame for the temporary problems being encountered. Thus, except for such luxury trades as the perfume industry, which the Communists were perfectly happy to see fade away, the government generally urged the workers to cooperate with the capitalists who wanted to contract their business and lay off people during this period.[8] Consequently, many capitalists began to see the trade unions as possibly beneficial to their own interests and accepted more readily their organization in the private factories.

The growth in trade union membership during June–December 1949 had been extremely impressive, and was caused largely by the wholesale recruitment of workers in the public enterprises and in the largest private firms. By early 1950, however, trade union growth had begun to slow down, averaging only 4,695 new members per month from January to March. Following the use of trade unions to persuade the workers to help the capitalists survive the recession, however, trade union growth quickly shot up to 8,089 per month and remained at that level for the rest of 1950. By the end of that year, Tientsin's trade unions had 285,000 members, 67 percent of the eligible labor force.[9]

These scattered measures to help the economy recover were

welded into a more coherent program in May 1950, at the height of the recession. The program stressed reforms in four areas: management and production within enterprises; relations between firms in the public and private sectors; production and marketing relations; and urban-rural relations. In most cases, specific elements of this program existed before the 1950 recession, and the May initiative simply accelerated policies already on the agenda. Overall, the program significantly enhanced the relative power of the public sector in Tientsin's economy.

That there was an undeniable need for management reform is illustrated by this description of the situation in the Tientsin and Shanghai cotton mills around 1930:

The whole system of management among Chinese owned mills is polluted by ignorance, favoritism, and squeeze. . . . The whole plant, worth millions of dollars, may be entrusted to a manager who knows nothing about spinning. The latter, usually the trusted appointee of the most influential stockholder, frequently has neither a grasp of the technical complexity of spinning and weaving, nor a knowledge of cost accounting, financing, and marketing. Instead, he delegates his duties to the subordinates, and relies upon the good turn of luck for the mill's profits. In such a mill, the head of the spinning or weaving department, oftentimes a close friend or relative of the manager or the stockholder, considers his job as the source of squeeze, but delegates his duties in turn to one of the foremen, who, although skilled in mechanics, lacks scientific training. Consequently, machinery is not well kept and is not running in an efficient order. Laborers are not well selected and trained, but recruited under the notorious contract system. The finished products deteriorate in quality, while their cost mounts higher and higher.[10]

Other accounts of pre-1949 management systems within large enterprises corroborate this description.[11] The Tientsin Communist leaders used the leverage they had gained in the recession to pressure the factory owners to reform their management and production techniques in order to increase productivity. They later took advantage of this reform process itself to expand and consolidate the power of the regime over the various enterprises concerned. Although roughly similar processes occurred in both the public and the private firms, it was in the private sector that these measures had the most direct effect on the extension of the CCP's power within Tientsin's society.

The typical pattern for the reform of a private enterprise consisted of, in this order: establishing at least a skeletal trade union organization; forming a labor-capital consultative body in which workers were represented by trade union cadres; signing various types of temporary agreements covering working conditions, promised levels of output, and other areas of concern to labor and capital in the firm; organizing production competition campaigns with the stated objectives of increasing productivity in the factory; and making changes in the wage, management, and technical production systems to eliminate the weaknesses that had been revealed by the production competition campaigns. Because the trade union represented workers in all of these transactions and itself assumed full responsibility for organizing and carrying out the production competition campaigns, this process inevitably led to the expansion of the role and consolidation of the position of the trade union within the enterprise concerned. The Communists, in turn, controlled the trade union organization.

Several of Tientsin's largest private firms, such as the Peiyang Mills, had begun organizing labor-capital consultative organs as early as November 1949,[12] but this movement did not spread to many other firms until the spring 1950 recession. Under the pressures of the recession, however, some 70 enterprises, two-thirds of them industrial, had established this type of body by mid-May.[13] The number of firms with labor-capital consultative organs climbed to over 100 as of mid-July,[14] and stood at 122 at the end of 1950.[15] Most of these organs assumed the title Labor-Capital Consultative Conference (LCCC).

A trade union effort to sign a wide range of "provisional agreements" with the factory owners accompanied the formation of these consultative bodies. These agreements, usually dealing with problems of immediate concern, were in force for very short terms, often less than three weeks. By negotiating and implementing these provisional agreements, the various trade union organizations both further secured their position

with the capitalists and became more familiar with the production process itself. In spring 1950, when the number of problems
in Tientsin's firms soared, the trade unions in over 700 private
firms managed to negotiate some type of provisional agreement
with the owners.[16]

Production competitions in private enterprises lagged considerably behind the formation of LCCCs because a production
competition generally required a fairly developed trade union
organization and a reasonably good working relationship between the trade union and the factory management. The first
two private enterprises held production competitions in March
1950,[17] 30 carried out such competitions in the early fall,[18] and
over 60 private enterprises engaged in production competitions
by the end of the year.* During 1951, the number of private
firms carrying out production competitions rose to 407.[19] These
production competitions usually occurred first in the largest,
most modern private enterprises, reflecting the Tientsin Communists' concentration on these firms. The two private firms involved in the March 1950 production competition were, for example, two of the largest private enterprises in the city: the
Peiyang and Hengyuan textile companies.[20] The 30 firms carrying out production competitions in the early fall employed a total of 2,200 workers, an average of some 73 per firm.[21] The 407
private enterprises carrying out production competitions in 1951
employed a total of over 27,000 people, an average of about 66
per firm.† Thus, the production competitions in Tientsin's private sector began in the largest firms and spread to smaller
firms. By the end of 1951, the competitions were still held in

---

*TC, 1.i.51. Reflecting the difference in degree of trade union development in
the public versus private enterprises, the figures on production competitions in
the public enterprises during 1950 show that these competitions occurred in
three waves: the first wave (Jan.–March) involved 72 factories with over 60,000
employees (CP, 19.vi.50, p. 2); the second wave (May–July) involved 107 factories and over 90,000 people (CP, 21.ix.50), p. 2; TC, 16.x.50, pp. 1–2, 19.ii.51, p.
2); and the final wave (in the fall) involved 60,000 staff and workers (TC, 1.i.51,
p. 1).

†CP, 21.i.52, p. 3. Since this figure almost certainly included all of the larger
firms engaged in production competitions both in 1950 and in 1951, the average
size of private firms engaging in production competitions for the *first* time in
1951 was probably in fact slightly smaller than 66 employees.

fewer than 1 percent of the city's private firms, although these firms employed 10 percent of the private sector's work force. These production competitions serve as a relatively accurate indicator of the development of the trade union organizations within Tientsin's various enterprises.

The municipal leaders felt that through the production competitions the trade union cadres would become more knowledgeable about the actual processes of production in their factories. In practice, as the trade union personnel became more experienced in running production competitions, the trend in the competition campaigns held in each factory changed from specifying general target goals for the entire factory or whole workshops* to establishing the desired output for each production team,[22] to determining the "struggle targets" for individual workers. At the same time, the trade union cadres tried to popularize successful methods by selecting model workers and then model teams. A longer-term goal was to develop model workshops. Other transitions characterizing the development of production competitions from spring of 1950 through 1951 were from rough quantitative to more detailed quantitative, to qualitative specification of goals; from productivity increases based solely on increments in effort to increases resulting from improved techniques; from subjective evaluation of work to objective standards for determining work performance; and from only rough accountability to specification of individual responsibility. These trends reflected the increasing familiarity of the trade union cadres with the production processes in the enterprises where they worked.

The basic operational principle of the competitions—that improved output should receive proportionate rewards—created pressures for the establishment of increasingly sophisticated statistical, inspection, and accountability systems.[23] These sys-

---

*A workshop (*ch'e-chien*) could vary greatly in size but usually was organized around a particular production area, such as a repair and maintenance workshop in a watch factory. A workshop usually had a director and sometimes deputy directors and subordinate sections. See Barry Richman, *Industrial Society in Communist China* (New York, 1969), pp. 773, 789; and H. Franz Schurmann, *Ideology and Organization in Communist China* (Berkeley, Calif., 1971), p. 249.

tems, in turn, gradually provided the trade union cadres in the private enterprises with the information they needed in order to recommend changes in personnel, wage, and production systems. Many of these personnel and wage recommendations aimed at undermining the favored position of people who had received special treatment because they were relatives, friends, or co-provincials of the owners or managers.[24] Such series of changes generally took well over a year in any one enterprise and typically began during the "readjustment" program initiated by the Tientsin authorities in May 1950. They resulted in private firms whose trade union cadres possessed intimate knowledge of the working of the firm and whose owners retained fewer people with special loyalty to them in positions of responsibility.

The Tientsin MPG's efforts to "readjust" the relations between the public and private sectors began with the establishment of a Public-Private Relations Mediation Committee (*kung szu kuan-hsi t'iao-ch'u wei-yuan-hui*) in early May 1950. The government soon thereafter greatly increased the amount of business it conducted with private firms, giving numerous contracts to them for processing goods and for supplying the publicly run companies with materials. The government also contracted to buy many products manufactured by private firms. By the end of the recession, for instance, the MPG had contracted to buy all of the output of the four largest privately run cotton mills in Tientsin.[25] On May 23, a National Machine Manufacturing Conference in Peking decided to place an order that involved purchasing 60–80 percent of the Tientsin machine industry's output for the remainder of the year.[26] Tientsin's metal, flour, weaving and dyeing, coal, rubber, and woolen textile industries also received large government orders during this period, and by the late summer of 1950 almost all of these industries depended on state orders for more than half of their output.[27] In addition, starting in July 1950 all orders placed by public enterprises for goods from the private sector had to be codified in detailed contracts that contained penalty clauses. Each of these contracts had to be approved by the MPG Bureau of Industry and Commerce, which subsequently supervised their implementation. The government claimed that prior to this time some private firms had been taking advantage of loosely drawn agreements for orders with the public firms, and that this had frequently resulted in disputes. This new system helped to guarantee the position of the public firms in their dealings with the capitalists.[28] Simultaneously, the People's Bank in Tientsin undertook a program of loans to privately run enterprises that were experiencing financial difficulties. While helping the companies involved, these loans also enhanced the leverage of the public sector over the major private firms.[29]

The Tientsin Communists' "readjustment" of production and marketing relationships focused on a series of problems that H. D. Fong had analyzed in Tientsin's industries during the 1920's and 1930's. Fong had concluded that the most intractable obstacle to economic development in Tientsin was the minuscule size of most firms and the lack of organization and cooperation among various firms in the same trade. He argued that this extreme fragmentation perpetuated inefficient production techniques, precluded the adoption of uniform standards of quality (and sometimes of measurement) within a given trade, and made the procurement of raw materials and marketing of finished products a haphazard and wasteful process. He felt that it also prevented long-term production planning within the trades.[30]

To cope with what the Communists described as the "blind" nature of production and the "anarchic" process of procuring raw materials and marketing finished products, the Central People's Government and the MPG convened conferences of enterprise representatives in a number of trades and promoted various types of joint management* ventures among the scattered tiny enterprises of Tientsin. These meetings brought together people in the same trade from all over the country; they speci-

---

*In most cases, these joint management (*lien-ying*) ventures involved only private firms in the same trade. They should not be confused with the "public-private joint management" (*kung szu ho-ying*) arrangement that characterized the later socialist transformation of industry and commerce during the mid-1950's.

fied a production quota for the item concerned for each area of the country and established zones within which the tradesmen of one area were permitted to enjoy a monopoly for that item. Through this process, the government hoped to rectify the situation that existed, for instance, in the Tientsin match industry, where production and marketing possibilities had little relation to each other.[31]

For its part, the municipal government had started encouraging the owners of small factories and workshops to establish various types of joint management relationships as early as the latter part of 1949.[32] Subsequently, it sought to have these same firms actually merge to form companies. The authorities felt that the federation of small firms enhanced the opportunity for specialization of labor, created the conditions necessary for joint purchasing, borrowing, and marketing, and facilitated the consultation and unified quality control systems necessary for product standardization.[33] The first major effort in this direction in Tientsin occurred during the "readjustment" program, during which roughly 5,000 firms in 51 trades established some type of cooperative buying, selling, or production relationship.[34]

The "readjustment" of urban-rural relations closely paralleled the measures taken in production and marketing. The government prodded the public and private enterprises involved in urban-rural trade to form teams to make joint purchases of both foodstuffs and industrial raw materials. As an incentive for private businesses to participate in these teams, the government permitted higher-than-normal profit margins to the private firms involved.[35]

The significance of these measures for increased government control over the scattered private firms came into sharp focus a year later. In early 1951, the MPG decided to establish an Urban-Rural Commodity Exchange Direction and Guidance Committee, which in turn convened various conferences for individual trades in order to develop urban-rural trade. By the end of September, this committee had already convened 14 conferences involving such trades as egg products, metals (those specializing in agricultural implements), and paper.[36] These conferences brought together the producing agents, commercial firms, appropriate government departments, publicly run enterprises, and private firms—in short, all units directly involved in producing and marketing a given item. As of late September 1951, people from 99 government departments, state enterprises, and cooperatives had participated in these 14 trade conferences along with delegates representing over 6,000 private industrial firms and 10,000 private commercial establishments.

The typical trade conference met for about a week and carefully reviewed the production and marketing problems within the trade(s) concerned. A significant amount of business often took place at these conferences, and numerous participants left with contracts in hand for future production. More important, however, the trade conference afforded the government both a forum in which to communicate its policies to the private businessmen and an opportunity to put pressure on them to readjust production and marketing through the use of uniform standards, a permanent organization to regulate quality, joint management programs, and so forth.[37]

The cotton weavers' trade conference, convened in Tientsin from March 28 to April 2, 1951, exemplified this process. During the six days of group discussions and seminars, conference participants signed agreements and contracts amounting to two months' average production. The conference resolved to establish a Tientsin Cotton Weaving Products Production, Selling, and Direction Organization under the leadership of the MPG. It required this organization to supervise and enforce the uniform standards of quality established at the conference; to organize a continuing exchange of technical information within the trade; to allocate the various processing contracts from the public enterprises; to advertise superior products; to promote marketing; to organize exchanges of management experience within the trade; and to perform other related tasks. The conference appointed a 16-man preparatory committee for this new organization. It also decided on measures to consolidate and develop the joint management systems that already existed and to form a large company for the trade that would eventually absorb many of the smaller production units.[38] This conference, in short, brought together representatives of the scattered firms in this trade and established an organizational framework for their future cooperation under government supervision.

The Tientsin MPG's finance and economics work report at the end of 1951 spelled out the government's intentions in promoting these changes. According to this report:

Tientsin is a city with a relatively large private sector, and therefore how the public sector can lead the private sector is a question of the utmost importance. The main way for the public sector to lead the private sector is for it to guide the private sector along the path of increasingly planned production and marketing. According to our experience of the past year, a really excellent method of having the public sector lead the private sector is to convene trade conferences centered around one or several items. The trade conferences bring together economic sectors with different components, various economic departments, different trades and localities within the city, public and private firms, and industry and commerce. They specify clearly the conditions in the trade(s), ferret out the problems, stipulate production and marketing plans, and establish an executive organ to function after the conference has adjourned. Through these measures, it is easier to carry out investigations and revise plans expeditiously as conditions change. By carrying through on policy and making relations close, these measures have greatly heightened and strengthened the leadership function of the public sector.[39]

The Communists also launched a propaganda drive to present the readjustment program in a way that would rally support for the regime's initiatives. A May 19, 1950, directive addressed the two major weaknesses of Tientsin's propaganda network: the lack of coordination among the Party, trade union, government, and Youth League in large enterprises; and the minimal penetration of the medium and small private enterprises, where the regime had not yet developed these bodies.[40] The May directive ordered the Party, trade unions, government, and Youth League organizations within each public enterprise to establish a joint propaganda committee under the leadership of the Party. In private firms, this directive simply called for the Party to decrease its own propaganda work and direct its efforts toward coordinating the work of the Youth League and trade unions. Henceforth, the Party cadres should rely completely on the trade union cadres to do all the actual propaganda work within the private firms. The broader effort being made at that time to strengthen the position of the trade unions in the private firms undoubtedly influenced the decision expressed in the May directive.* Not surprisingly, the directive strongly emphasized the need to convey to the workers the importance of increasing production and bearing sacrifices in order to end the economic recession.

The directive offered no solution to the problem of an inadequate propaganda capability in the smaller private enterprises. This could only come after adequate Party and trade union organizations had been developed in these firms—and this in turn depended on the authorities' broader strategy toward Tientsin's economy.

The May 19 directive proved difficult to implement, especially because Party committees in the enterprises typically failed to strike a good balance between "leading" propaganda work and leaving it to the trade unions to carry out this work. Some Party committees simply neglected propaganda entirely. Others gave orders but did not supervise their execution. Still more arrogated to themselves both the planning and the implementation of propaganda. In each of these cases, the resulting propaganda effort was not satisfactory.[41]

The Communists thus enjoyed only modest success in strengthening their propaganda capabilities during the May 1950 recession and the following months of "readjustment." In the long run, however, the regime's propaganda capabilities were a function of the development of the various mass organizations, and the readjustment measures, as noted above, had the effect of speeding up the development of these very organizations.

The components of the readjustment program significantly increased the MPG's administrative responsibilities over the city's

---

*Indeed, during the 1950 production competition campaigns, the Party was ordered to carry out *all* work among non-Party workers only through the trade union organization in that enterprise. *TC*, 16.x.50, p. 1.

economy, and the government accordingly moved quickly to expand its organizational capacity to cope with this additional burden. The radical centralization of administration that had been implemented on Liu Shao-ch'i's orders in June 1949 had been in part a response to problems created by the Communists' dearth of reliable cadres in Tientsin. For this reason, some subsequent decentralization could have been expected as the new municipal leaders witnessed an expansion in the human resources at their command. Personnel recruitment proceeded apace during the first few years after liberation, as indicated by the addition of 3,600 administrative personnel to the MPG payroll in 1950 alone.[42] Relatedly, the municipal leaders found that as the public security operations expanded and became more complex, the police administration was increasingly burdened with responsibilities for which it was not prepared. The policemen who staffed the precinct stations were simply not adept at handling political assignments such as judging the reactions of the local populace to the various policies of the government and communicating these sentiments to higher authorities. The precincts' mishandling of these tasks in turn bred resentment among the people who suffered as a result of their ineptitude.[43] In response to these conditions alone, the MPG had on March 2, 1950, decided to augment the government's political organization on the ward level. It had at that time increased both the power and the functions of the ward offices, and had concomitantly raised the number of staff from 7 to 24–34 in each of these offices. At the same time, the MPG made the ward offices more specialized, having each one establish a secretarial office and sections for civil affairs, mediation, hygiene, culture and education, guidance for cooperatives, and (where necessary) agricultural lands.[44] With the sharply increased responsibilities stemming from the readjustment program, however, the Tientsin MPG Council decided just four months later to strengthen once again the government organs on the ward level by adding still more personnel, by increasing the functional specialization, and by stipulating a more active role for the ward level in both policy coordination and policy implementation.[45] Indeed, this decision

(July 20) re-established the Ward People's Governments and also called for organizing ward-level All Circles People's Representatives Conferences (ACPRCs),[46] the first of which was convened in the No. 9 ward on August 25, 1950.[47]

Developments in Tientsin's trade union structure paralleled the MPG's organizational development on the ward level in mid-1950. Almost all trade union work had been concentrated until this time in the large public and private firms and had been carried out by the municipal Trade Union Council and its subordinate unions for each trade. The readjustment initiatives, however, began to bring the smaller firms within the active concern of the trade union organizers, and this in turn considerably expanded and complicated the tasks of the union organization in the city. In mid-1950, therefore, the Tientsin Trade Union Council established a trade union ward office in each of the city's 11 wards and in the T'ang-ta district.* Each ward office assumed responsibility for developing and coordinating trade union activities in all of the *smaller* private firms located in that ward. This division of labor in turn allowed the manufacturing trade unions to concentrate on programs for the larger enterprises.[48]

Tientsin began to recover from the recession in July, and by the end of August most of the city's firms were beyond the crisis point. A good fall harvest in Hopei in 1950 contributed to the recovery efforts, and at the end of the year the city's economy was sharply improved. The government consequently began to move beyond its readjustment measures, principally by increasing its control over the available investment capital and financial institutions in the city's now accelerating economy. This new focus on the realm of finances, like the earlier development of the readjustment program, received its initial impetus from Peking. There, in August 1950, the CPG had convened a National Financial Conference that had decided the People's Bank should play a more active role in "leading" the country's other financial institutions. In Tientsin, this Peking initiative led to the formation

---

*T'ang-ta was geographically separate from Tientsin. It was put under the control of the MPG because it included port facilities at the mouth of the Hai-ho that formed an integral part of the Tientsin economy.

of the Financial Trade Association in which the State Bank participated and, indeed, immediately assumed a leading role.[49] While increasing their own control over the city's financial institutions, the municipal authorities in September initiated a series of related measures to induce the 93 percent of Tientsin's industrial and commercial firms that had never relied on banks for credit to turn more readily to the banks for needed capital. Chief among these was the decision to have the Federation of Industry and Commerce (FIC)* establish a Finance Committee, which in turn convened four seminars for industrialists and businessmen on September 28–29, 1950. The authorities followed up these seminars with new measures to facilitate bank loans to smaller firms.[50]

In 1951, the Tientsin authorities sought to control the lion's share of private investment capital in the city through the establishment of the Tientsin Investment Company. The National Financial Conference had envisioned setting up such a company, and concrete preparations for it began before February 1951 in Tientsin. Capital for this company was acquired through the sale of shares to over 4,000 enterprises. The People's Bank alone, however, contributed a full 25 percent of this capital, enough to assure government control over the Investment Company's decisions. Through this device, therefore, the government managed to gain control over a great deal of the private investment capital in the city. The Tientsin Investment Company was formally inaugurated on June 10, 1951, with a capitalization of 30 billion *yuan*. From that time on, it represented the major source of long-term investment capital in the city.[51]

In sum, Tientsin's government successfully used the econom-

---

*In early March 1950, the Tientsin MPG's Finance Committee established a Municipal Federation of Industry and Commerce Preparatory Committee. This committee completed its work in late April 1950, at which time the Tientsin Chamber of Commerce was abolished and replaced by the government-organized Federation of Industry and Commerce. The available data do not permit an analysis of the extent of personnel changes that accompanied this shift, although prevailing united front policies at the time limited the degree to which the Communists could determine the membership of the new body. *TC*, 12.iii.50, p. 2, 29.iv.50, p. 1, 30.iv.50, p. 1. For information on the internal organization of the Municipal FIC, see *T'ien-chin kung-shang*, 1(12): 10 (15.vi.51).

ic recession brought on by national economic policies to extend its leverage over the private sector of the economy. Under the guise of rationalizing production, improving efficiency, and increasing output, the process actually expanded and consolidated trade union organizations and specified management's responsibility to make production competitions more realistic. It also sponsored conferences of entire trades. It encouraged greater use of guaranteed supplies and buyers through long-term contracts between the public and private sectors. And it amplified the role of the state banking system. These measures increased the state's penetration of the private sector and yielded valuable information that would later be used to undermine the economic and political strength of the capitalists and their enterprises.

The Party thus capitalized on a temporary crisis to develop a rationale that tied economic prosperity for the capitalists to an expanding role for the state and the trade unions in private firms. The government, in turn, expanded the MPG's administrative apparatus at the ward level to cope with the increased demands that state intervention in the economy entailed. The Three Anti Five Anti campaign of 1952 would later produce a quantum leap in the state's power over the private sector, but the groundwork for that dramatic transformation was laid during two years of "readjustment" in Tientsin's industry and commerce.

Two major national events directly affected the program outlined above and further challenged the local authorities to devise means of turning the pressures and constraints imposed by Peking to their own advantage. The first was China's entry into the Korean War in October 1950 and the second was the Suppression of Counterrevolutionaries campaign in the spring of 1951. We turn now to the interaction of these national events with the unfolding revolution in Tientsin.

CHAPTER 6

Capitalizing on Korea

While Tientsin's leaders wrestled with the recession in the early summer of 1950, events of major importance for the city were unfolding on the Korean peninsula across the Pohai Gulf. On June 25, 1950, North Korea's army launched an attack against Syngman Rhee's forces in the South,[1] thus beginning a war that was fought up and down the Korean peninsula for the next three years. The Chinese authorities at first did not show deep concern over the events in Korea, but they became increasingly alarmed as the U.N. forces committed to the South Korean side turned the tide and marched up the peninsula toward Manchuria. In October 1950, they ordered the PLA, under the fiction of acting as "people's volunteers," to intervene on behalf of the North.[2] These events had profound consequences for the Communists' process of consolidating power in Tientsin, and created problems and opportunities that they could neither put off nor ignore.

The immediate consequences for Tientsin were highly unfavorable, but in the long run they proved a boon. A brief digression into Tientsin's foreign trade experience during the previous two years will put the economic impact of the Korean War in better perspective.

As a port city, Tientsin's economic health depended heavily on its ability to carry on foreign trade. As of 1948, about two-thirds of this trade was done with the United States.[3] Following liberation, no commercial vessels called at Tientsin until the end of March 1949. During the late spring and summer of that year, however, trade through Tientsin picked up fairly rapidly because the Nationalists blockaded the port of Shanghai and a great deal of the Shanghai import and export trade was therefore routed through Tientsin.[4] Tientsin was also included on the KMT list of blockaded ports, but the Nationalists did not have the naval strength to enforce this policy vigorously in North China. In addition, there is evidence that the British used their own naval power in the area to protect ships coming into and out of Taku Bar.[5]

The Communist government had moved quickly to acquire control over Tientsin's foreign trade by establishing domestic trade monopolies over some of the city's major export items and by either selling these items to private exporters or dealing directly with buyers abroad. By the end of 1949, Tientsin had government trading monopolies for pig bristles, fur, skins, wool, hair, eggs and egg products, oil and fat, general produce, and salt.[6] Private traders who were given contracts by those monopolies were permitted only a small profit margin; and there were complaints that government mismanagement and uncertainty had frequently caused private firms to lose their profit completely and, on occasion, to take a net loss for a transaction.[7] As a result, both foreign and Chinese private traders fared badly until mid-1950.*

The spring 1950 recession added to the woes of the private importers and exporters, especially since at this time the prices for some of China's major export commodities dropped sharply on the American market.[8] These difficulties were compounded by trade restrictions on some 600 items imposed by the United States government at that time. The Tientsin importers and exporters thus faced a rapidly contracting market for many of their goods and decreased prices for a substantial portion of the items

*Most of the foreign businessmen in Tientsin were involved in the import and export trade, with very little foreign investment in manufacturing industries. It was, therefore, easier to eliminate foreign business from Tientsin than from cities like Shanghai, where foreign ownership of manufacturing industries was more prevalent. In Tientsin, some foreign economic presence remained until 1952, but by the end of 1950, most foreigners were looking for ways to leave the city. See the documents for this period (1949–52) in the China Association Archives for a graphic portrayal of the foreigners' waning confidence that they would be able to retain a portion of the market in the New China.

on which they could place orders. Under these conditions, the firms competed fiercely for a place in the shrinking market and thereby drove prices still further down. The government decided to step into this rapidly deteriorating situation, and from April to July 1950 the MPG organized 15 export and 7 import "trade groups," each specializing in the trade of a particular type of major commodity and including representatives of both the public and private firms involved. The stated purpose of these groups was to present a united front on the international market.[9]

With the outbreak of the Korean War, the United States increased the number of restricted goods from 600 to over 1,100. Fearing increasing trade difficulties in the future, Peking responded by ordering the Tientsin authorities to give full play to the capabilities of the city's private importers and exporters and to work hard to increase both imports and exports. This trade offensive continued through October 1950. Somewhat paradoxically, the government authorities at the same time enforced the trade-inhibiting policy of insisting that China receive the foreign goods ordered before sending out Chinese goods in return.[10] For all exports that could not be done on such a barter basis, the Chinese government required that the foreign buyer deposit the full amount of the payment due before the goods left China's ports.[11]

In November 1950, following China's military intervention in Korea in late October, the United States imposed a full blockade on China's ports, cut off all Sino–U.S. trade, and urged other Free World countries to cease doing business with the Chinese. On December 16, the United States additionally froze all Chinese assets in America, and the Chinese retaliated in kind on December 28. That these measures inflicted serious losses on Tientsin's economy is clearly reflected in the fluctuations of the city's volume of foreign trade. As Table 4 shows, foreign trade grew briskly during the first half of 1950 and picked up even more with the Chinese trade offensive following the outbreak of the Korean War. The fact that foreign trade through Tientsin historically went up during the latter half of each year undoubtedly

TABLE 4. *Amount of Sea Transport to and
from Tientsin, 1950–1951*
(*July–December 1949 = 100*)

Period	Index of sea transport	Change from previous period (percent)
Jan.–June 1950	142	+42%
July–Dec. 1950	227	+60
Jan.–June 1951	160	−30
July–Dec. 1951	130	−19

SOURCE: *CP,* 29.xii.51, p. 4.

helped this upward trend. The new sanctions applied by the
United States and adhered to by other Free World countries at
the end of 1950, however, completely reversed the favorable
trend in these foreign trade statistics, causing a 30 percent decline for the first half of 1951 and another 19 percent for the second half. Tientsin's losses would undoubtedly have been more
severe had it not adopted the pay-in-advance and barter policies
of 1950. During the course of 1951, the Tientsin authorities consolidated the initial 22 export and import trade groups into 14
jointly managed import and export companies. More important,
they turned to the Soviet Union and East Europe as the major
sources of industrial supplies and the primary markets for some
exports. These countries managed to supply Tientsin with many
of the imports it required, but were unable to replace satisfactorily the export market on which the city depended.[12]

As the hub of North China's foreign trade, Tientsin was seriously injured by the Korean War. But as the largest manufacturing and trade center north of the Yangtze, Tientsin reaped
considerable economic benefits from the fighting in Korea. Geographic considerations favored the city in the allocation of government contracts for war materials, and these contracts in turn
gave a substantial boost to the city's entire economy. The value
of processing and procurement contracts for private firms in
Tientsin for the first half of 1951, for example, rose 50 percent
higher than for the second half of 1950, and commentaries at the

time attributed this sizable increase primarily to "military and state" needs. The amount of private production done under state contracts continued to increase throughout the year.[13] By the end of 1951, largely as a result of these measures, the state trading companies had contracts for marketing all of the output for major industries such as cloth, coal, cement, glass, and matches. In addition, processing contracts from the publicly run enterprises tied up 83 percent of the city's flour industry pro-duction, 82 percent of the output of the textile-finishing indus-try, 85 percent of the telephone machinery, 73 percent of the canvas industry, 59 percent of the rubber soles production, and similarly high percentages of a number of other products.[14] The groundwork for this system of public-private contracts had, of course, been laid during the readjustment of industry and com-merce during 1950.

Overall, then, the Korean War had a mixed impact on Tien-tsin's economy, hurting the foreign trade sector, but attracting public funds to the city, and by late 1951 creating conditions bordering on an economic boom. In both the foreign trade and the domestic sphere, the war accelerated the speed with which the state sector of the economy gained leverage over the private sector—through the consolidation of the 14 trading companies in the foreign trade sector and through the greatly increased need for processing and procurement contracts with the private sector.

The Korean War posed contrasting political problems for the Tientsin authorities. On the one hand, it provided them with an issue of potentially great use in trying to rally the people to their political program. On the other hand, it naturally increased the Communists' concern for security and compelled them to take potentially unpopular measures to minimize the chances of sabo-tage and subversion. At the same time, the war undoubtedly gave heart to anti-Communists in Tientsin who viewed it as a means by which Communist rule might be overthrown. The war also gave the Communist leaders an *excuse* to suppress individu-als and groups whom they had distrusted in the first place. Overall, the war had the effect of greatly speeding up the Communists' expansion and consolidation of power in the city of Tientsin.

The Tientsin leaders at first responded to the Korean War by modifying their propaganda so as to lay heavier stress on nationalist themes and current political events. Concomitantly, they shifted their propaganda efforts from the city's modern enterprises to a more even balance between places of work and residential areas. Shortly after China's commitment of "people's volunteers" to the fighting, Peking launched a nationwide Resist America, Aid Korea campaign. Because the Tientsin authorities directed this propaganda campaign at the entire population, including non-working women, they moved the organizational locus for the campaign from the modern enterprises to the ward level of administration. This change could capitalize on the measures already taken in mid-1950 to strengthen the ward level of government and to convene ward ACPRCs. The MPG assigned 742 municipal-level cadres to the ward governments to organize and implement the Resist America, Aid Korea campaign. By the end of 1950, these cadres had established propaganda teams in the residential areas and organized propaganda brigades in various government organs.[15] On January 1, 1951, the Party Center in Peking announced its decision that the various localities should enhance their propaganda capabilities and firmly assert Party leadership in the propaganda field. Almost seven weeks later, Tientsin revealed its own concrete plan to implement this central directive.[16]

The Tientsin plan called for a Party-run propaganda organization that functioned outside of regular bureaucratic channels and could convey government policies to the populace in a lively and interesting way. This plan envisaged using February–April 1951 as an experimental period during which to establish trial propaganda organizations in areas where previous propaganda organization work had been successful and thus where conditions were most favorable. The plan further stipulated that in May–July the authorities would use the experience gained from this "keypoint" experimental work to establish propaganda nets in all other areas where such an endeavor was feasible.[17] The plan provided for the appointment during this second stage of "reporting personnel" (*pao-kao yuan*) at both the munici-pal and the ward level to coordinate the program between them.

The subsequent development of a Party propaganda net in Tientsin in 1951 proceeded according to schedule. February through April was utilized for experimental work, and then the Party launched a broad campaign to expand its propaganda net-work. The propagandists combined their patriotic Resist Amer-ica, Aid Korea appeals with exhortations from the Suppression of Counterrevolutionaries and Withdrawal from Superstitious Societies campaigns (discussed below) being waged at this time.

Nevertheless, this campaign to build a Party-led propaganda network enjoyed only modest success. For instance, as of late August 1951, less than one-third of the 150 factory Party branches in the Nos. 3, 6, 9, and 11 wards had established propaganda nets. Moreover, this factory record surpassed the results in the residential districts, where in the same wards only 27 percent of the 44 street Party branches had established propa-ganda nets—and these wards were singled out for mention in the Tientsin press because they had done a better job than the city's other seven districts.[18] This effort had evidently faltered because many Party cadres had disdain for propaganda work, which they considered less important than their other leader-ship duties.[19] The Party nevertheless continued its drive to es-tablish an effective propaganda network through the fall and winter of 1951. It succeeded best in the publicly run enterprises, less well in the private sector, and very little in the residential areas (see Table 5); and within the private sector, it accom-plished most in the larger enterprises.

The Tientsin Party's ability to organize a propaganda network closely followed the contours of its general capacity to carry out other kinds of programs in the city. A person's encounter with the Resist America, Aid Korea propaganda, like his exposure to virtually all of the regime's initiatives, depended largely on whether he held a job and, if so, in what kind of enterprise. In other words, those who worked in small firms or who did not hold jobs remained beyond the reach of the regime's ability to

TABLE 5. *Distribution of Propagandists in Tientsin,*
December 1951

Sector	Number of propagandists	Percentage of total
Publicly run enterprises	3,198	48%
Private firms and residential areas	1,901	28
MPG organs and mass organizations	1,022	15
Schools	582	9
TOTAL	6,703	100%

SOURCE: *TC*, 7.i.52, p. 2.

communicate its political message.* There is little question,
however, that the Korean War accelerated the Communists' efforts to create an extensive propaganda apparatus. The war also
provided a more effective emotional focus for this campaign
than the themes of increasing production and class struggle.

The war-related propaganda drive, of course, extended beyond the organizational program. The Tientsin press gave extensive coverage to the war effort throughout late 1950 and 1951.
Cultural workers in the city put on plays and skits with patriotic
themes about the war. Workers who participated in regular
study groups were supplied with information on the war to
serve as the focus of much of their discussion. The rapidly increasing number of people engaged in spare-time study programs received war-related propaganda as a part of their
courses.[20] Tientsin's youth were encouraged to enroll in a
newly established military training school, and the authorities
launched a signature campaign for peace among the adult populace.† The various sessions of the municipal and ward ACPRCs
became, to a significant extent, government propaganda forums
for the Resist America, Aid Korea campaign.[21] Perhaps most

*Indeed, by the end of 1951, some 60 percent of the propaganda nets in Tien-
tsin did not function regularly, and most of these defective units were in the
small enterprises and residential areas. *TC*, 7.i.52, p. 2.

†This campaign, which was claimed to have produced 1.5 million signatures,
was also directed against the rearmament of Japan. *CP*, 28.xii.51, p. 4.

importantly for the people in the city, the government launched a "patriotic contributions" campaign that put great moral pressure on people to contribute money to the war effort. These contributions were expressed in terms of the number of bombers that contributions could buy, at the rate of 1.5 billion *yuan* per plane.[22] A similar "victory bond" campaign had been waged in the city during the spring of 1950, and the two campaigns together succeeded in soaking up a substantial amount of the idle private funds in Tientsin. The patriotic contribution campaign also allowed poorer people to show their patriotism by pledging to do such tasks as saving raw materials in the production process or helping to keep the neighborhood clean. The government gave all of these efforts wide publicity.

Thus, Tientsin's leaders used the Korean War to mobilize the city's populace around patriotic themes and to identify the CCP more closely with China's international integrity. The war was a mixed blessing, however, in that it also made the Communists more nervous about espionage and sabotage. This growing concern for security was fully shared by the leadership in Peking. A month after North Korea's army invaded the South, the CPG's Government Administrative Council and Supreme People's Court in Peking issued a joint directive containing the most severe and far-reaching measures against counterrevolutionaries yet undertaken by the government.[23] During the fall, Peking ominously cautioned that "boundless magnanimity" in the treatment of counterrevolutionaries remained too common a phenomenon.[24] Finally, on February 21, 1951, the CPG issued its "Regulations of the People's Republic of China for the Suppression of Counterrevolutionaries," and launched a mass campaign to suppress counterrevolutionary activities throughout the country.

Responding to these national initiatives, Tientsin made preparations for the Suppression of Counterrevolutionaries campaign at the Second Session of its Third Municipal All Circles People's Representatives Conference, convened on February 28, 1951. At this meeting, Public Security Bureau Chief Hsu Chien-kuo stressed the connection between counterrevolutionary ac-

tivities in the city and the Korean War. He argued that these activities were designed to weaken the rear areas and pointed to
significantly increased instances of sabotage, including 83 cases
of wrecking machinery and carrying out anti-CCP propaganda
in the factories and 112 cases of cutting long-distance telephone
lines. He concluded that under wartime conditions a greatly increased effort to suppress counterrevolutionaries "is a necessary
policy for protecting the interests of the people and the political
power of the people's state."[25]

In March, preparations for the security campaign began with
preliminary organizational activities, testing techniques, and
background investigations of some suspected enemy agents. On
March 13, the MPG announced that it had smashed an espionage plot that had been using the Catholic Church as a cover.[26]
In mid-March, Tientsin's Railroad Bureau launched a campaign
to break up the quasi-religious societies such as the I Kuan Tao,
in order to try out techniques that might later be used on a wider
scale.[27] The Municipal Government Council and the Consultative Committee of the Municipal ACPRC on March 20 approved
a report on the proposed measures for carrying out the Suppression of Counterrevolutionaries campaign.[28] On March 23 and
March 26, two of Tientsin's democratic parties, the China Democratic National Construction Association and the Kuomintang
Revolutionary Committee, held meetings to endorse the need
for suppressing counterrevolutionaries.[29] And from March 16 to
26, ward ACPRC meetings convened in seven wards. Each of
these meetings heard a report on the suppression of counterrevolutionaries by the relevant Public Security District Branch
Bureau chief.* This series of lower-level meetings was capped

---

*Notice of these meetings is given in *CP,* 27.iii.51, p. 2, while detailed reviews
of several of the individual meetings are available as follows: No. 11 ward, *CP,*
17.iii.51, p. 2; No. 4 ward, *CP,* 19.iii.51, p. 2; and No. 10 ward, *CP,* 20.iii.51, p. 2,
21.iii.51, p. 2. These meetings undoubtedly served a preparatory propaganda
function. Similar ward ACPRCs convened in the Nos. 9, 1, and 5 wards during
the March 8–15 period had restricted their attention to the housing question in
Tientsin and did not bring up the question of the suppression of counterrevolution at all. Information on the meetings is available in *CP,* 9.iii.51, p. 2, 10.iii.51,
p. 2, 12.iii.51, p. 2. Thus, mobilization for the campaign began on a substantial
scale only in the latter part of March.

by an enlarged meeting of the Municipal Consultative Committee on March 27 to discuss the general topic of suppressing counterrevolutionaries. This enlarged meeting in turn announced plans to convene an enlarged ACPRC session on March 29, 1951, to be attended by all delegates of both the Municipal ACPRC and the ward ACPRCs.[30] It was this later meeting that in fact initiated the Suppression of Counterrevolutionaries campaign on a city-wide scale in Tientsin.

The meeting itself was a mobilization rally of considerable proportions. Some 15,000 people, representing the Municipal and ward ACPRCs, democratic parties and personages, people's groups, various government organs, factories, and schools, attended this gathering, and Tientsin radio broadcast the proceedings live. Participants heard reports by Tientsin's Party Secretary and Mayor, Huang Ching, and by Hsu Chien-kuo; unanimously passed a "Decision on Resolutely Suppressing Counterrevolutionary Elements"; and recommended the death sentence for 193 counterrevolutionaries who were brought before the gathering and accused of crimes by their former victims in the crowd.[31] The police publicly executed all 193 people two days later.[32]

Reports from other parts of China indicate that the Communists used the Suppression of Counterrevolutionaries campaign both to rid themselves of people actively engaged in counterrevolutionary activity and to do away with many of the former members of the KMT who had been tricked into revealing their past affiliation by earlier CCP promises of leniency.[33] The purge of this latter group hit the civil service the hardest, for the Communists had by 1951 built up sufficient cadre resources of their own to be able to do without many of the KMT holdovers. In these cities, the press never revealed the full extent of this suppression of former Nationalist officeholders, bringing to public trial only those who were sufficiently corrupt and unpopular that their punishment would probably win support for the regime.[34] A substantial proportion of those brought to public trial in Tientsin were likewise former KMT members, but without more evidence it is impossible to ascertain whether the campaign in Tientsin also included a secret purge of former Nationalists. Tientsin's campaign was, however, as ruthless as those in Shanghai and Canton. There were 492 public executions of accused counterrevolutionaries between March and early July 1951, and most of these took place with a good deal of fanfare.[35] The media during this period spared no words in trying to strike terror into the hearts of all who contemplated or had engaged in acts of disloyalty to the new regime. Many people in Tientsin must have emerged from this nightmare with greater respect for the determination of the Communists, if not any increased affection for their methods or goals.

For most people in Tientsin, however, the Suppression of Counterrevolutionaries campaign was of less immediate concern than another political campaign being waged in the name of wartime security. This was called the *t'ui-tao yun-tung*—the Withdrawal from Quasi-religious Societies Campaign. The MPG Council initiated the *t'ui-tao* campaign on April 6,[36] and its goal was to destroy the I Kuan Tao (IKT), the World New Buddhist Association, and all similar millenarian societies in the city. Because the IKT was the most powerful of these societies, it received the brunt of the Communists' attack. It had collaborated with both the KMT and the Japanese against the Communists during the 1930's and 1940's and had actively opposed the Communists' rule after January 1949.

According to the CCP, during 1949–51 the IKT priests had slandered the PLA and continued to praise both Chiang Kai-shek and America. The priests had claimed, in essence, that the Communists would not be able to maintain their hold over China. They asserted that once the PLA had crossed the Yangtze River, the United States would use nuclear weapons and defeat the CCP. Following the PLA's successful capture and retention of cities below the Yangtze, the IKT leaders warned their flock in Tientsin that Chiang Kai-shek had allied with the Japanese and that two million Japanese troops fighting for the Nationalists were landing in Manchuria. They also whispered that when World War III broke out, North and Northeast China would be targets for nuclear attacks. All of this intimidated the people and cast some doubt over the permanence of Communist control of Tientsin. It was a stratagem well suited to frighten the numerous people in Tientsin who had close ties with the rural areas where disastrous consequences had befallen peasants who had openly committed themselves to the Communists during the civil war, only to have the KMT regain control over their locality.[37] The Communists also claimed that the IKT clergy exploited the society's membership,[38] and that it and the other millenarian societies in Tientsin created artificial cleavages and barriers among the masses.[39]

More fundamentally, the Communists realized that anyone who believed in the IKT's theology could not possibly accept the Communists' world view.* The IKT preached a harmony and fatalism that led its members to respond passively to the hardships and discrimination they encountered. The CCP, however, had devised a revolutionary strategy in the rural areas that converted the peasants' traditionally passive fatalism into an active approach to problem solving,[40] and the Communists hoped to transfer this aspect of their rural strategy into the cities. In addition, the IKT's organizational strength and large membership were sufficient obstacles to the CCP's control over the populace that the Communists had strong incentives to disband this quasi-religious society.

The Communists had in fact made a policy decision to suppress the IKT throughout North China even before they liberated Tientsin. Their North China government had issued an order on January 4, 1949, calling for the investigation and dissolution of the IKT,[41] and by December a campaign against the society had been launched in the Northeast.[42] On December 15, 1949, the Tientsin MCC proclaimed a ban on all IKT activities in the city.

*The IKT's complex view of history divided the past into cosmic periods (*t'ien-hui*), each of which consisted of 12 periods (*hui*), each period being made up of 30 eras (*yun*), and each era encompassing 12 generations, or 360 years. Each era had its own characteristics. The change from the seventh to the eighth period took place, coincidentally, in 1948–49, at the time of the Communist victory in Tientsin. See William A. Grootaers, "Une Société secrète moderne: I Kuan Tao," *Folklore Studies*, 5 (1946), p. 324. This division of historical epochs, of course, sharply contradicted Marxist historical analysis.

Not surprisingly, this decree drew a careful distinction between the IKT leaders, who were branded as criminals liable for
punishment, and the society's rank-and-file members, who had
been "deceived" and were therefore not culpable for their actions. These rank-and-file members, allegedly constituting over
90 percent of the total membership, were assured that they were
actually being "liberated" from the clutches of the IKT clergy
and were urged to tell the authorities all they knew about the
society's organization and activities, to denounce the crimes of
the "leading criminal elements," and to assist the government
in destroying the IKT. The same decree informed the society's
clergy that they were guilty of crimes, but that the MPG was
willing to permit them to reform themselves. They need only
quickly confess and register, provide the MPG with full information on all IKT organizations with which they were familiar,
hand over all sacred implements and all public property, and
cease all organizational activities.* These provisions followed
precisely the method used to break up other counterrevolutionary organizations in 1949–50.

After publishing this decree, the Tientsin authorities arrested
some 25 IKT leaders and registered several hundred more.[43] As
in many other instances, however, the decree and the efforts to
implement it were only preliminary moves designed to make
clear the Communists' position and to permit them to test their
approach by carrying out the provisions of the decree in a selective way. During 1949 and 1950, the Tientsin leaders were not
yet ready to make a major effort to destroy the IKT, although
their rhetoric remained menacing.[44] With the announcement of
the *t'ui-tao* campaign in April 1951, however, the government fi-

*A full text of the Dec. 15, 1949, MCC decree is available in *CP*, 15.xii.49. Because the IKT was a totally indigenous phenomenon with no constituency outside of China, the CCP did not feel constrained by world opinion in dealing with
this organization. Such larger considerations did dictate that the Communists
"remold" the Christian and Buddhist associations in China rather than simply
suppress them. A brief introduction to the Communists' approach to the Catholic Church in Tientsin is presented in *T'ien-chin T'ien-chu chiao ko-hsin yun-tung
ti ch'eng-chiu* (Peking, 1951). On Chinese sensitivities concerning the opinions of
Buddhists outside the People's Republic, see Dick Wilson, *Anatomy of China: An
Introduction to One-Quarter of Mankind* (New York, 1969), p. 98.

nally launched the type of attack that was required in order to destroy such organizations.[45]

The *t'ui-tao* campaign combined mass mobilization from below with police actions from above to break up the quasi-religious societies. Mobilization served three goals: to generate vital information about those who participated in and who led the societies; to tell the rank-and-file members that the societies had been declared illegal; and to break the back of the societies financially. This mobilization "from the bottom upwards" required that the government utilize a wide range of techniques to reach the members and convince them to participate in the campaign. At the same time, the government security organs proceeded "from the top downwards" and focused, in the words of a subsequent report, on "making the leaders earn merit"—i.e., on intimidating the clergy who had not registered with the authorities to the point where they felt compelled to become informers and witnesses for the government.[46] In this way, the government carefully sowed dissension in the societies' leadership ranks and reaped the benefits of the resulting suspicion and fear.

The government sought three levels of response from the IKT's general membership. The first was simply to announce one's withdrawal from the organization. The second was to participate actively in an "accusation meeting" and denounce in front of one's peers the evil deeds of the local IKT leader. And the third was to make demands for "reparations" from the IKT leaders for the funds that, as the Communists claimed, the organization had stolen from the members.[47] The first of these responses required acknowledgment but no real commitment; the second demanded action; and the third sought to foster animosity between the poverty-stricken members and the IKT clergy by permitting members to "recover" money from the clergy in proportion to the intensity of their struggle for these funds.

The government faced a particularly difficult problem in mobilizing the members of the IKT because most of them were either women or uneducated men who worked in small enterprises and lived in the traditional sphere of Tientsin's society.

The women were basically a conservative force. Almost all of them stayed at home and had little contact with the outside world. Likewise, the typical worker in a small enterprise worked more than 12 hours a day, often ate and slept in the room where he worked, and had few holidays and almost no regular days off. In addition, Liu Shao-ch'i's strategy placed this type of enterprise beyond the reach of the programs the leaders in Tientsin had undertaken since liberation. Consequently, both the workers and the women who participated in the IKT presented special communications problems for the Communists.

The Municipal Trade Union Council, as the government-sponsored organization with the closest ties to the city's workers, immediately brought its resources to bear in the *t'ui-tao* campaign. On April 8, the Council publicly called upon all of the city's staff and workers to unite to destroy the quasi-religious societies.[48] Thereafter, the member trade unions used their organizations' skills and connections with the workers to convene meetings, carry out propaganda, and organize people to listen to relevant radio broadcasts.

The municipal authorities made use of the radio as a convenient, if superficial, means to familiarize people with the campaign. For instance, a *t'ui-tao* campaign radio broadcast on April 14 exposed the crimes of the quasi-religious societies and appealed to members to withdraw from and oppose these organizations. The broadcast ran for three hours and included speeches by Party Secretary and Mayor Huang Ching, and by the heads and representatives of the Trade Union Council, the Tientsin branches of the Youth League, the Federation of Students, the Federation of Industry and Commerce, the Federation of Women, and the People's Broadcasting Station. It also contained accusations against the quasi-religious societies by their members. The announcer invited the listening audience to call in their own opinions and accusations, and promised to broadcast these over the radio. The authorities utilized every means at their command to inform people of this broadcast and to organize them to listen to it, and they subsequently estimated that the listening audience totaled 460,000 people—almost one-quarter of the city's population.[49]

Another propaganda ploy took the form of an IKT Criminal Evidence Exhibition that displayed the money and goods that the IKT clergy had fleeced from the people. This exhibition ran from April 20 to May 17 and was attended by 260,000 people.[50]

The accusation meeting, however, was the most widespread and effective method used during this campaign. Almost all of these meetings had the same scenario. Cadres first told the audience about the IKT's evil deeds and about the threat it posed to the security of China. They then brought forward one or two members of the local IKT clergy and described their crimes to the assembled crowd. Not infrequently, they also displayed luxury possessions of the accused as evidence that the clergy had cheated the masses. Next, either another local IKT leader denounced the crimes of his colleagues or relatively "conscious" members of the audience stood up and made accusations based on their personal experience. At this point, the accused usually confessed, and as a finale, people who belonged to the IKT were asked to sign a statement declaring that they had withdrawn from the organization and would work to destroy it.[51] The cadres also invited denunciations of "hidden" IKT members and clergy at these meetings. In addition to factories, schools, and other units, each of Tientsin's public security precinct stations convened such accusation sessions.[52]

In early May, the authorities injected an important new element into the *t'ui-tao* campaign. Whereas throughout April the major object of mobilizing the IKT members had been to convey the government's message and persuade the members to withdraw from the society, the focus now shifted to encouraging society members to struggle against the local IKT leaders in order to regain the money and goods of which they had been cheated. Everywhere, people who had formerly withdrawn from the IKT joined "Committees to Recover Cheated Property." In contrast to the rest of the campaign, which had tended to be organized solely on the basis of police administrative boundaries, these committees were set up along the lines of both the IKT parish and the police precinct—but more commonly the former.* Whenever possible, these committees were also established in units such as factories. The actual struggles to recover cheated property were organized either by the public security precinct station or by the trade union in an enterprise. Thus, by May 4, 118 police precincts had raised the demand to "recover" the property that the IKT clergy had obtained through deception. A total of 1,745 members of the society had by that time already "recovered" a portion of their property.[53]

The implementation of this campaign in the Hengyuan Cotton Mill illustrates how the authorities wanted the *t'ui-tao* campaign to operate in economic enterprises. The trade union in this privately run factory had begun carrying out daily propaganda in the form of broadcasts and plays as soon as the campaign was announced in early April. This propaganda stressed the reactionary nature of the IKT. At the political classes attended by the staff and workers, a Guardian of the Three Powers† revealed how the local IKT clergy had cheated its members out of money and then used these funds for personal enrichment. Gradually, the workers who belonged to the IKT absorbed this propaganda, and one after another they agreed to withdraw from the society. Following this, the workers denounced a colleague who was trying to conceal that he was a Chief of the Altar. Finally, when almost all of the IKT members had pledged to withdraw from the organization, the trade union organized them to launch a struggle to recover the property they had lost to the IKT, "so as to make firmer the determination of those who withdrew from the organization." A total of 270 workers from this factory withdrew from quasi-religious societies,

---

*TC, 9.v.51, p. 1, 6.vii.51, p. 1. The IKT in Tientsin was organized into 18 territorially defined *ta-t'an* (large altars), each of which was divided into 18 sections (*ta-tsu*); beneath each section were a number of *t'an* (altars). The *t'an* were the basic-level organizational units in the Tientsin IKT, and the membership of each *t'an* constituted a parish. *CP*, 15.xii.51, p. 2.

†The Guardians of Three Powers were a middle-ranking group in the IKT hierarchy. Most of them were women. The lowest-ranking position in the IKT hierarchy was the Chief of the Altar.

TABLE 6. *Withdrawals of Tientsin Residents from Quasi-Religious Societies, April–December 1951*

Time period	Number of withdrawals	Average number of withdrawals per day	Total withdrawals to date
April 6–14	70,000	8,750	70,000
April 15–16[a]	30,000	15,000	100,000
April 17–May 4	55,000	3,055	155,000
May 5–June 10	54,000	1,459	209,000
June 11–Dec. 28	71,000	355[b]	280,000

SOURCES: *TC*, 17.iv.51, 18.iv.51, 8.v.51, 6.vii.51, 28.xii.51.

[a] Following the radio broadcast on the evening of April 14.

[b] The campaign formally ended on July 6, but no figures for the number of withdrawals as of that date are available. In all probability, the average number of withdrawals per day was very much higher than 355 for the June 11–July 6 period and was considerably lower than this figure for the remainder of the year.

and two leaders of these societies registered at the public security precinct station.[54]

Workers in smaller enterprises and non-working women could be reached effectively only through meetings convened by the public security precinct stations. The Communists later claimed that the Federation of Women had also played a major role in involving women in this campaign,[55] but there is no evidence in the press to support this assertion, and the Women's Federation itself was a relatively weak organization at that time in Tientsin.*

The statistics on the authorities' effort to mobilize people to withdraw from the IKT are impressive. Excepting only the Railroad Bureau where, as noted above, earlier experimental work had been carried out, the campaign began on April 6, 1951. As Table 6 reveals, within the first eight days, 70,000 people pledged to sever their ties with Tientsin's quasi-religious societies.[56] During the next two days, which followed the major April 14 radio broadcast, 30,000 more members announced their decision to withdraw from these societies.[57] Predictably, this

*CP, 24.ix.52, p. 1. The Women's Federation probably became stronger as a result of this campaign (which did manage to draw many women out of their homes to attend meetings) rather than itself promoting the campaign in a major way. Some evidence to this effect is furnished in CP, 28.xii.52.

hectic pace could not be maintained, but the figures for withdrawal remained high. By May 4, a total of some 155,000 people
had committed themselves, of whom 112,606 were former IKT
members.[58] As of June 10, 209,000 people had withdrawn from
the quasi-religious societies, of whom "over two-thirds" were
formerly affiliated with the IKT.[59] Even after the conclusion of
the campaign on July 6,[60] considerable pressure remained for
those who had stood on the sidelines to come forth and make
their declaration. A report at the end of the year referred to
the "over 210,000" people who had withdrawn from the IKT
alone.[61] At least 70,000 more people withdrew from Tientsin's
other quasi-religious organizations between April and December 1951. Half of those who withdrew from the IKT were
women, and a little over one-third, including both women and
men, received some flour and/or money as a result of their participation in the struggles to recover property from the disgraced
millenarian society leaders.[62] This effort to have people withdraw from the IKT was only a part of the Communists' attack on
the organization, however. The other part consisted of intensive
efforts by the public security organs to intimidate and suppress
the IKT clergy.

When the MPG Council proclaimed the beginning of the campaign on April 6, it set down the following requirements for registration and punishment of the IKT leaders: all Chiefs of the Altar and higher-level leaders must register; the most evil leaders
would be punished severely; those whose crimes were less serious would be sentenced to prison terms according to the law;
even Chiefs of the Altar with a relatively inoffensive record
would be subject to a fixed period of "control"; and those who
"earn merit" would have their punishments reduced or eliminated. The Council also pointed out that the broad group of
people who were "taken in" by the IKT need only cease their
activities to avoid arrest and prosecution.[63] Perhaps to lend
force to these regulations, the government had included a number of IKT leaders among the 193 counterrevolutionaries it had
publicly executed on March 31.[64]

This policy of having registration lead to possibly mild punishment achieved substantial initial results, and by April 15, 1,189 IKT leaders of Chief-of-the-Altar level and above had registered.[65] However, the rate of registration fell rapidly from the 132 per day achieved in these first nine days to an average of only 34 per day for the following 19 days.[66] Consequently, on May 8 the authorities decided to escalate the campaign by publishing a decree directed specifically at the lower and middle levels of the IKT. This required that people in these levels of the hierarchy register by May 20 or face severe punishment. The press carried frequent reminders about the May 20 deadline during the next 12 days, as illustrated by two articles in the May 15 *Tientsin Daily*. The first announced the release on bail of 28 IKT leaders who had earlier failed to register or registered "falsely" (i.e., had continued their organizational activities after registration), but who had fully confessed and "gained merit" after their arrests. The second reviewed the overall handling of IKT leaders, noting that some had been executed and others had suffered mild penalties or been freed. Both articles warned that any middle and lower IKT functionaries who failed to register by May 20 could not possibly receive lenient treatment.[67] As before, registration explicitly involved registering oneself and informing authorities about the parish's organization, property, accounts, and sacred implements; handing over a list of names and addresses of all personnel above and below one's organizational level; denouncing hidden "criminal" elements; and ceasing all personal participation in the IKT.[68] In this way, the authorities bore down heavily on splitting the lower levels of the IKT clergy and making them turn over needed information on the organization's leadership and activities.

The MPG's May 8 initiative brought dramatic results as the rate of registration of IKT clergy shot back up to about 132 per day and remained at that level for at least eight days.[69] By June 10, the authorities had registered 5,743 leaders of Tientsin's various quasi-religious societies, about 4,000 of whom were probably affiliated with the IKT.[70]

The government continued to apply police pressure to the former IKT clergy after the campaign; public security organs maintained supervision over all IKT leaders who had registered. The authorities also recommended that every people's group, factory, government organ, and so forth continue to "educate" and "help" confessed IKT members so they would not revert to their former practices. The press made clear that re-establishing IKT ties would in the future be a punishable crime, and it called on all responsible people to convey this fact clearly to all former IKT participants.[71] These warnings were reinforced by the last major public execution in the drive to suppress counterrevolutionaries, which took place in the period July 10–12, directly after the conclusion of the *t'ui-tao* campaign. Among the 277 people who were shot, 17 were identified as former leaders of the IKT.[72]

Through the Suppression of Counterrevolutionaries and Withdraw from Quasi-religious Societies campaigns, the Communists in Tientsin took harsh measures to reduce the threat of subversive activities during the spring of 1951. Neither of these campaigns was designed to win ideological converts to the Communists' cause, and it is unlikely that either increased the popularity of the authorities among the people. Even the *t'ui-tao* campaign, with its efforts to reach the many tens of thousands of women and employees in small private firms, had attempted almost exclusively to destroy the hierarchies of the various millenarian societies rather than subject their rank and file to an intense political experience. Indeed, despite the impressive statistics on the number of accusation meetings convened and the number of people who withdrew from the societies, for the average person the campaign merely meant attending one or two meetings and then foreswearing future participation in the quasi-religious society concerned. The fact that later the Communists never referred to any activists who had "emerged" during the course of the campaign indicates that few citizens were really mobilized by the movement.[73] For the *leaders* of the quasi-religious societies, however, the *t'ui-tao* campaign had been a searing experience that few could ever forget. The MPG had made it impossible for the hierarchies of the millenarian societies to function in an organized way again.

The 1950 unification of finances and attendant "readjustment" of the industry and commerce, the repercussions of the initial year of the Korean War, and the related Suppression of Counterrevolutionaries and *t'ui-tao* campaigns had the effect of significantly accelerating the Communists' consolidation of power in Tientsin, and by late 1951 they had achieved a position of considerable security and strength in the city. All organizations that opposed them had been attacked and disbanded. Foreign trade and the transport industry were completely under their control, and they had acquired important leverage over key sectors of the privately run economy, such as the textile industry. Through the development of trade unions and the utilization of production competition campaigns, they had achieved a position of considerable power in almost all of the large enterprises in the modern sector of the economy. Their Investment Company controlled a substantial proportion of the long-term investment capital in the city, and their tax and bond drives had soaked up much of the remaining idle funds from the private sector. They had accomplished all of this, moreover, while maintaining a remarkably good record for economic recovery and growth. The rate of inflation for 1951 totaled only about 15 percent, a near miracle when compared with the disastrous inflationary spiral that had gripped the city over the previous five years. By the second half of 1951, the city's industrial production was booming and its domestic trade volume was setting new records.[74] Indeed, interviews suggest that by this time many of the Tientsin businessmen who had moved their capital and firms to Hong Kong on the eve of liberation were now reinvesting in their native city.

The Communists had not ignored the educational system in Tientsin during these years. Rather, they had from the start viewed the city's schools and universities both as a potential source of skilled manpower and as the center of China's budding liberal tradition in intellectual thought. Their policy stressed taking maximum advantage of the former while stamping out the latter. To this end, they kept constant pressure on the teaching faculties to study Marxism-Leninism and Mao Tse-tung's Thought and to learn the Party's line on current matters of political and pedagogical concern. They also revamped school curricula in favor of technical courses and tried to introduce new textbooks that embodied the desired political outlook as well as the substantive technical material necessary for the various courses. The regime's efforts in the educational sphere were at this time very much limited, however, by the Communists' strong desire to win over the intellectuals as allies and by their inability to replace teachers on a large scale should these people become disaffected and decide to retire. Until the fall of 1951, therefore, the authorities applied strong pressure to the educational system but tolerated faculty members who showed independence of thought as long as these people did not become overtly anti-Communist.[75]

During 1950–51, a basic strategy shaped the contours of the regime's policies toward the various segments of Tientsin's society. This pattern of interaction had been determined by Liu Shao-ch'i during his April–May 1949 visit to the city, when he had suggested to the municipal leaders that they marshal the regime's resources and expand their programs only as the necessary resources became available. He had specified as their starting points the modern sector of the economy and the municipal level of government and had advocated a subsequent strategy of organizing "from the top down." Tientsin's leaders followed Liu's advice, and their organizational efforts in the city proceeded from the municipal level to the ward level and from the larger, more modern economic units to the smaller firms in the traditional sector of the economy. By the end of 1951, this process of organizational development was still far from complete. Indeed, the regime enjoyed a major organizational presence only in the public enterprises and the largest private firms, each of which boasted fairly well-developed Party, Youth League, and trade union organizations. The Youth League also extended into enterprises beyond the reach of the Party, and the trade unions existed in firms untouched by the Youth League. But effective trade union organizations outside the large enterprises were confined to only a small proportion of the medium-sized firms and a very tiny part of the small enterprises.

Outside the economic sphere, the regime had concentrated its efforts during 1950–51 on reforming government organs and consolidating its position in the city's schools. This order of priorities left the programs directed at people working in small enterprises and at those who stayed at home starved for cadres. Propaganda carried out among these people was usually conveyed at mass meetings because there were too few cadres available for a more personal approach.[76] The effectiveness of mass meetings undoubtedly varied among individuals, but on the whole the Communists with good reason regarded this as a relatively unsatisfactory way to communicate with the populace.*

This state of affairs meant that by the end of 1951 a person's perception of the Communist government largely depended upon his job. While the capitalists, staff, and workers in the modern firms had generally received rather systematic exposure to the CCP's policies, the situation was markedly different in many neighborhoods, as revealed by two government investigations in April 1951.

The Hsin Ma-lu police precinct in the No. 9 ward contained 118 blacksmiths and rope-twisting handicraft workshops that employed a total of 720 people, including managers. These workshops were generally somewhat larger than the average workshop in the city. Government investigators checking on the effectiveness of the Resist America, Aid Korea campaign in April 1951 found that:

Most of the workers in these workshops have not participated in any trade unions. Their workday is relatively long, especially some of the rope-twisting workers who work 17 or 18 hours per day. They fundamentally do not have any time to participate in study or in social activi-

*Tientsin's leaders were particularly concerned about the possible ineffectiveness of mass meetings because so many of the speakers were from areas other than Tientsin. *T'ien-chin hua*, or Tientsin dialect, differs considerably in both tones and idiom from Peking mandarin, even though Tientsin is located very near the capital. For an example of the CCP's sensitivity to this question, see *CP*, 1.xii.52.

ties. Add to this the fact that these small workshops have been under the direct leadership of the [ward] Industry and Commerce Branch Bureau but that due to its small number of cadres this Branch Bureau could not look after them, and the result is that a "blank spot" in the Resist America, Aid Korea campaign has been created.[77]

The No. 9 ward Party committee decided to make these handicrafts workshops a "keypoint" for Resist America, Aid Korea propaganda work. This effort consisted of convening three meetings in the space of two days—one among the managers and two among the workers.

Before the managers' meeting, because some of the managers had received relatively little education, they had placed obstacles in the path of the workers and apprentices who wanted to participate in social activities. Some even did not permit their workers to read and ridiculed and beat the workers, saying, "Can you eat by gloriously convening meetings and looking at books?" "Are you thinking of becoming cadres?"[78]

At each meeting, several hundred people discussed a broad range of topics, including the new position of the working class in society, the Americans' aggression in Korea, the re-arming of Japan, the campaign to withdraw from the IKT, and the suppression of counterrevolutionaries. The investigators subsequently listed the deficiencies of these meetings as follows:

(1) At the managers' meeting the cadres did not arouse the more active ones to speak up so that the masses could educate the masses; (2) each of the meetings for the workers and apprentices lasted from 7:00 P.M. to 10:00 P.M., and this was too long; and (3) in some instances the speakers did not speak in a sufficiently lively, earthy, and concrete way: some of the workers complained that the speakers spoke in an accent so heavy that they could understand only a small part of what was said.[79]

Nevertheless, the press cited this example as a model for others to follow.

A second investigation of the Resist America, Aid Korea campaign looked into the situation in the Ta Yao Wang Miao police precinct in the No. 8 ward. The investigation report stated:

The Ta Yao Wang Miao precinct station has in the past done quite a bit of Resist America, Aid Korea propaganda work. According to summary statistics, it has convened at least 50 large and small *p'ien* meetings and has carried out three mobilizations—for contributions, for extra work to comfort the People's Volunteers, and for organizing parades. It has also organized over 4,000 people to listen to each of the recent radio broadcast meetings for Suppression of Counterrevolutionaries and for abolition of the I Kuan Tao. According to our investigation, however, the workers and apprentices in quite a few of the small workshops have not participated in a single meeting and fundamentally do not know what Resist America, Aid Korea is. [For instance], among the 40 households in the Ch'ang-chia *hu-t'ung*, 10 percent of the residents have not participated in a single meeting, 20 percent of the residents can only recollect the characters "K'ang-Mei Yuan-Ch'ao" (Resist America, Aid Korea) [but do not know what they mean], and 50 percent of the people know only whom Resist America, Aid Korea is against and whom it is for but do not know where Korea is. These facts explain that our past propaganda work has not been sufficiently universal and penetrating.

In this area there are 201 households and firms. Aside from the 33 commercial firms, the vast majority of the rest are the homes of pedicab drivers, freight workers, and people with street stalls. The men work outside all day, while the women stay in all day and do housework. Very few have in the past participated in propaganda activities or heard the rationale for Resist America, Aid Korea.[80]

The Hsin Ma-lu and Ta Yao Wang Miao experiences are cogent reminders that surface appearances are poor indicators of the degree to which a revolution has penetrated the various segments of an urban society. More than mass rallies and rousing speeches, concrete organizational and resource development dictates the impact of a revolutionary movement. Massive doses of written propaganda do not change the ideas of semi-literate people whose work keeps them closely confined to narrow quarters, and rhetoric rings hollow when it is pronounced by speakers with strange accents and is isolated from the daily problems and prospects of the listeners. In practice, there is a dialectical tension between this need for organizational capabilities and the spontaneity verging on anarchy that imparts to revolutionary change much of its soul-searching character and energy. Without careful preparation and husbanding of resources, the bursts of revolutionary fervor burn themselves out and leave disappointment, alienation, and apathy in their wake. But without surges of revolutionary energy, organization rapidly produces bureaucratic inertia and vested interests in the *status quo*. Effective revolution demands both aspects of the dialectic.

In the fall of 1951, echoes were heard in Tientsin of a campaign that had been launched in Manchuria in late August against corruption, waste, and bureaucratism.[81] At the same time, people involved in the city's educational system experienced a sharp increase in the level of pressure applied to the schools and universities.[82] During the winter of 1951–52, these scattered rumblings grew in intensity and then exploded across the city's political landscape in the form of three mass campaigns—the Three Anti (*san-fan*) campaign against cadres in the government and the mass organizations, the Five Anti (*wu-fan*) campaign against the bourgeoisie, and the Thought Reform campaign against the professors in the universities. Through these campaigns the Communists in Tientsin temporarily abandoned their methodical policy of marshaling their resources and gradually expanding their control in favor of a radical breakthrough to a new level of penetration of Tientsin's society. Put differently, by the early fall of 1951, most people in Tientsin still viewed the Communist regime as a very strong reformist government. A mere six months later, there were few individuals in the city who were not profoundly aware that they had been caught in the grip of a revolution.

CHAPTER 7 *The Second Revolution*

Revolutions ultimately seek to change popular views about such fundamental issues as the way people relate to each other in personal as well as political and economic terms. By this criterion, for most of the citizens of Tientsin, the revolution came not in 1949 but in early 1952, when the ferocious Three Anti (*san-fan*) and Five Anti (*wu-fan*) campaigns washed over the city. These massive political movements, accompanied by the Thought Reform Campaign aimed at the intellectuals in the city's education system, brought a dramatic, indeed a qualitative, change in the Communists' interaction with Tientsin's society. This monumental onslaught would have been largely self-destructive, moreover, had it not been prepared for by years of effort accumulating data, training cadres, constructing an administrative apparatus, and so forth. For, beneath the sound and fury of the campaigns, only this preparation permitted the leaders to capitalize on the social breakdown produced by their initiatives in a way that transformed and consolidated their position in the city.

These campaigns had two major targets: the urban bourgeoisie, who were the objects of the Five Anti, and the cadres in the basic-level units of the city's public organizations (the government, trade unions, and so forth), who bore the brunt of the Three Anti. Pre-1949 urban values predominated among the former group and to an increasing extent were seducing the latter. This chapter examines the campaigns in microcosm, as they intruded upon and transformed the lives of the assistant manager of a medium-sized chemical company and the overseers in the city's construction industry. Chapter Eight then provides a larger overview of the origins, development, and effects of these campaigns in the city.

The following two case studies also highlight some of the underlying costs of the strategy that Liu Shao-ch'i had proposed in April–May 1949. His reforms and his emphasis on economic expansion had sharply limited the degree to which the Communists could restructure the functioning of the city's myriad economic units. Those who possessed scarce and vital technical and commercial skills had to be persuaded, not coerced, into submitting to Communist organizational discipline. As a result, the CCP had to elaborate an economic and organizational structure that was grounded in commercial mores predating the Communist period, and that often utilized personnel who shared little of the CCP's vision. The Three Anti and Five Anti campaigns confronted this problem head on and sought to lay a firmer foundation for the establishment of a socialist society in Tientsin.

The Five Anti Campaign in the China Chemical Company

The Firm Before 1949

The China Chemical Company was established in Tientsin during the Japanese occupation. Mr. Wang, the interviewee upon whose information this study is based, began working as the firm's assistant manager at the time of its founding and continued without interruption until the socialization of industry during the mid-1950's.*

The China Chemical Company had over 100 stockholders, most of whom were very wealthy men. It was nominally headed by a Board of Directors with over a dozen members, which in turn selected a standing committee of three men. This committee assumed day-by-day control over the financial affairs of the company and directly hired and supervised the firm's two ac-

---

*This Five Anti case study is based on extensive interviewing of the assistant manager of the firm involved. All names, including that of the firm, have been changed.

countants. Under the Board of Directors, there was a manager, an assistant manager, and a head for each of the firm's departments (wholesaling, retailing, purchasing, stockroom, and so forth). The manager was a wealthy man with good connections in Tientsin. He did not participate in the actual operation of the firm. Rather his sole responsibility was to use his good name and his not inconsiderable connections to keep the company out of trouble and to make certain that the company never had to pay excessive taxes. The person who actually ran the firm was the assistant manager, Mr. Wang. Wang exercised control over all aspects of the company's management except finances. He had the power to hire and fire all employees other than the company's two accountants and to supervise the firm's day-to-day operations.

Most of the company's 30 to 40 employees were skilled women who synthesized the chemical compounds that the firm produced. Several male clerks ran the retailing department, which accounted for the bulk of the firm's income. The company also did a small volume of wholesale business, for which it employed several men. The company also had seven servants— two cooks, two drivers, a housecleaner, a young handyman, and the "No. 1 boy." Mr. Wang personally hired each of the firm's employees, all of whom had some type of personal relationship, or *kuan-hsi,* with him. Some were relatives, others were close friends, and the rest were relatives of close friends. The servants presented a special case. The "No. 1 boy" in 1952 was over sixty years old and had worked for many years in Mr. Wang's household before joining the Chemical Company. All of the other servants were relatives of the "No. 1 boy."

The China Chemical Company was considered to be a rather modern medium-sized firm, and it did very well financially. It used a portion of its high profits to provide unusually good salaries and living facilities for its staff and workers. The remainder was used to reimburse the stockholders and to undertake the various activities that would ensure the company's continued financial well-being.

The China Chemical Company had several ways of guaranteeing a good profit at the end of each year. Virtually all of the stockholders were men who could influence the chemical purchases of other firms in Tientsin and could occasionally arrange for these firms to buy chemicals they did not really need. In these instances, the Chemical Company sold almost useless, inexpensive compounds and received high prices for them. Stockholders received a 20 percent kickback on any business they directed toward the company.

In general the company overcharged for its products. Even after paying the kickback, it rarely made less than a 300–800 percent profit on each transaction, and it never permitted itself to make less than 100 percent profit. At the same time, the company produced mainly those chemical compounds that could be made most cheaply, and that brought in the greatest profit. The high position and good reputation of the stockholders guaranteed that the company never lacked business.

Making a substantial profit was only part of the problem. Keeping it was the other part. Government exactions and inflation were the two main dangers. The Chemical Company reduced its taxable income by the simple expedient of keeping two sets of books. The accountants put exactly half of the gross income into a bank account under a fictitious name, while they entered the other half on the books as the total income. Mr. Wang was not himself responsible for this policy, since he had no control over the accountants. He nevertheless knew about the policy and fully approved of it, for as he said, "All firms used this type of device and everybody knew about it." In addition, the titular manager regularly presented appropriate gifts to influential men and maintained social contact with relevant government and non-government figures in order to lighten the tax burden. Although Mr. Wang knew few of the details of these activities, he was aware that the Company had paid no taxes under either the Japanese or the KMT government. This remained true during 1949–51.

While the company could evade taxes, inflation presented a more difficult problem. The solution was to convert cash into gold bars and foreign currencies, a practice that continued after

1949, even though the People's Government passed laws forbidding it.

The Firm in 1949–1951

During the shelling of Tientsin by Communist forces in January 1949, the Chemical Company sustained some damage. The day after liberation, PLA soldiers called Wang and all of the other businessmen in his neighborhood outside to inform them in courteous but stern language that the entire city was now under new control, that the People's Government would work to restore order to the city's economy, and that nobody would be harmed so long as they obeyed the laws of the new government. Wang had friends who were asked to billet PLA soldiers in their homes during the following few weeks, and they were very impressed with the discipline and honesty of the soldiers.

Wang was vaguely aware that the new government professed to protect private industry and commerce, but he had no other knowledge whatsoever about any policies of the People's Government between 1949 and 1951.* He heard from relatives about the Youth League, the CCP, and the Suppression of Counterrevolutionaries campaign, but he did not bother to learn anything concrete about any one of these. He was, of course, cognizant of the general improvement of the economy in late 1950, and he gave the new gvernment fairly high marks on economic policy. Since none of these policies affected his firm *directly*, however, he remained oblivious to their actual content. At no time did he discuss any government policies with his employees. The internal operation of the company did not change in any way. The basic principles guiding the relationship between the firm's manager and the municipal government—using entertainment and maintaining good personal relations in order to keep out of trouble—also remained the same, and, as noted

*The degree of Wang's ignorance about government policies may be somewhat atypical. Wang himself was not in charge of the financial affairs of the company, and thus it was not he who had to maintain the social contacts with government bureaucrats. The principle that businessmen would learn only about those government policies that actually affected the daily operations of their own firms does, however, seem to be a generally applicable one.

above, the China Chemical Company paid no taxes during 1949–51. After the PLA soldiers left the company on January 16, 1949, no official government cadres came to the company's doors until the start of Three Anti Five Anti.

Thus, by December 1951, Wang regarded the Tientsin MPG as a good reformist government under which business could prosper. Because he had no interest in political philosophies, he did not read the political pronouncements of the new government. Since none of the economic policies touched him directly, he had not bothered to educate himself on the concrete economic laws passed by the new government. The Chemical Company continued to do well, and Wang was confident about the future.

The Five Anti Campaign

One day at the end of 1951, a group of about 20 young men came to the China Chemical Company. They asked Wang whether they might come in and talk with him about the company's business operations. He replied that he was too busy to speak with them and that, in any case, it was none of their business. They responded, "We are from the Tax Bureau. Do not shut the door on us so quickly. We want to talk with you." This was the beginning of the Five Anti campaign for Mr. Wang.

The group of young men who came to Wang's were in fact a Five Anti work team. This team was composed in part of cadres from the MPG Tax Bureau and in part of young employees from other chemical companies and other young cadres in Tientsin. They spent the next few weeks at Wang's firm.

The Tax Bureau cadres immediately began going over the company's accounts, and they kept at this day and night for two weeks. At the end of this period, they concluded that the accounts were in good order. Wang felt that it would have been difficult for them to reach any other conclusion for two reasons. The company's accountant, Mr. Kuo, was one of the best in Tientsin. And more important, Kuo had previously taught accounting, and several of the cadres sent from the Tax Bureau turned out to have been his former students.

While some members of the work team pored over the accounts, others questioned Mr. Wang about the general affairs of the company. Wang answered these questions without much anxiety because he was confident that he had done nothing wrong in running the firm. One day a rather large group from the work team came, and they said they wanted to explain "policy" to Wang. They declared that they recognized him as the sole responsible person in the company, and that "thus, the problems of the company are your problems and the problems of anyone who works in the company are your problems." After repeating this statement several times, they asked Wang whether he understood it. He felt this way of viewing things was rather unfair, but since he did not want to argue with the large group before him he indicated his assent. The cadres then asked him whether he had ever sold opium. He said he had not. They had him write a statement that, "I, Wang I-ling, have never sold opium. If I have ever sold opium, I am willing to suffer . . . punishment." Wang then signed the statement and placed the fingerprints of his two forefingers at the bottom. He felt this was strange but did not want to argue. A cadre took the statement and put it in his pocket. He then led in one of the company's drivers and asked him whether he had ever sold opium. The driver answered in the affirmative and was taken out. The cadre then asserted that the driver's problems were Wang's problems, as Wang had just affirmed. Wang felt a sense of panic well up inside him.

When the cadre saw that Wang was shaken, he told Wang that the government's policy was one of leniency toward someone as long as that person honestly confessed his crimes. Wang responded that he would say anything the cadre asked him to.

Following this incident, the cadres from the work team questioned Wang about the company's business affairs for several more days. They then insisted that he write an autobiography, reviewing his life from boyhood. This autobiography had to include all major events in his life and all of his social relationships since the age of eight. When Wang handed in the autobiography the cadres went over it and asked him to write about a given section of it in more detail. For several weeks, each time he handed in this report he was asked to make another supplement. He found this experience very trying. By the end of it, the work team had a considerable amount of information about every relative, friend, business associate, and employee Wang had.

When Wang finally handed in a "satisfactory" autobiography, the cadres asked whether he "dared" to participate in a meeting. He replied that he had nothing to hide. On the following day, he began his participation in a Five Anti Chemical Industry Study Group. He attended meetings of this study group for an average of over 13 hours a day every day for the next three months. It was, by his own account, the most traumatic experience in his life.

Wang's study group consisted of 30–40 managers of various chemical companies in Tientsin. The composition changed slightly as several members were added and others dropped, but for the most part the membership remained constant. Aside from these managers, two to four cadres from the work team sat in the corner and listened to every meeting.

The group chose a chairman and two secretaries from among their number. The chairman ran each meeting, and the two secretaries took notes on all the proceedings. Wang served as one of the secretaries, and for this reason, he was able to do a little less talking than others. He handed in his notes to the two cadres at the end of each meeting. He never saw any of the notes again.

The study group met in a very small and stuffy room in a building near Wang's company. Everyone smoked heavily. Wang, who had never smoked before, took up cigarettes during those meetings—a habit he has subsequently been unable to give up.

At the first meeting, each member of the study group received a six-page booklet that spelled out in large characters the basic policies of the Communists: "benefit to both capital and labor," "favor industry over commerce," and so forth. On most days the study group began with a discussion of one of these policies.

The first major "crime" tackled by the study group was tax evasion. A discussion of selling chemical compounds that did not meet the specifications claimed for them followed. An extensive analysis of the business and personal relations among people in the chemical industry was next on the agenda. And so it went. During the course of these meetings, Wang readily "confessed" to all of the shady business practices in which his company had engaged.

The typical meeting began at 8:00 A.M. with the chairman stating the subject of that day's study, for instance, tax evasion. After reading the relevant CCP pronouncement on tax evasion, the group discussed it for a short time. The chairman then called on one of the managers to talk about his own past in relation to this issue. After the person had complied, he had to listen to all the other people discuss his testimony. At this time, everyone had to speak up, for "there was no freedom to keep silent." At the end of this general discussion, which might well last several days, the original "target" manager was asked whether he recognized the validity of the critical points the others had made against him. If he did, the chairman expressed satisfaction, and the study group moved on to the next question. If he did not, there followed a prolonged series of discussions about the issues in dispute until either he recognized his errors or the group gave up.* Once someone had acknowledged a charge, he encountered a great deal of trouble if he subsequently tried in any way to deny or retract this affirmation. The cadres immediately added each charge that a person acknowledged to his "confession."

Mr. Wang listed five characteristics of the Communists' basic strategy in conducting the Five Anti study group. (1) Only one representative of each chemical factory participated in a given study group; this separation put great pressure on the individual concerned to confess quickly to everything before his business partner confessed in another study group. (2) Different firms had different methods for making high profits and avoiding taxes; the general discussion of each firm took advantage of jealousies and feelings of disapproval among the managers to elicit greater information about each "target" manager and to in-

---

*The documentary evidence indicates that during this time, unknown to the target manager, an investigating team would go to his factory to gather evidence concerning the charge under discussion.

crease the severity of the criticism. (3) Each participant received strong encouragement to make detailed accusations against other managers even if he was not at all sure of the accuracy of his charges. (4) Anything that was admitted during the discussion could not be denied subsequently without a great deal more trouble. (5) All confessions and criticisms had to be related to one's own *concrete* experience, and the group required full details of every instance.

In illustration of the last point, when the group asked Mr. Wang whether he had illegally bought and sold gold since liberation, he replied in the affirmative. He was not permitted, however, simply to give an arbitrary figure for the amount involved. Rather, after declaring the amount to be 33 ounces, he was required to state from whom he bought each ounce of the gold and to whom he sold it. He was questioned and prodded for three straight days and nights until he could recall each transaction.

The Communists used other tactics to make the study group a more effective tool for eliciting information and confessions. Not infrequently, one of the work-team cadres in attendance stopped a discussion to take the chairman out of the room for a short talk. During this time, he instructed the chairman on how best to proceed with the discussion. People who "performed well" in the study group were used to maximum advantage. If the cadres though that a person was progressing well with the discussion of a problem, they often asked him to attend a secret meeting with several other members of the study group outside of the regular group meeting. They encouraged the people attending this small caucus to raise questions about the problem with respect to a particular person at the next regular meeting. Mr. Wang knew about this arrangement only because he was once asked to participate in one of these meetings. Moreover, if a manager was especially vociferous in his questioning of others, he might well be transferred to a second study group of chemical industry managers, where he could bring his experience to bear among a new group of people.

The cadres had to deal with the problem of informal alliances and cliques among the participants in the study group. Although Mr. Wang himself did not know any of the other participants in his particular group, it was clear to him that some of the members were acquainted with each other. To cope with this problem, the cadres usually noted who seemed to know whom and then concentrated on having these people criticize each other. Since the authorities in this case knew that the two people had some knowledge about each other, the pressures on each to denounce the other became particularly intense. If this tactic failed, one of the parties to such a relationship was actually transferred to another study group.

Psychological pressures within the study group grew almost unbearable. The cadres constantly warned the participants that the government's policy was to be lenient to those who confessed and severe to those who refused to confess. A manager would fare badly if he was denounced for a crime before having admitted it himself. Each participant had no idea what denunciations the government might have received against him. The atmosphere in the study group was kept tense by the active encouragement of denunciations, even when they had little basis in fact. There was no real punishment for a false accusation—only for refusal to anticipate the accusation with a confession.

The cadres were careful not to let someone know how he was doing over the course of the study group meetings. For instance, Mr. Wang first got an inkling that he might be progressing well when he was asked to participate in the small secret meeting mentioned above. This occurred after Wang had been participating in the study group for several months.

People in the study group did not know how many types of crimes there were to which one should confess. Wang never heard the term *wu-fan* (Five Anti) before the end of the campaign. He felt that within the study group there were *"pa-fan-to"* (more than eight anti's), and in fact, that there was no practical limit to the number of "anti's" with which one could be charged.[1] Similarly, the participants had no sense of the possible duration of the campaign or of the severity of the punishments that they might face. They knew only that every admission was noted down and added to their confession, that every sign of reticence was taken as a deliberate attempt to "obstinately refuse to confess," and that doing what the cadres wished, in terms of both confessions and denunciations, might bring leniency in the final judgment.

During the course of this period, the managers received no succor outside the study group. Every one of their workers, servants, and casual acquaintances absolutely refused to speak a word to them, and they were consequently in a very real way cut off from effective contact with the outside world. It was like slipping into a dark hole with nothing to grab onto but with a vague sense that acting in a certain way might some day permit one to climb up into the daylight.

Wang continued to manage the China Chemical Company until the socialist transformation of industry in late 1955, and during these few years after the Five Anti Campaign, he learned a bit about what had transpired at his company while he had participated in the study group. He is certain that before the Five Anti campaign the CCP did not have any informers or even strong sympathizers among his employees. There had never been any talk of forming a trade union within the company. Very early in the Five Anti campaign, however, the CCP did manage to recruit the youngest person in the company—they young handyman Hsiao Yang, who was the nephew of the "No. 1 Boy." This young man was in his middle teens. Until that time, he had served simply as a helper around the company, pouring tea when guests came, running errands, and so forth. But after the campaign, Hsiao Yang served as the eyes, ears, and mouthpiece of the regime inside the company.

During the course of the Five Anti campaign, the employees of Wang's company spent most of their time in production and part of their time attending various meetings. They attended these meetings together with employees of other chemical companies. Only Hsiao Yang attended separate meetings, about which nobody knew any details.* By the end of the campaign, every one of the staff and workers of the China Chemical Company had been recruited into the Chemical Workers' Trade Union.

During the campaign, the cadres treated all of the employees of the company other than Wang as members of the working class. This included even the accountants and the head of wholesaling, who, according to Wang, had engaged in corrupt activities outside of the company to make extra money. Wang alone was considered to be a "representative of the capitalist side" and thus was ineligible to participate in the trade union or other activities of the workers.

Toward the end of March, people from Wang's study group began to be called up individually to try to "pass through the gate" (i.e., to prove that they recognized their errors and were fully repentant). Wang was about the eighth member of his study group to be summoned for this ordeal. Many staff members and workers from a number of chemical factories participated in the meeting where Wang passed through the gate. The meeting took place fairly late at night in a large hall packed with people. Wang's own employees occupied the front rows.

Wang and the head mananger of the China Chemical Company, whom Wang had not seen since the start of Five Anti, both faced this meeting at the same time. The personnel of the China Chemical Company directed harsh questions at each of them, with Hsiao Yang obviously taking the lead. Several times, after Wang had responded to important questions, the chairman of the meeting made him leave the room for a moment. Upon his return, the questioning shifted to another topic.

The people were in general more severe toward the head manager than toward Wang, and at the conclusion of this meeting, they decided that Wang had successfully passed through

*It is possible that he was attending one of the training classes the authorities were running for future trade union cadres at this time. On these training classes, see *CP*, 29.iv.52, p. 2.

the gate, but that the manager had not. The manager had to return to his study group and some time later attempt again to pass through the gate.

When Wang went home after the meeting, some of his employees followed him and engaged him in some brief conversation. This was the first time since the start of the study group that they had said a word to him. It indicated to Wang that he had now been accepted back into society. He still did not know, however, what his punishment would be.

Within a few days after passing though the gate, Wang received a form from the authorities. He had to fill out this form with all of the pertinent information about his supervision of the company that had emerged during the course of Five Anti. This form then served as the basis for the final judgment of his case.

After completing the form, Wang again had to participate in a study group. This new group devoted all its time to the study of the Common Program (which served as the equivalent of a constitution in China during 1949–54). This new group, like the old one, consisted of 30-40 managers of chemical companies. All these managers had passed through the gate, but they were not the same people as had been in Wang's previous study group. Although the mechanics of the new group were very similar to those of the old one, the style of the new group was notably more relaxed. The group met every morning but did not take up the whole day. The participants went over the Common Program article by article, and they were required to relate each article to their personal experience. There were neither confessions nor denunciations, although all remarks were recorded and the notes of each meeting were given to the work-team cadres. This study group met until it had thoroughly reviewed every article of the Common Program. It stopped meeting only in the middle of the summer of 1952.

At the end of this period, Wang and all other responsible people from the chemical companies in Tientsin were summoned to attend a mass meeting at the largest theater in town. There, a report was given that explained the five-category classification for Five-Anti offenders. The name of each chemical company together with the category into which it had been classified, was then read out.* The China Chemical Company, which had admitted keeping a false set of books, corrupting tax officials, and so forth, was classified as a "basically law-abiding firm," and did not have to pay a fine.† Wang believes the company received this lenient treatment because he had tried to be very cooperative in the study group.

The Effects of the Five Anti Campaign

Socially, the Five Anti had the effect of separating Wang from his employees. Even though most of the China Chemical Company's employees were Wang's own relatives, they and their families maintained only minimal social relations with him after the campaign. Wang attributes this ostracism to the fact that all of them knew that any unnecessary contact would immediately be reported to the authorities through Hsiao Yang. This situation did not change appreciably during Wang's remaining few years with the company.

After the Five Anti, Wang felt that the regime could restrict and interfere with the internal affairs of the company almost at will. For instance, Hsiao Yang continued to play an active role in the company, and his position became virtually unchallengeable because everyone assumed that what he said reflected the regime's policies. He continued to attend meetings on almost a daily basis, and nobody dared to ask him what kind of meetings these were. The rest of the staff and workers believed that he regularly reported on the internal affairs of the company, and they treated him with appropriate caution. Over the course of

---

*The documentary evidence indicates that Wang is probably confused in his timing. The normal pattern was for the Five Anti targets to receive their classifications and then to participate in the systematic study of the Common Program. This section follows Wang's chronology, though.

†For reasons that do not concern us here, Wang, as distinct from the company, received a more severe classification and had to pay a rather substantial fine out of his own pocket. Wang's personal activities could be judged separately from those of his company because the company was owned by the stockholders. The vast majority of firms in Wang's trade, however, were family-owned. In these firms, the activities of the company could not be judged separately from those of the owner/manager.

the next six years, Hsiao Yang became both a member of the CCP and an important cadre in the Chemical Workers' Trade Union.

After the campaign, every morning from 7:00 A.M. to 8:00 A.M. the staff and workers of the China Chemical Company participated in a "newspaper reading group" or a "study group." Wang knew that these meetings took place but was barred from them himself. Sometimes the employees called a meeting of the company's trade union, to which everyone belonged. Again, Wang could not participate.

Perhaps most importantly, a Labor-Capital Consultative Committee was organized in the China Chemical Company. This committee met at fixed intervals of several weeks, and all meetings were attended by Wang and every other employee of the firm. In theory, the LCCC was established to discuss how to increase the volume of the company's business while cutting its costs. In fact, however, Wang perceived this committee as the primary way in which the government conveyed new policies to him. He assumed that virtually all suggestions made by the employees in these meetings were first given to them at their trade union meeting. Furthermore, Hsiao Yang tended to dominate these meetings, and no one would quarrel with his suggestions. Consequently, Wang feared the LCCC and tried to minimize its role. He adopted the strategy of agreeing readily to every suggestion made by the committee and in this way letting the committee make its own mistakes. He hoped in this way to demoralize this body and gradually undermine its authority.

After the Five Anti campaign, the government placed numerous restrictions on the China Chemical Company. In some cases, these restrictions were embodied in official directives; in other instances, they were conveyed only through a "suggestion" raised by Hsiao Yang. The LCCC was charged with supervising Wang and making sure that the company in fact faithfully obeyed these restrictions. For instance, during one of the committee's meetings Hsiao Yang expressed the conviction that a 20 percent profit on each transaction was a proper amount to make. Everyone realized that this represented government policy, and the meeting immediately agreed to the suggestion. Thereafter, all of the company's prices were lowered so that it made no more than a 20 percent profit on each sale. Later, the committee persistently questioned Wang about prices and profit margins to ensure his continued compliance with this guideline.

Other restrictions prohibited Wang from firing any of his employees, reducing the scope of the company's operations, cutting back on salaries, or engaging in any wholesale transactions that did not go through the government-run Credit Company. The Credit Company, which made the arrangements for all wholesale transactions, allowed only a very small rate of profit. As a consequence, the costs of the Chemical Company remained constant while the firm experienced a sharp decline in income. Wang soon perceived that it would be only a matter of time until the firm went bankrupt, and he therefore assumed as passive a role in managing the firm as he dared without risking serious trouble.

After the Five Anti, the Board of Directors and its standing committee lost interest in managing the China Chemical Company, and they ceased to follow the affairs of the firm. For all intents and purposes, therefore, the company became independent of its own general governing body at the same time that Wang lost much of the initiative in running the firm on a day-to-day basis.

The Five Anti campaign was the first penetration of the China Chemical Company by the new regime, and it transformed the lives of everyone in the firm. Before the campaign, the firm had been held together by common economic and social ties and a shared indifference toward politics. By the end of the campaign, the regime had succeeded in opening a gulf between the manager and the other employees, in recruiting a member of the firm to serve as the government's unofficial agent, in organizing all of the employees to carry out the will of the authorities, and in creating a situation where both the owners and manager were either too cowed or simply too tired to care seriously about the firm's future financial well-being.

The government also acquired a very substantial amount of information about the past practices of this company and about the relationships among the people in the chemical industry. It succeeded in convincing the manager of the company to cease practicing the "normal" business activities of the past, which had involved corruption, tax evasion, cheating on materials, and so forth. Finally, it also succeeded in conveying the substance of its political outlook to both Wang and the entire staff of his company. It was unlikely that either Wang or his staff could ever again be totally ignorant of, and oblivious to, the policies of the Communist authorities.

The Three Anti Campaign in the Construction Industry

The Three Anti campaign was roughly concurrent with the Five Anti and focused on corruption, waste, and bureaucratism within all public institutions—government offices, public enterprises, and mass organizations. Its primary object within the government organs and public enterprises was to tighten up discipline. And in mass organizations, as this study of the construction industry shows, it aimed at consolidating the control of the higher leadership over the primary-level organs.

Background

Shortly after liberation, Tientsin had only 30,000–40,000 construction workers,[2] a figure that was unusually low because the unsettled economic situation had brought about an unwillingness or inability to invest in the normal range of capital construction projects. By late 1951, with the economy experiencing robust growth, the number of construction workers had grown to 60,000,[3] and the more than 220 construction firms in the city had been united into a Building Industry Trade Association.[4]

The construction industry in Tientsin used the overseer (*pa-*

t'ou)* system for hiring workers. Under this system, when a construction project was being planned, a company agreed to undertake the work at a given cost. The company then hired one or more foremen to carry out the actual construction work, while the company itself assumed responsibility for supplying the raw materials and providing other related services. Each foreman contracted to perform the work on a project for a fixed payment.

Having assumed the obligation to do a construction job, the foreman took complete responsibility for finding and hiring the necessary workers and for supervising the actual construction work at the building site. Some foremen personally discharged all of these obligations, but most hired lower-ranking foremen to carry out the actual recruitment and supervision. As a *Tientsin Daily* editorial explained, for a single construction project, frequently "the *ta-kuei* [big devil] submitted the bid, the *erh-kuei* [little devil] contracted to do the work, the *ta-t'ou* [big boss] found the workers, the *hsiao-t'ou* [little boss] supervised the workers, and the workers did the work"[5]

The foreman exercised complete control over his workers. It was not unusual for foremen to travel into the rural areas of Hopei and recruit peasants with promises of high salaries and good working conditions. Commonly, a foreman recruited people from his own village, and he personally arranged their passage into the city and their lodging once they arrived. After they entered the city, the foreman typically had these new recruits at his mercy, for it was only through him (or another foreman) that they could find employment.

Usually the foreman's agreement to do a given construction job made no mention of the number of workers he should employ or the salaries he should pay them. Since the workers themselves had no idea how much money the construction company

Pa-t'ou has a distinctly negative connotation and is best translated as overseer. *Kung-t'ou* is a more neutral term, usually translated as foreman and customarily used for the foremen in factories. Articles concerning the overseers in the construction industry usually used *pa-t'ou* when stressing their negative functions and *kung-t'ou* when adopting a more positive attitude toward them. These terms are used interchangeably in this study.

was paying the *pa-t'ou,* they had no basis upon which to demand a given wage. In addition, the foreman usually arranged for the workers' food at the site, for which the workers had to pay higher-than-market prices. At the end of a construction project, it was not unusual for the foreman to withhold a substantial portion of the wages he had promised to pay on the pretext of docking the workers' wages for insubordination, tardiness, or poor work. The great tension that characterized the exploitative relationship between a foreman and his workers virtually guaranteed that the foreman would have incidents to which he could point as an excuse for not paying the workers their full wages.[6]

The Communists described the relationship between a foreman and his charges as "feudal," because the obligation of the workers to their foreman often included presenting him with gifts, taking care of his chores, and paying obeisance in ways that went far beyond a simple contractual relationship.[7] The foreman's hold over his workers was based on their fear of starvation. And because an original contract was typically subcontracted to three or more middlemen, each of whom took a percentage, only a very meager wage remained for the workers.

The Communists had begun to organize the construction workers into a trade union in early 1950. In the spring of that year, the Construction Trade Union arranged for some of the unemployed construction workers to take minor jobs by contracting directly with their employers, thereby eliminating the middlemen and preserving higher wages for the workers. The trade union quickly realized, however, that the essential problem was a lack of leadership among the construction workers engaged in collective contracting, as the system of direct contracts with employers was called. This problem reflected the fact that the overseers not only recruited the necessary labor, but also planned, assigned, and supervised the construction tasks at their work sites. Furthermore, only the overseers had sufficient stature among the workers to discipline and instruct them, for most of the workers came straight from the fields and were unaccustomed to a non-agricultural regimen. The trade union lacked cadres with either this technical competence or stature among the workers, and it soon discovered that the workers it recruited to participate in the collective contracting system were unable to do even small jobs satisfactorily. Consequently, when in May–June 1950 the Construction Industry Trade Union began to establish a publicly run Tientsin Construction Workers' Co-operative Construction Company (CCC) the trade union cadres made a conscious effort to recruit overseers into the company.[8]

During the remainder of 1950, the number of workers participating in the CCC continued to grow, and by the end of the year the company had completed 168 construction projects, almost all of which were in the public sector of the economy and were very modest in scope. The CCC took responsibility in each instance for making cost estimates, assuming contractual responsibility for the work, purchasing raw materials, supplying the tools, and organizing and administering the workers. The company made all of its accounts public, and the workers themselves decided on the most equitable scale for wages at the site.[9]

During the winter of 1950–51, the Construction Trade Union reviewed its work and recognized two major flaws. First, the union had been organized "from the top down" on the basis of the workers' place of residence. The union leaders determined that this system weakened the union because the workers at any given site came from different neighborhoods and belonged to different local union organizations. As a consequence, the union had no effective control at the work sites and in a real sense simply lost contact with its members.[10] Second, by spring 1951 the CCC had only 28 higher-level administrative personnel,[11] and all control over the actual operation of the CCC, devolved upon the leaders at the various work sites—i.e., upon the former overseers.

The Construction Trade Union corrected the first flaw in March 1951. It changed the basis of union organization from a worker's residence to his work site and reorganized the union "from the bottom up. " The union transferred 70 percent of its administrative cadres from the ward offices to the four main construction sites in the city. This virtually destroyed the union organization between the union's central offices and the construction sites and permitted most of the union cadres to gain firsthand experience. All subsequent union organization took the work site as its starting point.[12]

On July, 1, 1951, the Construction Trade Union and the Building Trade Association signed a collective contract aimed at undercutting the destructive influence of the *pa-t'ou* throughout the construction industry. (A different collective contract between the CCC and its workers signed that spring had anticipated this action. It had called for the establishment of a Democratic Management Committee at each work site to oversee administration there and to enforce the workers' right to set the scale of their piece-rates. However, this contract had covered only those in the CCC, and the fact that there was no mention in the press of a campaign to enforce it suggests that it remained more a statement of goals than a reflection of reality.) The new contract outlawed the subcontracting system in both the public and the private sector of the construction industry. The June contract forbade private construction companies to farm out their obligations and required that their own employees complete all work at any construction projects undertaken. The contract took a two-pronged approach to the former overseers, on the one hand forbidding them to engage in the exploitative subcontracting system, and on the other, encouraging them to remain as employees in the construction companies so that the industry could still benefit from their technical skills. This industry-wide collective contract also contained provisions for the establishment of a Democratic Management Committee at each of the CCC's sites and of a Labor-Capital Consultative Committee at each of the work sites of the private construction companies. In both cases, these committees were entrusted with, in essence, keeping tabs on the former overseers and ensuring that they did not cheat the workers.[13]

The Construction Trade Union announced a number of measures to ensure the thorough implementation of the June 1951 contract. It initiated a campaign to familiarize the construction workers with the guarantees and protection provided them by the new contract. It also declared its intention to establish a temporary trade union committee at each work site to supervise the implementation of the contract's provisions. It affirmed that in the future workers and management at each site would sign their own collective contract giving concrete substance to the general provisions of the all-industry contract. And finally, it pledged to the foremen that workers would be educated concerning the "indispensable" leadership role that these traditional leaders still had to play and the consequent necessity of obeying their orders. The overseers, having been formally stripped of the power to hire and fire workers and abuse the subcontracting system, under the new contract received high wages as an incentive to contribute their skills toward making the new system work.*

The shortage of cadres and the technical nature of construction work thus forced the CCP to devise a program for the construction industry that preserved the pivotal position at the work site of the very person whom the authorities least trusted—the foreman. Because the new regulations did not establish a separate personnel assignment office, each overseer in the private sector retained his own group of workers, who now formally became employees of a private construction company rather than of the overseer. This distinction, however, was often lost on the peasant boys who made up the construction gangs. And although legally removed, the crucial power to hire and fire in both the public and private sector remained *de facto* in the hands of the overseers. Also, at the end of the 1951 construction season, the private construction companies were still responsible for almost half of the construction work in the city.

In the fall of 1951, the publicly run CCC still had only 28 ad-

*TC, 4.vii.51, p. 1; see both the editorial and the accompanying feature article. There were two essential differences between the construction industry's overseers and the transport industry's coolie bosses: the overseers had a far more indispensable economic role to play than the coolie bosses; and the overseers had only monetary ties with their workers, while the coolie bosses' ties with their workers were reinforced by strong secret-society relations. Therefore, the initial Communist policy in the transport industry could aim at removing the coolie bosses from management positions, while the policy in the construction industry had to be directed toward winning over and utilizing the overseers. Also, cleaning out the ranks through criticism by fellow workers stood far less chance of success in the transport industry than in the construction industry.

ministrative personnel above the level of the work site. All operational authority, therefore, remained with the overseer. Under the new system, the only possible check on the overseer became the trade union and the site democratic management committee or labor capital consultative committee. The union, however, had by late 1951 recruited only about 25 percent of the construction workers as members.[14] In addition, the workers proved unwilling to oppose the overseers very strongly, which in turn undermined the independent position of the management and consultative committees. Indeed, the trade union cadres were themselves admonished to "learn modestly from the overseers."[15]

By the beginning of Three Anti Campaign, therefore, much of the CCP's work in the construction industry had come to naught. Superficially, one mass organization—the trade union—now had a broad cross-section of one-quarter of the workers in the industry, and one public institution—the Cooperative Construction Company—now handled over half of the construction undertaken. In reality, however, the distribution of power within the industry had not changed very much, for underneath these organizational superstructures the overseers still ruled the construction sites and retained the vitally important power to hire and fire. A Tientsin construction worker's lament in January 1951 that "the trade union is ours and is good, but if you rely on the trade union [as opposed to the overseer] then you are out of work"[16] was as applicable at the end of that year as it had been at the beginning. As a later report noted, prior to the changes effected during the Three Anti,

the publicly run construction companies assumed responsibility only for making plans for a project. They completely relegated to the overseers the right to hire workers, to assign the labor, and even to supervise the work. This gradually led to a situation where the state and public construction companies could not fire workers without going through the overseers. Because of this, the overseers cruelly exploited the workers in this arrangement, colluded with the dishonest businessmen in the construction companies, to a serious degree cheated on work and materials at the sites, gypped the builder, stole large amounts of state property, and harmed the basic construction of the state.[17]

To undermine still further the effectiveness of the trade union, many overseers took advantage of its continuing weakness at the work site to enter the union and assume a leading position in it. For instance, by February 1952, the chairmen of five out of the nine basic-level construction union organizations in the No. 1 ward were former *pa-t'ou*. In their usurpation of the legitimate functions of the trade union, the *pa-t'ou* were, it seems, aided by the preference of a number of construction company owners and merchants for continuing to work with people they already knew.[18] The only real possibility of future change stemmed from the pressure on the overseers to give technical training to the ordinary construction workers, and thus to relinquish their monopoly of technical and administrative knowledge—the basis of their power to date.

The Three Anti in the Construction Industry

During the Three Anti campaign the Communists launched a multifaceted attack on the *pa-t'ou*, seeking to destroy their power and enable the upper levels of the trade union and the CCC to gain firm control over the basic-level units. At the same time, the Communists took measures that, linked with the Five Anti campaign, increased the strength of both the trade unions and the CCC vis-à-vis the rest of the construction industry.

The Communists initiated the Three Anti campaign in the construction industry by establishing political study classes for over 2,000 workers. These classes began on January 3, 1952, and lasted for two months,[19] and because winter is the slack season in construction, they did not interfere with normal work assignments. They were one of the ways in which the Communists sought to build a group of potential leaders from among the rank-and-file.

The cadres fired the enthusiasm of the construction workers by having them participate in the Five Anti struggle against the dishonest businessmen who had colluded with the overseers during the previous months.[20] Through the accusation and struggle meetings accompanying this campaign, the workers gained both a greater sense of their own strength and a confirmation of the fact that they had continued to receive lower wages than they were entitled to.[21] Having imparted these lessons through the Five Anti struggle, the cadres led the workers to launch a Three Anti struggle against the overseers.

The Three Anti campaign against the *pa-t'ou* in the construction industry assumed several forms. The construction workers in each ward formed "workers' fighting teams" to force the overseers to confess to their crimes. The municipal authorities stepped in and arrested some of the most notorious overseers, and the trade union expelled from its ranks all *pa-t'ou* who were found to have committed serious crimes. The guiding principle, nevertheless, was to permit the relatively "good" foremen to continue in their jobs once they had been sufficiently frightened and knew that they would be susceptible in the future to control from above and below. The authorities dismissed and punished only those foremen whose past record showed that they probably would become recidivists if allowed to.[22]

Once these measures had greatly weakened the authority and position of the overseers, the MPG administered the crushing blow against them on March 26, 1952, with its announcement of the "Temporary Method for the Unified Assignment of Municipal Construction Workers."[23] These regulations decreed the establishment of a Unified Assignment Office in each ward. This new organizational network took as its first order of business the registration of more than 15,000 construction workers in the original Construction Trade Union and their reorganization from the top down.* The office registered skilled union members according to their type of skill, while it registered all other workers simply according to their work site.

The reorganization placed these workers in a three-level hierarchy: *chung-tui* of 45–90 workers, *hsiao-tui* of 15–30 workers, and *hsiao-tsu* of 5–10 workers. The relevant ward Construction Trade Union appointed the head of each *chung-tui*; the basic-level trade union appointed the head of the *hsiao-tui*; and the

---

*Actually, this registration also included crippled revolutionary soldiers, veterans, and the immediate relatives of revolutionary martyrs; but these categories did not significantly expand the number of people eligible to register.

members of each *hsiao-tsu* elected the head of their own small unit. The Unified Assignment Office itself had to approve the appointment of each of these unit leaders. By April 15, 1952, the end of the initial period of registration, the Tientsin construction industry was divided into 211 *chung-tui,* 649 *hsiao-tui,* and 1,959 *hsiao-tsu.* [24]

The trade union leadership intended this reorganization to undercut the power of the overseers by making the hierarchy of units independent of, and not coterminous with, the work site. The number of workers at a site varied, of course, according to the nature and size of the job at hand. Unlike previous arrangements, this one varied the real levels of operational power according to the number of workers, which were thus only rarely if ever coterminous with the work site. These new organizational units were assigned to exercise the foreman's previous functions of organization and leadership and thereby to prevent re-emergence of the *pa-t'ou.* The authorities thoroughly purged and tightened up the entire trade union organization as an integral part of this reorganization work. [25]

The main obstacle to doing away with the overseers had once been their virtual monopoly of leadership and technical skills. The special political training classes set up in early January 1952, however, helped to develop the necessary leadership talent among the rank-and-file union members, and the 2,000 graduates of these training classes undoubtedly figured prominently among the 15,000 union members who registered during March 26–April 15. At the completion of this registration period, the authorities ruled that only technically skilled construction workers—such as non-union carpenters, masons, and stone-cutters—could register with the Unified Assignment Office. [26] With the great weakening of the financial resources of the private sector during the Five Anti campaign,* it became increasingly obvious to the skilled workers that the public sector would

---

*The private sector of the construction industry came under particularly strong attack during the Five Anti campaign, as attested by the fact that the Building Trade Association was one of the first trade associations to be abolished during this campaign. This trade association was replaced by a seven-man "temporary work committee" on Feb. 1, 1952. *TC,* 2.ii.52.

finance most construction jobs in the near future, and that the work would therefore be given to those who were registered with the Unified Assignment Office. The Communist authorities made certain that the workers did not miss this message; they openly announced that the large-scale construction of workers' dormitories and of a machine-making factory would commence as soon as the registration process was completed.[27] In this way, the Unified Assignment Office may soon have registered virtually all of the technically skilled personnel who had not been seriously compromised during the Three Anti.

At the beginning of the Three Anti campaign, the two major public institutions in the construction industry—the Construction Trade Union and the Cooperative Construction Company— were administratively weak, dominated at the key work-site level by the overseers, and claimed as members a fairly random sampling of about 25 percent of the people engaged in construction work. These organizations did not have a dominant position in the construction industry and within each of them the upper-level Communist cadres exercised little control over the basic-level units. By the end of the campaign, the Communists had broken the power of the overseers, assumed effective control over their basic units, weakened the private sector of the economy, and recruited virtually all of the scarce, technically skilled personnel into the public institutions, which they now had firmly under their command. All of this in turn established a firm basis on which to make these two public institutions the dominant organizations of the industry in time for the large-scale economic construction scheduled to begin in 1953.

CHAPTER 8

The Campaigns in Perspective

The traumatic experiences suffered by Mr. Wang and the construction industry overseers in early 1952 were part of a group of national campaigns that swept China from the northeast to the southwest in the winter and spring of 1951–52. It is to this larger context, and to the unfolding of these campaigns within Tientsin municipality, that we now turn. This perspective reveals preparations for and stages in the campaigns that individual participants could perceive only dimly, if at all. It also brings in a third campaign—the Thought Reform of the intellectuals—that occurred simultaneously with but fell beyond the compass of the case studies in the previous chapter.

Background

The rationale for the campaigns of 1951–52 came from a speech made by Mao Tse-tung just as the Communists were beginning their task of governing China's major cities in 1949. His speech anticipated the dilemmas that urban rule would pose for the CCP, and revealed his dread that the revolution would degenerate once it entered China's cities. He saw that the boundary between stability and change, incremental technical development and revolutionary mobilization, would require that Party cadres master the specialized knowledge necessary for economic development without losing sight of the revolution's long-term goals. The peasant-based revolutionary movement, Mao noted, would have to enlist China's intellectuals in the cause of socialist construction, even though liberal ideas among the urban intelligentsia would inevitably dampen their enthusiasm for some Communist programs.[1] The Party Chairman also cautioned that monied interests in the urban areas had long experience in the art of winning friends in the government bureaucracy and dulling the cutting edge of government programs and policies that might threaten their welfare. The revolutionary cadres, therefore, would have to beware of the "sugar-coated bullets of the bourgeoisie." Mao also sensed that many cadres viewed seizing state power as the ultimate goal of the revolution, after which they would be rewarded for their efforts with positions of responsibility and prestige in the New China.[2] He pointedly reminded these people that capturing political power would be "only the first step in a march of 10,000 *li*," a stricture that he must have known he would have to repeat frequently in the future.[3]

By late 1951, Mao's fears were being realized. Revolutionary élan had by no means disappeared, but many cadres were becoming enmeshed in the nets of personal relations that underlay Chinese urban society. Official policy since Liu's 1949 visit to Tientsin had stressed economic recovery and expansion of the urban united front. Under these circumstances it was not difficult for cadres to view close ties with intellectual, commercial, and industrial interests as wholly consonant with the dictates of the revolution. As revolutionary vigilance became distracted by pressures for harmonious cooperation, the traditional means of fostering smooth working relationships through gift-giving, entertainment, and other favors increasingly characterized the relationships between the Communist cadres and the still non-revolutionized Tientsin society. The protracted Korean War, with its widespread opportunities for profiteering by taking advantage of the government's urgent need to purchase supplies, provided the private sector with additional resources and incentives to corrupt members of the Communist bureaucracy. And while the government was engaged in an intensive campaign to raise the level of enthusiasm for the war, numerous university professors remained more pro-American than pro-Soviet.* The intellectuals' liberal conceptions of the university's role in society were also sadly out of tune with the Communists' view of the universities as institutions whose existence was justified by their ability to turn out the politically loyal technical specialists needed for the task of economic construction.

These factors made Peking decide toward the end of 1951 to launch the Thought Reform, Three Anti, and Five Anti campaigns. (The fact that land reform had by this time been completed in the areas surrounding China's major cities may also have influenced the timing of these CCP urban initiatives.) These campaigns dealt devastating blows against three sectors of the urban population: the Thought Reform campaign engulfed the university professors (and subsequently, the middle and primary-school teachers); the Three Anti campaign encompassed civil servants, members of the Party apparatus, and cadres in the mass organizations and public enterprises; and the Five Anti campaign targeted members of the national and petit bourgeoisie. Although these initiatives began separately, by February 1952 they had essentially merged into one all-encompassing campaign.†

Chou En-Lai presaged the Thought Reform campaign in his September 29, 1951, speech on the problem of reforming the intellectuals.[4] Just two days after Chou's speech, the CPG's Government Administrative Council promulgated a "Decision on the Reform of the Educational System," which stressed the importance of technical and political education.[5] Within a week, the Ministry of Education established a subordinate "Study Committee for Teachers of Institutes of Higher Learning of Peking and Tientsin,"[6] and this body in turn set up a branch com-

---

*Many professors in Tientsin had received training in America. The documents from the Hundred Flowers campaign in 1957 indicate that at that time many Chinese intellectuals were still skeptical of the alliance with the Soviet Union.

†The Thought Reform campaign officially became a part of the Three Anti, while the Three Anti and Five Anti became for all intents and purposes a single campaign.

mittee in each of Peking's and Tientsin's universities and related institutes of higher learning.[7]

Throughout October and early November, professors in Tientsin participated in small meetings and seminars to discuss the issues raised by Chou's speech, but for a number of reasons, these discussions got off to a slow start. Many professors felt that through their teaching they had all along been "serving the people," and thus that they had no need to undergo thought reform. Others viewed themselves as progressive, and concluded that their participation should be limited to helping their colleagues reform. Most felt inhibited from participating fully in the criticism and self-criticism process by what the Communist press described as "unnecessary scruples."[8] To make these faculty members view the campaign with a greater sense of urgency, the authorities elicited abject public self-criticisms from Chairman Yang Shih-hsien of the Nankai University administration committee and by President Chang Kuo-fang of Tsin Ku University. This tactic seems to have borne some fruit.

By mid-November, these initial efforts in the Thought Reform campaign had familiarized the Tientsin university faculty with the CCP's basic ideas about the need for, and directions of, thought reform for higher intellectuals; they had also made a start toward translating the campaign's ideas into specific modifications in the teaching methods of the professors concerned. Perhaps most importantly, these early efforts had provided the cadres leading the campaign with concrete experience upon which to implement what for the Communists was an essentially new program—the "remolding" of intellectuals of all political persuasions in China's best universities.[9]

On November 18, P'eng Chen made a speech in Peking that propelled the Tientsin campaign into its second stage. Having been exposed to the general process of study, the Tientsin faculty members were now urged to criticize the thoughts of certain widely known people, such as the recently deceased Chang Po-lin, former president of Nankai University, and to relate this criticism directly to their own political viewpoints and to suggestions for curricular reform. At this time, the authorities anticipated that the third stage of the campaign would narrow the focus of acceptable viewpoints to Marxism-Leninism, and that on this basis attention would be devoted to separating enemies from friends. The two final stages of the campaign were to consist of discussions of the reform of higher education in connection with the needs of national defense and economic construction and of making an overall summary of the campaign's progress.[10] In fact, however, these last three stages became submerged in the frenzy of the Three Anti campaign that rocked Tientsin society from early January through the spring of 1952.

During the Three Anti campaign, all of Tientsin's universities were closed, and the faculty suffered severe criticism at the hands of students and colleagues. As the campaign progressed, it increasingly focused on ridding the universities of bourgeois notions of education (stress on the arts, on freedom of inquiry and expression, on maintaining the university as a relatively protected enclave in society, and so forth) and on removing or downgrading those professors who were least willing to accept the Communists' view of the university.[11] By the end of the campaign, university curricula had been substantially revised in favor of economics and the physical sciences, and all graduates of Tientsin's higher education institutions in June 1952 became subject to unified assignment to jobs by the CPG's Ministry of Personnel and Ministry of Education.[12] In education, the Communists then turned their attention toward thought reform of teachers in Tientsin's middle and primary schools.[13]

Preparation for Three Anti and Five Anti

The Three Anti campaign began in Manchuria at the end of August 1951, and did not spread south of the Great Wall in a significant way until the late fall of that year.[14] Because the Three Anti focused on corruption among state employees, it inexorably widened to encompass the source of the alleged corruption—the urban bourgeoisie. After several months of gradually increasing pressures on the capitalists, in early January 1952 official policy shifted so as to include members of this class squarely within the campaign's scope.

Within Tientsin, late 1951 had witnessed a government initiative against corruption, waste, and bureaucratism among cadres, and against bribery among private industrialists and businessmen. Although this drive had produced some strong rhetoric and several cases of bribery and related activities,[15] it seems to have been intended primarily to sensitize Tientsin's populace to the Communists' growing concern over the problem of corruption. The various trade associations had spearheaded this effort, each one setting up study classes and relating this issue to its own trade. The municipal authorities ordered three weeks of such study for each capitalist.[16] On December 7, 1951, the Government Administrative Council of the CPG called on the various localities to escalate sharply the Three Anti campaign. Seven days later, the Tientsin MPG formally adopted a resolution to carry out this campaign "with fanfare" throughout the city. This resolution provided for the establishment of a special administrative organ—called the Austerity Investigation Committee (*chieh-yueh tiao-ch'a wei-yuan-hui;* AIC)—to carry out the Three Anti.[17]

On December 16, the MPG convened a large Three Anti "mobilization meeting," at which Mayor Huang Ching decried the slackening of revolutionary vigilance during 1950–51 and admonished the leading cadres in each organ to promote the campaign by engaging in self-criticism before their subordinates. He also outlined the goals and principles of the campaign and predicted that the Three Anti would run its course in four months.[18]

The Tientsin leaders devoted most of their efforts during the last half of December to organizing the apparatus that would run this campaign. They announced the formal establishment of the Municipal AIC on December 18, 1951. The first meeting of the committee in turn set up various internal organs and decided to establish branch committees in 12 functional areas. It at the same time called for sub-branch AICs to be organized beneath each of these branch committees.[19] This was the beginning of the establishment of an extraordinary number of bodies set up explicitly to carry out the Three and Five Anti campaigns, including fighting squads (*chan-tou-tui*),[20] ward-region work teams (*ch'ü-yü kung-tso hsiao-tsu*),[21] investigation teams (*tiao-ch'a tsu*),[22] an evaluation organ (*p'ing-i chi-kuan*),[23] arbitration committees (*p'ing-tuan wei-yuan-hui*),[24] reception teams (*chieh-tai tsu*);[25] visiting groups (*fang-wen t'uan*),[26] and People's Tribunals (*jen-min fa-t'ing*).[27] Throughout the campaigns, however, the AICs remained the core organizations that directed and controlled this plethora of auxiliaries.

Although some initiatives to promote criticism and self-criticism in public bodies accompanied these organizational efforts, there was little sense of urgency apparent in these activities. Many cadres simply did not think that their conduct had been improper and thus assumed that they did not have an important role to play in the campaign. Others felt that because they worked in organs that did not handle large sums of money, the campaign did not really relate to them. As reported in the contemporary press, the general sentiment among cadres at the end of December was that, "to spend four months of time [in this campaign] is a waste."[28]

Carrying Out the Campaign in Tientsin

In January, in response to pressures from Peking, the tempo of the campaign picked up markedly and its focus rapidly shifted. On January 5, Chou En-lai made a report to the 34th meeting of the Standing Committee of the Chinese People's Political Consultative Conference in which he called for the large-scale mobilization of "all circles," but particularly of the people engaged in private industry and commerce.[29] Four days later, Po I-po reiterated this appeal and enumerated the five "crimes" that many members of the bourgeoisie had committed: bribery, tax evasion, stealing state property, stealing state economic secrets, and cheating on government contracts. He warned all law-breaking industrialists and merchants to confess their crimes to the government and noted that this problem amounted to "a serious class struggle in which we must win victory."[30]

From the outset, the Tientsin authorities had recognized that the Three Anti campaign required the participation of people in the private sector—women, youth, and especially industrialists and merchants. Their mobilization, however, had been at best half-hearted during December.[31] Now all this suddenly changed. Between January 5 and January 13, shop personnel,[32] party cadres,[33] Youth League members, and people in the sundries trade, in the warehouse industry, and in many other branches of the economy convened "mobilization" and "denunciation" meetings. On January 9 alone, for instance, the Tientsin press reported that Three Anti meetings had been convened by the following groups: store personnel in the Nos. 1,4,7,10, and 11 wards: foodstuffs industry people in the No. 1 ward; warehouse and trade industry people in the No. 8 ward; confederation of manufacturing industries people in the No. 8 ward; sundries trade people in the No. 10 ward; the CCP committee and all Youth League committees in the No. 1 ward; the Federation of Industry and Commerce and the heads of 35 trade associations; and a joint meeting of the MPG Tax Bureau, FIC, heads of the trade associations, representatives of industry and commerce, activists from among the tax collectors, and store personnel representatives.[34]

This massive mobilization initiated a period of intense political involvement that was to affect profoundly the lives of almost every working Tientsin resident during the next six months. It was the first time since the early spring of 1949 that the Communists had openly attacked industrialists and businessmen. Likewise, for many workers such as those in the China Chemical Company, the campaign provided their first intense exposure to the policy demands of the regime, especially insofar as these demands impinged on the traditional system of social relationships in their firms. The major beneficiaries of the "revolution from above" were the Communist authorities themselves, for by the end of the campaign they had vastly increased their leverage over *both* the workers and the capitalists in the city.[35]

In a general sense, the Three Anti and Five Anti campaigns in Tientsin passed through four fairly distinct stages: initial mobil-

TABLE 7. *Timing of Stages in the Tientsin Three Anti and Five Anti Campaigns*

Stage	Three Anti	Five Anti
Initial mobilization	Dec. 15, 1951– Jan. 25, 1952	Early Jan.–Jan. 25
"Tiger beating" (*Ta-hu*)	Jan. 25–late March	Jan.25–late March
Evaluation and disposition	Late March–late April	Late March–late April
Establish new systems, promote new cadres	Late April–late May	Late April–late May

ization and investigation; "tiger beating";* evaluation and disposition; and establishment of new systems with the attendant promotion of cadres. Table 7 gives the approximate timing of these stages. Although this division of the campaigns follows the Communists' own analysis, it is somewhat misleading because it masks important changes in the tempo, intensity, and techniques of the campaigns that occurred within each stage. It also disguises the fact that in general the Communists dealt first with the smaller firms and only later with the larger ones.

A joint meeting of the MPG Council and the Municipal ACPRC Consultative Committee on January 14 marked the moment when the Five Anti campaign in Tientsin officially became more than simply the mobilization of people in the private sector to assist in the Three Anti. Obviously in response to Po I-po's speech of January 9, this meeting proclaimed that the Three Anti campaign alone would prove ineffective because corruption could not be eliminated without a major campaign to reform the capitalists.[36] At a mass mobilization meeting on January 16 convened ostensibly to push forward the Three Anti campaign, Huang Ching for the first time mentioned the "five poisons" that Po I-po had enumerated seven days earlier in Peking: bribery, tax evasion, cheating on state contracts, stealing state property, and stealing state economic secrets.[37] The

*Major offenders during the Five Anti campaign were called tigers, and the attacks on them, tiger beating (*ta-hu*).

meeting also passed the "Principles for Disposing of the Problems of Corruption and Bribery," which had been formulated at the third meeting of the Municipal AIC. These principles stressed the standard CCP tactic of rewarding cooperation and punishing resistance.[38]

On January 20, the Shopworkers' Trade Union formed 276 "fighting teams" to intensify the Five Anti investigation of large commercial firms. Before the formation of these teams, the campaign in most commercial trades had only mobilized workers to make denunciations and pressured the owners to make confessions. After January 20, however, the fighting teams followed up this mobilization with vigorous "keypoint" investigations of the bigger firms, thereby breaking up the areas of purported greatest resistance to the development of the campaign. The fighting teams combined the talents of technically skilled personnel, such as accountants and purchasing staff, and politically reliable personnel, such as relatively high-level trade union cadres. In each investigation, the team first ascertained background information on a firm, such as previous capital-labor relations and earlier experience with the state trading organs, and then sought to convince the firm's high-level staff to cooperate. The Communists relied on the shared background of the technical personnel in the team and in the firm under investigation to promote cooperation between them.* These elite teams prepared for the tiger-beating stage, when the thorough investigatory work was used to launch "ferocious, many-sided attacks" on the heads of the firms. In these attacks, the fighting teams applied tremendous pressures on their targets, frequently grilling them for days on end. By February 9, the shop workers' fighting teams had uncovered 177 companies that owed the state more than 500 million *yuan* apiece.[39]

On January 25, a joint meeting of the MPG Council and the

---

*According to Olga Lang's investigation in the mid-1930's, the technical staff of a large commercial firm was almost certain to have had a modern education, while the other employees of the firm almost equally certainly did not have such an education. *Chinese Family and Society* (New Haven, Conn., 1946), p. 93.

Municipal ACPRC Consultative Committee raised the pitch of the campaign to a new height. The meeting declared that all obstacles to the Five Anti campaign should be swept away, and the campaign now entered the tiger-beating and tiger-catching phase. It also decided that within a week the authorities should arrest and punish 32 "law-breaking" capitalists as an object lesson to the other capitalists in the city.* The same meeting also established an "evaluation organ" directly under the Municipal AIC, marking the beginning of the gradual shift from securing denunciations and confessions to setting up the necessary machinery for evaluating and disposing of crimes after they had been discovered.[40]

The January 25 meeting also changed the authorities' strategy with respect to utilizing the Tientsin FIC and the trade associations. Although throughout January the FIC and the trade associations had played a major role in organizing the meetings at which capitalists were denounced and forced to confess, they continued to be dominated by the same "big tigers" who were themselves the chief targets of the campaign. The authorities resolved, therefore, to bypass the industrial trade associations completely and place the Five Anti campaign under the direct leadership of the various territorially defined ward AIC branch committees. The 32 men arrested after this meeting were leaders of various trade associations,[41] and during the following weeks many individual trade associations were dissolved and replaced by "work committees."[42] By the end of the Five Anti, at least 53 of Tientsin's 108 trade associations had been dispatched in this way. In the late spring, the authorities decided to re-establish the trade associations, and announcements began to appear heralding the formation of "reorganized" trade associations.[43] The extensive efforts made by the authorities in 1949 and again in 1951 to remodel the trade associations had evidently not suc-

---

*While this was not the first arrest of the Three and Five Anti targets, it was the largest such arrest and received unmistakably threatening treatment in the Tientsin press. See *TC*, 1.ii.52, for the initial stories on 13 of these arrests, all of which were made on Jan. 31, 1952.

ceeded in making these organizations into sufficiently pliant tools of the regime, and a campaign strategy based on these associations had therefore proved inadequate.[44]

During February, the emphasis gradually shifted to disposing of cases rather than soliciting more denunciations. Most Tientsin capitalists suffered a routine of denunciation, study, confession, and final disposition similar to that which Mr. Wang of the China Chemical Company endured. The victim began by participating in a study group made up of other capitalists in his own trade.* Within this group, each participant confessed his past transgressions and subjected this confession to scrutiny by his peers. If someone had serious "problems" and refused to confess them, an "investigation team" visited the person's firm and carried out an appropriate inquiry. If this inquiry proved the crime but the capitalist still refused to confess, he was arrested and punished severely. When it was felt that the individual concerned had made a full confession, he was permitted to fill out a "disposition form." After his study group had evaluated and approved his disposition form, the form was sent to the relevant ward AIC branch committee for review. The AIC branch committee then passed the form back to the staff and workers at the capitalist's firm who, after reviewing and checking the facts, summoned their boss to a meeting. There he had to face them and answer sharp questions about his previous activities and future intentions. Party members, Youth League members, and labor union cadres spearheaded this questioning. If the capitalist responded to the workers' satisfaction, they accepted his confession as adequate, and he was proclaimed to have "passed through the gate."[45] The staff and workers returned the disposition forms of all who had passed through the gate to the relevant ward AIC branch committee, which decided on the proper classification for the culprit and his punishment. These final decisions, called "summaries," were read to the capitalists who had passed through the gate at a general meeting convened for this purpose.[46]

---

*Strictly speaking, the CCP included both capitalists and "representatives of the capitalist side"—usually the managers—in the Five Anti target group.

Even after a capitalist had successfully completed this evaluation procedure, the authorities strongly encouraged him to remain active in the campaign by denouncing others and assisting the authorities in ferreting out and evaluating the crimes of his peers. The CCP spoke of this recruitment of confessed offenders in terms of forming and expanding a "Five Anti united front." The authorities began pointing to this ever growing Five Anti united front to show holdouts that they would inevitably be found out, and should therefore confess without further delay. They indicated that active participation in the united front qualified one for a more favorable final classification and thus for a lighter punishment. Newspaper articles in late February stated that most capitalists had already made confessions, and that a sizable percentage had received their summaries and joined the Five Anti united front.[47] By this time, then, the campaign had begun to narrow its focus and marshal its resources to concentrate on the most difficult cases.

Meanwhile, the authorities also began to narrow the scope of the Three Anti campaign. Reminding the cadres that the purpose of *san-fan* was to increase rather than obstruct production, the MPG in late February castigated the neglect of economic affairs that had accompanied Three Anti. The combined effects of the Three and Five Anti campaigns had brought most branches of Tientsin's economy to a complete halt. The authorities now ordered three changes: one-third of the people in each publicly run factory or enterprise must stop participating in the campaign and begin drawing up plans, restoring production, and overcoming production-related difficulties; all units must implement the system of spending half of each day beating tigers and half of each day doing normal work; and the purchasing and marketing departments of each unit must be rectified or reorganized, and personnel gaps in these departments must be filled immediately—i.e., departments should not wait until the end of the Three Anti campaign before promoting new cadres.[48] Thus, by the end of February 1952, the authorities were taking significant steps toward economic recovery and the consolidation of their political gains.

March proved the pivotal month in Tientsin's Three and Five Anti campaigns. At the beginning of the month the Communists were still trying mainly to elicit confessions from a majority of the capitalists and erring cadres. By the end of the month, most confessions had been accepted, and cases had entered the "disposition" stage. Not surprisingly, the impetus for this shift came from Peking. On March 8, 1952, at the meeting of the CPG's Government Administrative Council, P'eng Chen proposed a set of standards for the classification and disposition of Five Anti cases, and the CPG's AIC reported on the disposition of Three Anti cases. Three days later, the GAC recommended these two reports as the basis for handling Three Anti and Five Anti cases throughout the country.[49] On March 21, 1952, the GAC ordered the establishment of special Five Anti People's Tribunals (*jen-min fa-t'ing*) to handle particularly serious Five Anti cases,[50] and one week later it ordered the establishment of similar Three Anti People's Tribunals.[51]

The Three and Five Anti campaigns in Tientsin immediately reflected these decisions by the CPG. The Tientsin authorities convened mass meetings of the capitalists in each ward and conveyed the substance of the GAC directives to them. They asked the capitalists to make one last confession that would wrap up their cases. In the vast majority of cases, this last confession proved rather *pro forma*, since within 10 days of the GAC decision over 17,000 firms in the Nos. 2, 4, 7, 8, 9, 10, and 11 wards had made their confessions, and the disposition of most cases was completed.*

Politically, the GAC's regulations were a mixed blessing for the authorities running the Three Anti Five Anti in Tientsin. On the one hand, the regulations permitted them to settle most cases with confidence that their standards of evaluation and punishment did not differ sharply from those of the CPG. This in turn allowed them to focus even more on the most serious offenders. On the other hand, the regulations told those people

---

*CP, 1.iv.52, p. 1 In many cases, this "last" round of confessions followed the acceptance of a previous confession; and not infrequently, capitalists added a little to their list of crimes in this final confession.

who were still trying to conceal something that the campaign was rapidly drawing to a close. They almost certainly strengthened the resolve of some of the remaining "big tigers" to hold out.

On March 26, a Joint Meeting of the MPG Council and the Municipal ACPRC Consultative Committee summed up the past experience of each campaign and declared that both should now move rapidly into the disposition stage. The meeting also ordered the establishment of separate Three Anti and Five Anti People's Tribunals and Arbitration Committees. The People's Tribunals assumed responsibility for the cases of the most serious offenders, while the Arbitration Committees, set up under the various AIC's arbitrated disputes over the technical aspects of Five Anti violations, classifications of crimes, and the size of repayments. Most of the cases that came before both organs were handled at the ward level.[52]

By March 26, the heads of some 65,000 industrial and commercial firms (including some street stalls) had participated in Five Anti study groups. Of these, 35,000 had already completed evaluation by their study group, and 25,000 had already had their summaries announced.[53] The authorities' estimates of the classification of firms into the five categories listed in P'eng Chen's report is shown in Table 8. The meeting of March 26 also noted that the owners of only 1,800–1,900 firms had refused to make satisfactory confessions and declared that future efforts would be concentrated on this small group. It asserted that the Five Anti campaign as a whole would be "basically completed" by mid-April.[54]

The Three Anti campaign lagged somewhat behind the Five Anti, and by March 26 only 20 percent of the units in the city had completed their Three Anti tiger beating struggles. Approximately 50 percent would "basically" complete their tiger beating by early April, and the final 30 percent were not slated to complete their tiger beating until mid-April.* The first 20 percent were by March 26 devoting almost all their efforts to dispo-

---

*In Communist usage, "basically" usually means 70 percent or more.

TABLE 8. *Estimated Five Anti Classification of Tientsin Firms, March 26, 1952*

Classification	Number of firms	Percent of total
Law-abiding	6,600	10.0%
Basically law-abiding	42,000	64.2
Semi-law-abiding, semi-law-breaking	13,700	21.0
Seriously law-breaking	2,300	3.5
Completely law-breaking	800	1.8
TOTAL	65,400	100 %

SOURCE: *CP*, 29.iii.52,p. 1.

sition of cases, the next 50 percent were expending half their energies on tiger beating and half on disposition, and the last 30 percent were still concentrating on tiger beating.[55]

In both the Three Anti and the Five Anti, then, the official move into the disposition stage came at a time when about half of the people concerned had already had their cases summarized. The campaigns had become so intense that entire trades and branches of industry had ceased to function. Moreover, the economic effects of the Five Anti had been compounded by the fact that the Three Anti concentrated on those state institutions most vital to economic recovery—the finance and economic system including the banks and the State Trading Company. These had been so severely disrupted that they were now unable to loan money, ensure a supply of materials from the rural areas, or provide marketing opportunities for goods produced in the city.

To relieve this economic paralysis, the March 26 meeting suggested such remedial measures as expanding state orders for goods from the private sector, increasing the volume of loans to the private sector, and harshly punishing capitalists who did not quickly resume production after receiving their summaries.[56] The meeting also indicated that extensive efforts had to be made toward promoting new cadres, establishing new systems, and developing a new work style in the public sector.[57] The government's progress in this effort was, however, far from satisfactory. On the one hand, the haste to rehabilitate the economy cut short the Three Anti in the public sector,[58] while on the other, the economy remained in a slump throughout the rest of 1952.

In line with the drive to achieve order, during April the Tientsin press announced that 70 percent or more of the cases in various wards had achieved final settlement. For instance, on April 7, the No. 10 ward announced final classification for 1,765 firms—70 percent of all firms in the ward. Of these 1,417 (80 percent) were "law-abiding," 295 (17 percent) were "basically law-abiding," and 53 (3 percent) were "semi-law-abiding, semi-law-breaking."[59] However, the cases of the seriously law-breaking and completely law-breaking firms were omitted from these figures.

In effect, the final stage of the Three Anti and Five Anti campaigns was divided in two parts. For the smaller firms and public institutions, it consolidated the new relationships that had emerged through the establishment and rectification of organs such as the LCCCs and through the signing of contracts with the state sector. For the large private firms, it meant going through a final period of intense pressure for confession before the new systems could be established. On June 5, 1952, the Tientsin authorities finally announced the "victorious conclusion" of the Three Anti and Five Anti campaigns, specified the means by which the gains of this campaign should be consolidated, and declared the newest slogan to be "the economy comes first."[60]

Significance of the Three Anti and Five Anti Campaigns

The Three and Five Anti campaigns were significant in part because they marked a drastic shift from the regime's limited penetration of Tientsin's larger economic enterprises to a more effective penetration of the city's numerous smaller firms. These initiatives restored the Communists' presence to a wide range of enterprises of various sizes, as had been somewhat the case during the January–April 1949 period. This time, however, the penetration was achieved by organizations controlled by the municipal leadership, coordinated on a city-wide basis; it entailed a tolerable level of disruption, and was linked to very important economic and sociopolitical changes.

Economic Changes

The Three and Five Anti campaigns markedly intensified the government's control of investment capital and use of public-private contracts to determine production in the private sector; they also increased its ability to acquire revenues through taxation. In 1951, the government had increased its leverage over potential investment capital by establishing the Tientsin Investment Company. During the Five Anti, the government soaked up a large part of the remaining private investment capital by imposing fines that firms had to pay for the "debts" growing out of their past "unsavory" activities.[61]

The campaigns' disruption of the economy combined with the Five Anti fines jeopardized the financial stability of many privately run firms. The government loaned money to and placed orders with these firms to save them from bankruptcy. Several figures indicate the magnitude of this rehabilitation effort. During the 18 months from the successful national unification of finances in June 1950 until the eve of Three and Five Anti campaigns in December 1951, firms in the private sector of Tientsin's economy had borrowed a total of 549.8 billion *yuan* from banks. By contrast, the figure for the eight months of January–August 1952 was 582.6 billion *yuan*. Moreover, because the economy was almost totally paralyzed in January–February, these figures indicate that the rate of private sector borrowing tripled that of the previous 18 months.[62] In all likelihood, this high level of borrowing continued because the government permitted most firms to defer payment of their fines until the end of 1952.[63] Many firms had to borrow money in order to make these payments.

Similarly, during the June 1950–December 1951 period, public firms wrote processing contracts worth 4,072 billion *yuan* with Tientsin's private firms. In July–August 1952 alone, however, contracts totaling 1,026 billion *yuan* were signed, a 126 percent increase over the previous monthly average.[64] Indeed, by the first half of 1953, approximately 66 percent of the total output of private industry in Tientsin was produced under government contract.[65] These post–Five Anti contracts, moreover, established standards that differed in important ways from their pre-campaign counterparts. While the standards for the pre-1952 contracts had been negotiated on an individual basis, those signed in June 1952 and later were pegged to the government's estimate of average costs and productivity for each branch of industry. The official rationale asserted that this new basis for standards would force inefficient private firms to increase their productivity and cut their costs.[66] However, after the Three and Five Anti campaigns, few private firms dared refuse a government offer of a processing contract, and the imposition of government-determined standards provided the authorities with an easy way to place private enterprises in an untenable economic position.

The campaigns also increased the revenue the government could acquire from taxation by increasing its collection resources and undercutting the private businessmen's ability to conceal company earnings. The major pre-campaign means of tax evasion had been to bribe collection officials and to keep two sets of books. But the bribe-giver and bribe-takers were attacked so fiercely during the Three and Five Anti campaigns[67] that bribery ceased to play a large role in tax evasion. Likewise, government audits of each firm during the campaign undoubtedly uncovered most cases of fraudulent bookkeeping and yielded sufficient information on each firm to make this a very risky stratagem for the future. The government had also recruited and trained additional tax collection personnel in late 1951,[68] and these people, along with many cadres, gained a great deal of practical experience during the first six months of 1952. Finally, the Communists devoted a major part of the Five Anti campaign to convincing high-level staff (such as accountants) in the private firms to side with the regime. Wherever they succeeded, the owner of the firm could probably no long conceal a substantial portion of the company's income. Combining the above factors with the post-campaign timidity that gripped large segments of the private business community,[69] tax evasion must have greatly diminished in the wake of the Three and Five Anti campaigns.

Estimates of pre-1952 tax evasion had ranged around some 30 percent of the value of total taxes collected.[70] The government also estimated that on average the private firms who were a party to processing contracts before 1952 had cheated the government out of 30 percent of the materials involved.[71] Now, with the government's increased auditing capabilities and the chastised capitalists' diminished control over their own staffs, future processing contracts would grow in number, and each of these might tie up roughly 30 percent more of the private firms' resources than had pre-1952 contracts.

The Five Anti campaign departed from earlier economic policies by undermining the financial position of the city's *larger* private enterprises. Most previous campaigns, such as the various production competitions, had increased the productivity and financial well-being of the larger private firms, albeit at the same time increasing the regime's leverage within these firms. The Five Anti campaign reversed this and marked the termination of the CCP's policy of uniting completely with the national bourgeoisie for the sake of economic recovery.

Overall, the Three and Five Anti campaigns gravely weakened the private sector of the Tientsin economy and especially the national bourgeois component of that sector. The government emerged with greater information, enhanced surveillance capabilities, more leverage through public-private contracts, better tax collection machinery, and vastly increased funds. In addition, the Five Anti campaign sapped the morale of most capitalists, making the overwhelming majority unwilling in the future to defend the private sector against further encroachments from the public sector. Indeed, after June 1952, it required a great deal of effort simply to convince many capitalists to return to work at all.[72]

Sociopolitical Impact

The Three Anti and Five Anti campaigns had wide and pro-found effects on the sociopolitical situation in Tientsin. They se-verely disrupted the web of social relationships that had pro-vided the underpinning for much of Tientsin's economy; they successfully injected the power of the regime into most of the medium and some of the small enterprises; they increased trade union membership and, more importantly, brought the basic-level units in these organizations firmly under the control of the higher authorities; they effected a revolution in the business practices of the medium and large-scale firms; and they made all sections of the people in Tientsin's economy more aware of the importance of politics and the Communist regime's revolution-ary goals.

Personal relations, generally based on family, native place, school ties and close friendship, had played two major roles within Tientsin's economy. Within enterprises, they had formed the basis for hiring staff and workers, and had therefore tended to make firms like the China Chemical Company somewhat self-contained social units. This was especially true of smaller firms and less so of larger ones. Among different enterprises, social relationships had determined with whom one did business, bor-rowed money, and so forth. On this level, they may have been more important for the bigger enterprises because these firms could afford to be more selective about the people with whom they would deal. Social ties thus had increased the internal co-hesion and isolation of smaller firms and at the same time largely had determined the patterns of interaction among the various larger economic units throughout the city. The Three Anti and Five Anti campaigns wrought major changes in both of these spheres.

By the end of 1951, very few of the CCP's policies had had any appreciable impact on the medium and smaller firms in the city, which were overwhelmingly in the commercial and handicraft sectors. The trade union network, the production competitions, the propaganda activities, and even the changes in the tax laws had barely touched the vast majority of enterprises that employed fewer than 50 workers.

The Three and Five Anti campaigns were directed primarily at the commercial sector of the economy, bypassing many of the smaller handicraft shops. They aimed at penetrating the shops, mobilizing the staff and workers to denounce the "illegal" activities of their employers, and recruiting at least one or more "activists" who could serve as reliable agents for future trade union organization activities in the firm. The various ward AICs and the shopworkers' trade union led this effort. According to official statistics, 95 percent of the 150,000 shopworkers in the city participated in the campaigns. Of these, 45,000 attended mass mobilization and denunciation meetings convened during January and February,[73] another 6,000 formally participated in special trade union training classes, and 10,000 more were involved in the investigation teams assigned to learn firsthand the organization and business affairs of their businesses.[74]

The Communists devoted their greatest attention in the commercial sector to the medium-sized shops, those with approximately 30–50 employees. They tried hard to win over the higher-level staff in these firms, and their effort proceeded in four stages: initial mobilization,[75] organization of 276 "fighting teams,"[76] week-long "Five Anti Campaign High-Level Staff Study Classes,"[77] and finally, face-to-face confrontations in which the staff questioned their employers sharply and accused them of improper activities. The regime viewed these face-to-face struggles between the high-level shop staff and the shopowners as "an important key in consolidating [the staff's] class consciousness."[78]

These efforts were carried out in conjunction with a wide range of other initiatives, including forcing the shopowners to participate in study groups for periods up to three or more months (thereby removing their authority from the firm for that time),[79] propagandizing and organizing the workers in the stores,[80] and recruiting individuals from among the staff and workers to become trade union and, on a more selective basis,

Party and League cadres.[81] In addition, because many lower-level workers were hired not on the basis of direct ties with the shopowner, but on the basis of their relationship with one of the higher-level staff, separating the higher-level staff from the owner reaped extra benefits for the government in terms of breaking the internal cohesion of the firm.

The Five Anti campaign also included a powerful attack on the webs of personal relationships that bound together the various businessmen in the city. Both the study groups and the interrogations of the shopowners had been designed to elicit information about these very webs. Whenever cadres in a Five Anti study group realized that two people had some sort of relationship between them, they made a special effort to find out from each person about the other. In every case, they constantly reminded each person that it was a sin not to tell everything he knew. In this way, the Communists at least temporarily transformed personal connections, which had previously provided a safe haven from the harsh demands of society, into vulnerabilities that exposed the parties concerned to special pressures and danger. Having been made aware of the potential danger of cultivating and using his *kuan-hsi* with someone else, the average businessman in all probability became somewhat more cautious about establishing such a relationship in the future. Thus, during the course of the Five Anti the regime demonstrated that personal relations were no longer a sufficient guarantee of united resistance to outside encroachments. In so doing, it undermined the social basis of economic organization and practice in Tientsin.*

The Three and Five Anti campaigns also enabled the regime to penetrate the medium-scale enterprises and to consolidate its power in both these and larger enterprises. In the medium-scale enterprises, mostly shops, this occurred initially by expansion of the trade unions. In the larger private enterprises, it occurred

---

*Of course, this need not have been the response in every instance. One interviewee said that after the Five Anti he was even more careful to deal only with relatives and close friends, since he now realized how menacing the regime could be.

through rectification of the extant trade unions and emphasized control over their basic-level units—very much as in the construction industry case already discussed. In both large and small firms, as soon as a trade union was firmly established, the cadres set up LCCCs through which the union could constrain and supervise the capitalists.

During the course of Three and Five Anti campaigns, then, most of the growth in union membership occurred in the medium and small enterprises. By early April 1952, for instance, membership had increased by over 2,000 in the No. 3 ward, over 800 in the No. 6 ward, over 2,000 in the No. 7 ward, and over 1,500 in the No. 8 ward. In the No. 10 ward, membership among high-level shop staff increased by 150 percent during January–April.[82] According to an article published later in April, over 4,000 shopworkers had applied to enter trade unions and were still awaiting approval of their applications.[83] While these increases were not very large in absolute terms, they usually represented the first penetration of the trade union into the firms concerned. They amounted, therefore, to a very significant extension of the government's effective penetration of Tientsin society. The spring 1952 campaigns succeeded in establishing the seeds of union organization in most—but not quite all—of the enterprises with 20 or more workers.[84]

As we have seen, the Communist authorities before 1952 had tried wherever possible to recruit local talent to lead the trade union organizations. But the nature of personal relations within Tientsin's firms, combined with the fact that most workers lacked administrative and organizational skills and retained their respect for traditional authority, meant that local leadership positions had become occupied by relatives and friends of the capitalists, by higher-level staff who had old ties with the owners, or by former overseers and pre-1949 KMT trade union leaders. Consequently, the regime had discovered by the end of 1951 that it lacked real control over many of its primary-level trade union units. To rectify this situation, the Communists removed cadres who were not sufficiently obedient and generally replaced them with the workers who had emerged as "activists" in the Three Anti and Five Anti campaigns. Indeed, the worker who became a cadre had often been the first to denounce the former occupant of his position.[85]

These policies of expansion and recitification produced a reasonably disciplined trade union network that encompassed most economic units employing more than 20 people. The Communists immediately began to involve the unions in enterprise management through LCCCs.[86] Unlike the LCCCs that had been formed in a small fraction of the private enterprises by the end of 1951, these new organs were established in order to provide a tool with which the workers could lead rather than merely advise the capitalists.[87] The China Chemical Company's experience illustrates how this leadership actually worked. Through the Three and Five Anti campaigns, therefore, the Communists managed first to put workers into trade unions that could be controlled from above and then to have these unions play a major role in the operations of private enterprises.

The Three and Five Anti campaigns also changed business practices in Tientsin. The Five Anti campaign had aimed at wiping out the "five poisons"—bribery, tax evasion, cheating on contracts, stealing state property, and stealing state economic secrets. While all of these may sound to a Westerner like unscrupulous activities, in China the first three were, prior to 1952, accepted as normal, and indeed essential, business techniques.[88] The Communists' sudden attempt to wipe out the five poisons amounted, in reality, to imposing a wholly new code of moral behavior. For this reason, the Communists' assertion at the beginning of the campaign that the Tientsin bourgeoisie had launched "wild attacks" against the People's Government was regarded by businessmen as inaccurate and unfair.[89] But the ferocity of the Five Anti campaign undoubtedly made Tientsin's businessmen understand the "criminal" (and dangerous) nature of these activities. The five poisons had indeed become lethal.

The war against bribery and tax evasion in the private sector was paralleled by an almost equally vociferous campaign against corruption among government officials. During the Three Anti campaign, for instance, the *Tientsin Daily* reported accusations of corruption against 63 government officials and 67 governmental units, including 21 municipal bureaus. While precise figures on the number actually demoted or purged are not available, the campaign produced an increased percentage of high municipal positions held by Party members.[90] The old type of relation between government officials and private citizens had received a rude shock and been largely, if not wholly, discredited.[91]

The last, but by no means least significant, accomplishment of the Three and Five Anti campaigns was that they made virtually all of the people in Tientsin's economy aware of the Communists' sociopolitical outlook[92] and policies; they also marked a turning point in the regime's ability to communicate political messages to the people on a continuing basis. The campaigns had employed every conceivable technique to convey their message: mobilization meetings, accusation meetings, radio broadcasts, press coverage, study groups, keypoint investigations, special organizations, trade union, Party and Youth League activities, official governmental conferences, special training classes, and so forth. It is, of course, difficult to judge the actual impression made upon the people who were exposed to these activities. There is little question, however, that the staff and workers in the medium and large enterprises bore the brunt of this propaganda offensive, and among these, it was in all probability the people in the medium-sized firms who experienced the greatest *increment* in propaganda exposure.

Toward the end of these campaigns, the Tientsin authorities tried to institutionalize some of the propaganda forms they had developed. At the end of 1951, Tientsin had only 6,703 propagandists, of whom approximately 3,200 (48 percent) were in publicly run factories and enterprises.[93] One year later, the number of propagandists in the city had more than quadrupled, to 28,856, with most of the increase having occurred during the Three and Five Anti campaigns. These campaigns had provided the major breakthrough for the propaganda apparatus into the private enterprises in Tientsin.[94]

Beginning in late April 1952, each ward resumed political

classes in the workers' spare-time schools. During May, many of the workers and shop personnel who had not participated in spare-time education were organized for political study. Finally, for the personnel in many small stores and handicrafts workshops and for scattered workers who could not participate in regular study, the Tientsin People's Radio Station began in June to broadcast special political talks on a scheduled basis. The small shop and handicrafts personnel and the scattered workers were then organized to listen to these broadcasts. As a result of all of these efforts, by mid-June 1952 a total of 248,000 staff and workers—over 55 percent of the total work force in Tientsin—were participating in some form of political study.[95] The Communists also launched a systematic study program centered around the Common Program for the capitalists.[96] The workers' program was intended to spread class consciousness among the workers and make them realize the necessity of their actively controlling the capitalists for the good of the country. The capitalists' program urged them to accept the leading role of the state sector of the economy and the need for obeying the laws and ethics of the People's Government—all of which had been clearly spelled out in the Common Program accepted by the First National Chinese People's Political Consultative Conference on October 1, 1949.[97] It seems that most capitalists simply had not believed the more ominous articles in the Common Program before the Five Anti campaign. But this optimistic attitude had, of course, been nurtured by the CCP's own united front propaganda.

CHAPTER 9 *Conclusion*

The above analysis of Tientsin in 1949–52 highlights the methodical approach the Communists took toward expanding their power after Liu Shao-ch'i's visit in April–May 1949. This strategy recognized the danger that the CCP's resources could easily become spread too thin, generating forces and demands beyond the Communists' control. It therefore focused on the basics: eliminating counterrevolutionary threats, bringing key economic enterprises under control, and gradually marshaling resources so that the new regime could expand its compass as the situation permitted. The initial attention to modern enterprises to the virtual exclusion of traditional firms and nonworking residents had two complementary rationales: the modern firms were the most important for securing the economic resources vital to the CCP's efforts; and the social environment of the workers in this sector made them more susceptible to Communist appeals, which meant these workers could more readily be recruited to increase the CCP's own limited ranks. This decision to penetrate and transform Tientsin "from the top down" of necessity placed a premium on organizational development and control versus spontaneity. It nevertheless still permitted ample use of mobilizational techniques and mass campaigns to achieve specific breakthroughs within the context of this organizationally oriented strategy. We now turn to the lessons of this early period for understanding Chinese politics since the 1950's.

Why look to the early 1950's for a better perspective on the politics of the 1960's and 1970's? First, because people and their social perspectives do not change fundamentally in a short time. Significant social developments do occur and can affect the way people view society, but their result is always a mixture of new and old, not a thoroughly new concept of human relationships. And although the Chinese media have overemphasized what is new in this composite we have seen that there are equally important legacies from the past. Second, one of the key debates in Chinese political leadership since the mid-1950's—that concerning mobilization versus organization as a means of bringing about revolutionary change—in fact surfaced during the period we have studied in the city of Tientsin. Tientsin's experience, moreover, provides a basis for evaluating the competing terms of this debate and for grounding this evaluation in an understanding of underlying social relationships in Chinese society. And third, the early revolution in Tientsin reveals some of the fundamental organizational problems that have plagued the Chinese Communists' efforts to transform their society over the past three decades. Thus, the value of this study lies not only in its specific historical treatment of Tientsin, but also in its illumination of issues that have enduring importance for the study of Chinese politics.

The system of *kuan-hsi,* as we have seen, traditionally delineates the social horizons of many Chinese citizens. In the Tientsin of 1949–52, its influence showed in the extraordinary degree to which policies could not spread beyond the specific groups at which they were targeted. Put differently, there was very little civic consciousness in Tientsin, very little concern with events and problems that fell outside one's own social web. *Kuan-hsi* meant that one's obligations toward others were based, not on a generalized principle of brotherhood, charity, or social consciousness, but rather on specific obligations defined by the particular type of personal relationship two people shared.[1] This central role of *kuan-hsi* largely solves an apparent mystery—that a Chinese might act in a seemingly altruistic way for some distant relative or a schoolmate of his father, but leave a starving man to die in the street without giving him second notice.[2] For most people, duties and concerns simply did not extend beyond the boundaries of their particular net of social relationships.

Social relations also defined interests and, with them, the effective channels of information. People had learned through long experience that governments profess high principles but spell only trouble, and thus they tried to minimize contact with all officials. Government propaganda, therefore, received little serious attention; the prudent man paid attention to politics only enough to learn how to avoid trouble.[3]

This situation, of course, was antithetical to the polity that the CCP wanted to create. *Kuan-hsi* obscured class relationships and made the concept of class struggle seem unnatural, even in a society scarred by extremes of wealth and poverty. The aversion to politics in general and the substitution of ritual for substance in political expression created a poor environment for changing men's consciousness through political propaganda.

The Communists' attack on the system of *kuan-hsi* took several forms, of which propaganda was only one. In part, the Communists tried to undermine the system by making close social relationships a source of vulnerability instead of a bastion of trust and confidence, as for instance, through the forced denunciations elicited during the study group meetings of the Five Anti campaign. At the same time, the Communists created impersonal organizations to fulfill many of the functions that *kuan-hsi* had traditionally performed. Thus, for example, the CCP developed rudimentary insurance systems, cooperatives, hiring offices, and other tools to supplant the roles that the secret societies had played in the lives of their members in the transport industry. These societies, as we saw, had in many ways replaced *kuan-hsi* among poor people in transport work. Looking at Tientsin's elite in 1952, the Communists instituted a system of unified assignments for university graduates so that these highly skilled people could no longer rely on personal connections to find employment after they had finished their training. The Communists also undertook massive propaganda efforts to change people's attitudes toward personal relations. The goal of this propaganda was to develop a common sense of comradeship among all citizens, one that would replace the far narrower social horizons etched on people's consciousness by the system of *kuan-hsi*.[4] Uncounted hours have been devoted to making China's citizens think in terms of class and civic relations rather than in terms of kin relations and other types of personal ties.

It is impossible to evaluate to what degree the Communists have succeeded in bringing about this fundamental transformation in the way people view their society. Undoubtedly, some significant changes have occurred, especially among China's youth. The development of large-scale industry has itself had a marked effect on workers' social attitudes. Still, notions of *kuan-hsi* continue to play an important role, as illustrated by the story of a former high-level provincial cadre who left China under attack at the height of the Cultural Revolution. This cadre had just entered a university when the Communists took over, and through the years imbibed a steady diet of indoctrination by the CCP, of which he had become a member. Nevertheless, when he fled to Hong Kong and needed a job, he immediately inquired whether any hiring agent for a major firm came from his native village in Kwangtung. When he heard of such a man, he called on him and ("of course") was given a job even though he possessed no background relevant to that position.[5] The noteworthy element in this anecdote is not that *kuan-hsi* continued to play such a strong role in Hong Kong, but that a Communist cadre so readily turned to this system of personal relations.

This anecdote illustrates a larger dialectic that seems to exist between institutional development and *kuan-hsi* in Chinese society. Strong and stable institutions are needed to undermine *kuan-hsi* because they must fulfill the tasks that *kuan-hsi* would otherwise handle. Additionally, when the propaganda apparatus breaks down, a substantial percentage of the Chinese population quickly slips out of reach of the regime's political messages. *People's Daily,* for example, is printed in only seven million copies. It exerts its tremendous influence in Chinese society largely because an extensive network ensures that key articles in the Party paper are discussed and studied in groups that encompass most Chinese adults. If these groups cease to function—or if they are no longer linked to the Party through a hierarchy of smoothly working propaganda and education of-fices—the power of the central authorities to speak to the aver-age person diminishes considerably.

Certain types of political campaigns—large-scale class struggle movements—decrease the leaders' ability to communicate with the populace in several ways. Such campaigns are times of dan-ger, when past practices may cease to be a sufficient guide to safe conduct and when institutional relationships become upset. Under these circumstances, some people turn to those they trust most—to those, in many cases, with whom they have some special *kuan-hsi*. The decreased efficacy of institutions during these periods simply reinforces the urge to turn to more tradi-tional private relationships. Thus, ironically, while these cam-paigns clearly intensify the political experiences of the target groups and give massive doses of propaganda to the society as a whole, many citizens not in the specific target groups may expe-rience the campaign as an event that decreases the govern-ment's penetration of their lives and that *de facto* encourages them to employ "old ties" when they might otherwise have turned to the authorities.

These observations suggest, then, that there is generally an inverse relationship between the strength and stability of the organizations that govern China and the importance of *kuan-hsi* in the lives of the Chinese people. Evidence from China has repeatedly confirmed the accuracy of this general proposition, although the facts we have do not permit us to specify the rela-tionship in a precise way. For example, institutional relation-ships broke down as China slipped into a severe recession to-ward the end of the Great Leap Forward in 1960–61. The causes for the failure of that campaign included poor weather and the withdrawal of Soviet advisors in 1960. One key ingredient, however, was simply that the Chinese had attempted too much institutional change too rapidly; the consequent confusion and overload of demands on newly established organizations ren-dered them ultimately ineffective. When this occurred, the CCP explicitly called upon the former capitalists in Tientsin to rely on their old nets of social relations in order to re-establish marketing and commercial networks that would set the country's economy going again.[6] Once the institutions had recovered, of course, these personal networks were again attacked by the authorities.

The political strife accompanying the succession struggle in China from 1966 to 1976 also decreased the efficacy of the country's institutions. Objective standards for recruitment to higher education, for hiring and promotion in factories, for payments for labor, and for many other activities and functions ceased to exist. Factional strife sapped organizations of their authority and their ability to function. One might anticipate that in this situation the importance of personal connections in managing one's affairs would increase, and the qualitative evidence from China suggests that this was indeed the case. Increasingly, students tried to enter the universities "through the back door" (i.e., by using personal connections). Indeed, the back door became a major path for obtaining scarce consumer goods, finding job opportunities, obtaining services, and so forth.[7]

It is impossible to ascertain to what degree the post-Mao Chinese press's stories about the prevalence of backdoor activities reflected a real increase in these activities over previous years rather than the authorities' decision in 1977–78 to try to crack down on the use of *kuan-hsi*. Our argument, however, based on an examination of the period before the Cultural Revolution, tends to substantiate the Communists' claim that backdoor methods became more pronounced during 1966–76. Put differently, post-Maoist leaders like Hua Kuo-feng are correct when they have argued that the "radicals" are in reality a conservative influence in China (that, in their terms, they are "Left in form but Right in essence") because the anarchism inherent in the radicals' program saps the ability of the Communists' organizations to penetrate and guide the society, and thus allows a resurgence of traditional attitudes and morals.

In Tientsin during 1949–52, it was primarily the CCP's organizational resources that breached the walls that *kuan-hsi* erected between people in different social groups. The Communists' effectiveness in conveying their message to the citizens of Tientsin depended more directly on their organizational development than on their control over the Tientsin media. To an unknown but probably significant degree, moreover, *kuan-hsi* continues today to define the limits of people's interests and, therefore, of their attention and concern. The more extensive organizational development of society has, of course, enabled the CCP to contour people's actions to a far greater extent than before. Organizational development in China remains, however, not only a stepping-stone from *kuan-hsi* to true civic consciousness, but also a partial substitute for that larger consciousness that is still only incompletely developed. The Chinese media have been highly misleading on this sensitive issue, especially during 1966–76, but it is a problem that analysts of China must confront directly if they are to understand the nature of the society that Mao Tse-tung's successors are trying to remold.

A second major lesson to be learned from our analysis of Tientsin is that organization is often more efficacious than mobilization in bringing about social change in the PRC. Here, large-scale class struggle movements and campaigns designed to bring about major sociopolitical change, such as the Great Leap Forward, the Cultural Revolution, and the Campaign to Criticize Lin Piao and Confucius, must be differentiated from the highly specific mobilization efforts that intensify pressure to achieve concrete targets, such as the almost annual production competitions and public health campaigns.* We are concerned here with the former type of mobilization, which is designed to change society.

The argument in favor of mass mobilization to achieve socio-

---

*Even the change-oriented political campaigns almost always build upon and intensify trends already under way. Such campaigns, like the Five Anti and the Great Leap Forward, require the political leadership to accumulate appropriate organizational and information resources before initiating a political upsurge. Only the Cultural Revolution and the campaign against Lin Piao and Confucius seem to have violated these principles to a substantial degree. Gordon Bennett reviews the range of types of political campaigns in China and their usual pattern of development in *Yundong* (Berkeley, Calif., 1976), pp. 38–74. For a more systematic treatment of the process of accumulating resources for the Three Anti Five Anti in Tientsin than is presented in this volume, see Kenneth Lieberthal, "Reconstruction and Revolution in a Chinese City: The Case of Tientsin, 1949–1953," Ph.D. dissertation, Columbia University, 1972, pp. 359–415.

political change is multifaceted. In part, it asserts that organizations are by their very nature conservative forces that acquire vested interests in the *status quo* and therefore become poor vehicles for fundamental change. To function effectively, organizations require people with organizational skills, people who are literate, good at summing up experiences and writing reports, and know how to maximize efficiency through rational choices. Cadres with these skills are unlikely to hail from the poorest strata of society. They are, moreover, almost certain to want to protect and preserve the basic order of things that brought them into their privileged positions of authority. Thus, though they may be willing and able to work hard to make the existing set of arrangements (with marginal changes) work more efficiently, they often resist the advance of society to new and higher levels. Only mass mobilization can break the conservative grip of these cadres over the lives of the citizens and create a situation where basic changes (such as the introduction of people's communes or the radical restructuring of the entire educational curriculum) can be brought about.

Mass mobilization, according to its adherents has inherent salutory effects for those who participate in it. Mobilization places masses of people into a *revolutionary* situation, where the rules of the game are uncertain and where a mistake can prove extremely costly. This atmosphere of crisis engenders an intensity of concern and a depth of commitment that no more orderly and incremental approach could possibly instill. Thus, the very act of mass mobilization creates a revolutionary élan and produces a profound commitment to ultimate Communist values, temporarily allowing the populace to set aside the values (hard work, discipline, material reward) of the long transitional period between the formal victory of the revolution and the advent of Communism. This rebirth of the revolution through periodic mass mobilization keeps the revolution from going astray and embracing as ultimate goals those transitional values originally thought necessary simply to bring about the rapid industrialization of the economy.[8] This subtle transformation of the transitional into the ultimate is exactly what the Chinese assert occurred in the Soviet Union, and it poses, for leftists, the greatest danger to the Chinese revolution.

These arguments in favor of mass mobilization have considerable validity and power, as the experience of Tientsin during 1949–52 indicates. During their first few years in power, Tientsin's leaders found that they had to staff their organizations with basic-level cadres who possessed scarce organizational skills, and that they subsequently became dependent on the information reported by these cadres. In the transport industry, however, many of these new recruits were in fact former coolie bosses; and in the factories, the former KMT trade union functionaries tended to assume the basic-level positions in the new Communist unions. Even when staunch Communists took such positions, they were not immune to conservative influences. The central policy demanding both change at a deliberate pace and the cultivation of a broad united front gradually forged links between these cadres and the sectors of the municipal society over which they had taken charge. These ties, in turn, bred an increasingly strong commitment among the cadres to some reasonable facsimile of the *status quo*. It took the startlingly effective mass mobilization of the Three Anti Five Anti campaign in early 1952 to alter these trends, at least temporarily.

Thus, mobilization as a strategy to achieve radical change makes considerable sense and has obvious advantages. Opponents of this strategy often do not dispute its effectiveness but rather decry the disruption and the inevitable instances of human tragedy that it entails. Our analyses of mobilization in Tientsin in early 1949 and 1952 suggest, however, the importance of another dimension of the argument over mass mobilization— that without extensive preparation and follow-through in the organizational realm, prolonged mobilization weakens rather than strengthens the Party's long-term ability to guide the transformation of society. Indeed, insofar as mass mobilization undermines the ability of the Communist governing organizations to function, it provides a portion of China's citizens with respite from, rather than increased exposure to, the pressures for change generated by the political authorities. Many of these people then insulate themselves from the campaign by minimizing their involvement in the issues it has raised and by retreating into a more traditional set of relationships based on *kuan-hsi* that provide protection from the demands of a suddenly unpredictable political system. Thus, for example, sympathetic chroniclers of the Cultural Revolution at Peking's leading higher educational institutions noted that by mid-1968 all but the most zealous and radical students abandoned the struggle and sat out the rest of the campaign in the privacy of their families. For this majority of students, then, much of the Cultural Revolution was not so much a searing exposure to new values and a test by fire, as a decreased exposure to new values and an enforced, prolonged stay with their families.[9] The fact that during the Cultural Revolution the birthrate soared in direct contradiction to the government's policy[10] provides yet another indication that the leaders' ability to convey new values to the populace actually decreased at the height of this massive political upheaval.

Naturally, not all people slip away during a massive political campaign. For an important minority, such campaigns have provided searing experiences that have had a major impact on their political consciousness. The problem, however, is that China cannot remain in a campaign phase indefinitely, but must at least alternate periods of mobilization with those of consolidation and quotidian administration.[11] As the country moves into a consolidation phase, those who were most acutely affected by the rhetoric of mobilization almost always fail to adapt to the new set of priorities They must be removed. In this sense, mobilization as a strategy to change political values is sometimes *too* effective, for it produces individuals unable to cope with a more disciplined environment. These individuals, in the final analysis, are likely first to impose impossible demands on the system and then to suffer disillusionment (and purge) when these demands are not met; this was the fate of K'uai Ta-fu and many other Red Guard leaders during 1968–70.[12] Activists who can adapt and provide a pool for new recruitment into the Communist Party and related organizations also emerge during the course of these campaigns. For the vast majority of Chinese, however, mass mobilization campaigns are relatively ineffective in bringing about major changes in their outlook—either because they have insulated themselves from the campaign or have suffered disillusionment as a result of the post-campaign consolidation.

A campaign approach to inducing large-scale change has the further drawback of becoming less effective with time. The campaign strategy must create a period of genuine uncertainty in order to bring about basic changes in values. Clearly, a person's first exposure to a major political campaign will be far more shocking than the second, third, or fourth. As people see how campaigns develop, they become increasingly able to structure their participation so as to achieve security in these periods of ostensible uncertainty.[13] The only way to shatter the security of China's millions of campaign veterans, then, is to make each new campaign qualitatively more forceful than its predecessors. The Cultural Revolution demonstrated the problems of this strategy and probably defined the outer limits to which it could be carried. The related problem of using political campaigns to change the views of youths who have grown up in a campaign environment poses similar difficulties.

For all these reasons, a strategy of relatively steady change under the firm control of the CCP and its organizations is probably the most effective way to change Chinese society fundamentally over the long run. This strategy permits government-sponsored organizations to play their full role in linking China's citizens to the national system and its goals as defined by the Party leaders. It is also the system most capable of bringing about China's rapid industrialization, a process that in every country has produced a profound transformation of man's conception of his fellow man, his work, and even his relationship with his natural environment.[14] In short, the strategy of demobilization and organizational development that Liu Shao-ch'i prescribed for Tientsin in April–May 1949 embodied a set of ideas that has continued relevance for the Chinese revolution in the 1970's and beyond. While mass mobilization can provide a corrective to some of the inherent problems in this strategy, it does so at potentially enormous cost and with considerably less effectiveness than its own sound and fury would indicate.

The experience of Tientsin suggests a third major lesson: that Chinese political organizations are neither as strong nor as unified as they seem. Lucian Pye has wrestled with the enigma that seemingly strong and durable Chinese organizations virtually disintegrate when under attack. Attributing this fragility to deeply rooted Chinese concerns about authority, Pye argues that the Chinese seek the security of stable hierarchies and abhor situations where social lines are blurred and confused. Therefore, they readily join organizations that seem to embody and reflect the underlying set of authority relationships in their society, but they with equal alacrity abandon an organization that seems to be in trouble and unlikely to provide a safe haven in the future.[15] Pye may be correct, but one need not look to cultural explanations for the phenomena he observes; the emphasis on organizational control demanded by Liu Shao-ch'i in 1949 contains elements that also contribute to the very outcome that Pye has tried to explain.

As noted above, when organizations impose their own demands for skilled manpower, they structure the requirements for recruitment to the political elite of society. They do so, moreover, in a way that demands that much of the political leadership even at the basic levels be drawn from groups other than the poor and the dispossessed who lack the necessary organizational skills. The case of Tientsin demonstrates how this led to the recruitment of many basic-level cadres who did not fully share the Communists' values or goals. Consequently, Tientsin's rapidly developing political organizations stood on feet of clay. The Three Anti campaign aimed in part at rectifying this situation. The dilemma, however, is perennial and does not stem simply from the difficulties of taking over a major municipality during a revolutionary political movement. Thus, for example, the editors of the *Tientsin Daily* should not have been surprised when, six months *after* the conclusion of the Three Anti campaign, they received a letter from a disgruntled worker in the construction industry revealing that a former overseer who had been a target during the Three Anti and had made a full confession, had already managed to take over the work at a major construction site and largely re-establish his influence. The overseer of 1951 had simply become a trade union leader of 1952, and in that capacity he had hired relatives, friends, and others with whom he had *kuan-hsi* to fill 80 of the 100 positions at the construction site. Two of his closest friends received appointments to the other two trade union positions at the site, and all of the 80 received higher pay than they should have.[16] The overseer had simply parlayed his skills in organization into a basic-level position from which he could control the flow of information to higher levels. Chinese organizations still must recruit heavily among those who do not fully share the leaders' goals—in the late 1970's, the intellectuals were the major embodiment of this phenomenon—and this in turn imparts a heterodoxy to the organizations that is not usually visible from afar.

This study of Tientsin also highlights the degree to which Chinese political organizations exist in a symbiotic relationship with their environment. Over time, a united-front strategy produces cadres who have become intimately familiar with the problems and perspectives of the particular groups with whom they have been forming ties. While this is good from the Communists' viewpoint insofar as it increases the effectiveness of communication between the political organizations and the key groups in the society, it also exacts a cost by bringing the tensions and contradictions of Chinese society into the political organizations themselves. Indeed, the strategy of proceeding "from the top down" virtually ensures that newly formed organizations exist initially as hollow shells that only over time will be fleshed out. This was, for example, the case in the socialist transformation of industry and commerce in Tientsin in late 1955 to early 1956. The ostensible socialist transformation of entire trades in a few months was followed during the next year by a long series of measures designed to make effective a "transformation" that in fact had not at all affected the operations of the vast majority of Tientsin's firms.[17] Older organizations, of course, have more substance than this, but scholars must always pay attention to sources of recruitment and related factors in order to fathom the degree to which any Chinese organization is strong and unified.

Finally, this study makes clear that there is little friction between the imperatives of rational organization and those of political dictatorship and revolutionary change.[18] Indeed, "rationalization," as pursued in Tientsin, provided a key link between economic development and political change. At its heart, the effort to rationalize Tientsin society focused on defining clear lines of responsibility and job specifications while establishing concrete standards for hiring, evaluation, rewards, and so on. Each component of this effort, however, provided an opportunity for the leaders to acquire more information about the populace and to pinpoint relatively quickly whether their preferences were being met.

Rationalization increases information and with it, the potential for control. Moreover, it does not in itself dictate that the decisions made by the system will cater to already entrenched interests or that they will conform to a relatively conservative line. Rather, rationalization's real effect is to broaden the range of choices available to political leaders by enhancing both their informational resources and their ability to implement and evaluate decisions without dictating the substance of the decisions themselves. The need for essentially *political* judgments—choices determined by value preferences and goals—remains even in the most rationalized political and social system.[19] The experience of Tientsin shows that even major efforts to increase society's subjection to rational rules and standards are perfectly compatible with tight political control over the society and with the exercise of that control to serve revolutionary goals.

This lesson of the Tientsin experience in the early 1950's is pertinent to the PRC as it embarks on its fourth decade, for it suggests that the splurge of rule-making that has occurred since the death of Mao Tse-tung and the overthrow of the radicals[20] will enhance rather than constrain the successor leadership's ability to transform Chinese society. Rationalization, in brief, can but need not be accompanied by liberalization; indeed, it can play a vital role in actually closing those gaps in the political control system that provide much of the discretion available to individuals in the PRC.

Notes

Notes

Complete authors' names, titles, and publication data are given in the Bibliography, pp. 217–25. The following abbreviations are used in the Notes:

CB	*Current Background*
CP	*Chin-pu jih-pao*
FBIS/PRC	Foreign Broadcast Information Service/People's Republic of China Daily Report
JM	*Jen-min jih-pao*
JPRS	Joint Publications Research Service
MK	*Min-kuo jih-pao*
NCNA	New China News Agency
NYT	*New York Times*
PKKKTT	*Pan-yun kung-jen kung-hui kung-tso ts'an-k'ao tzu-liao*
SCMP	*Survey of China Mainland Press*
SW	*Selected Works of Mao Tse-tung*
TC	*T'ien-chin jih-pao*
TCSCK	*T'ien-chin shih chou-k'an*
TKP	*Ta Kung Pao (Tientsin edition)*
TP	*Tung-pei jih-pao*

Chapter Two
1. *SW,* 4: 363–64.
2. Murphey.
3. Information on the concession areas is based on extensive interviewing and the following sources: *T'ien'chin chih-lueh,* pp. 18–21; Pao Chiao-ming and Ho Tz'u-ch'ang, pp. 54, 101–8 (of the translation); Nikitin and Feodorov, pp. 14–17; Ueda Toshio; and Jones, pp. 120–31. See also Prentice.
4. Jones, p. 131.

5. *T'ien-chin t'e-pieh shih,* Pt. 4, p. 7. See also Lieberthal, "Reconstruction," pp. 27–28.

6. *CP,* 3.iii.49, p. 4, 6.vii.49, p. 3.

7. Surveys of sources of labor for various Tientsin trades include Fong, *Hosiery,* pp. 57, 64; Fong, *Carpet,* pp. 44, 54; *Chung-kuo lao-tung,* 2: 133, for textiles; Fong, *Grain,* p. 598, for the grain trade and milling; Fong and Ku, p. 529, for shoemaking; and Li Pu-lung, p. 6, for the brick industry. Population figures for 1936–47 to determine rural-urban immigration can be calculated from *T'ien-chin cheng-fu,* June 1936; *T'ien-chin Shih chu-yao t'ung-chi,* 2: 2 (iii.48); and *TCSCK* 8: 5 (1.ii.47).

8. Fong, *Cotton,* 1: 115.

9. This is a common phenomenon in developing countries. On Latin America, see Huntington, *Political Order,* pp. 278–83.

10. Derived from interviews and from descriptions of Chinese village life in Fei T'ung, pp. 1–44, 51–69; and Fried, pp. 99–135.

11. See, for example, Fong, *Carpet,* pp. 44–45.

12. *Ibid.,* p. 51; Lang, pp. 82–83. Working in a retail store, of course, was less confining in this respect.

13. *CP,* 15.xii.49; *TC,* 6.vii.51, p. 1.

14. Delioussine, pp. 424–25, 431.

15. Grootaers, pp. 331–41.

16. Nathan, pp. 47–58.

17. *Chieh-fang hou ti,* p. 11; *Hsin-Hua yüeh-pao,* Feb. 1950, pp. 707–8, quoting *JM,* 1.i.50.

18. *CP,* 3.iii.49, p. 4, 6.vii.49, p. 3, 18.x.50, p. 1.

19. *TKP,* 23.iii.48, p. 5, 2.i.48.

20. Chesneaux, p. 62.

21. Fong, *Industrial Organization,* p. 56.

22. Fang Fu-an, p. 81.

23. Fong, *Cotton,* p. 170.

24. Chesneaux, p. 504; Ho and Fong, p. 27. A more general analysis of the obstacles to effective labor organization in China is presented in Fong, *Industrial Organization,* p. 60.

25. See, for example, Barnett, *China on the Eve,* pp. 53–54.

26. From interviewing. See also Lang, pp. 93–101.

27. *MK,* 3.x.46, p. 4, 17.v.47, p. 4.

28. *TCSCK,* 1(2): 4 (21.xii.46).

29. "Pen-hui chin-jung wei-yuan-hui," pp. 14–16.

30. See *T'ien-chin chih-lüeh,* pp. 322–44; Fong, *Carpet,* pp. 61–63; and Burgess.

31. For examples, see *MK,* 7.vi.46, p. 4; *TCSCK* 1(9): 9,11 (8.ii.47); and *MK,* 6.vi.46, p. 4, 3.x.46, p. 4, 7.xii.46, p. 4.

32. From interview data.

33. Lang, pp. 185–89.

34. *Ibid.,* pp. 92–93.

35. *PKKKTT,* p. 52; *JM,* 25.iii.50, p. 1.

36. *PKKKTT,* pp. 4–7; An Li-fu, p. 4.

37. *PKKKTT,* p. 6.
38. An Li-fu, p. 4; *PKKKTT,* pp. 13–15.
39. *PKKKTT,* p. 4.
40. Davis, p. 49.
41. *Chung-kuo pang-hui shih,* p. 198; Davis, p. 55.
42. Based primarily on interviewing.

Chapter Three

1. On the civil war in general, see Chassin.
2. On the refugee problem, see *MK,* 21.vi.47, p. 4; and *TCSCK* as follows: 3(10): 13 (2 viii.47); 3(12): 10 (16.viii.47); 5(4): 7–8 (6.xii.47); 6(4): 11; 7(1): 3 (1.v.48); 7(7): 6–9 (12.vi.48); 7(11): 9(10.vii.48); 7(12): 10–11 (17.vii.48).
3. See, e.g., *TCSCK,* 4(8): 2–3 (11.x.47), and 6(10): 6–7 (10.iv.48).
4. These and the following cost-of-living index figures are derived from *T'ien-chin kung-jen,* pp. 9–10. These indexes are based on constant dollars for July 1936–June 1937.
5. Chang Kia-ngau, pp. 78–81, provides details.
6. See also Campbell and Tullock, pp. 242–45.
7. *SW,* 4: 289–93.
8. Derived from *NYT,* 8.i.49, pp. 1–2, 11.i.49, pp. 1–2, and 12.i.49, p. 1; and from Whitson, p. 6.
9. *NYT,* 22.xii.48, p. 8.
10. *NYT,* 7.xii.48, p. 18, 24.xii.48, p. 3.
11. *TCSCK,* 9(7) (27.xi.48); *NYT,* 24.xii.48, p. 3.
12. *NYT,* 7.xii.48, p. 18.
13. *NYT,* 22.xii.48, p. 8, 6.i.49, p. 1, 8.i.49, pp. 1–2, 11.i.49, pp. 1–2.
14. The major sources on the events of Jan. 14 and 15 are Chang; Grace Liu, pp. 5–7, 19; *NYT,* 15–16.i.49; Gerstenzang, p. 15; *Hung-ch'i ch'a-shang T'ien-chin* (a book of memoirs of the battle for Tientsin by soldiers who participated in it); *P'ing-chin chan-i;* and the China Association archives for the period Jan.–June 1949.
15. The information summarized in the next three paragraphs is analyzed in greater detail and fully documented in Lieberthal, "Mao," pp. 496–509.
16. Firsthand accounts of the liberation of Peiping are available in Barnett, *China on the Eve,* pp. 315–37; and Bodde, pp. 100–115.
17. Good accounts of battles for major cities are given in *Chung-kuo jen-min; Hung-ch'i ch'a-shang T'ien-chin;* and Lai Chih-yen. For brief overviews of the civil war in 1949, see F. F. Liu, pp. 260–70; and Harrison, pp. 224–431.
18. For the texts of these decrees, see *Cheng-ts'e fa-ling hui-pien,* pp. 5–7. For the biographies of Huang K'o-ch'eng, T'an Cheng, Huang Ching, Hsu Chien-kuo, and Huang Huo-ch'ing, the most important people named in these decrees, see the appropriate entries in Klein and Clark.
19. The summary figures are taken from Tientsin Mayor and Party

First Secretary Huang Ching's first major report on the work in Tientsin from liberation to July 1949, *CP*, 6.ix.49, p. 2, and 7.ix.49, pp. 1, 4. On students returning to the Northeast, see *TC*, 1.ii.49, p. 2. On destroying suburban dwellings that might block the line of fire, see *China Weekly*, 1.i.49, p. 119. At least some of the relief food that the Communists distributed in Tientsin had been appropriated from the American Economic Coordination Administration *NYT*, 26.i.49, p. 12, 28.i.49, p. 7, 3.ii.49, p. 3. On small loans to help people in distress recover, see *TC*, 12.ii.49, p. 1. On the initial post-takeover policies in Peiping, see Barnett, *China on the Eve*, pp. 338–64.

20. On audits in the enterprises, see *Chung-kuo jen-min*, pp. 106–9; and Grace Liu, pp. 6–7. On completion of takeover work, see Grace Liu, pp. 6–7; and *TC*, 28.ii.49, p. 2. For the figures on the number of units taken over, see *TC*, 3.xi.49; and Wei Chin, whose article first appeared in *JM*, 1.i.50. The MCC Takeover Department had thirteen subdivisions (*ch'u*): industry, communications, railroads, finance, domestic trade, foreign trade, motors, telecommunications, irrigation, villages, warehouses, sanitation, and "residual." See *TC*, 18.ii.49. Other pertinent information is contained in the municipal government work report in *CP*, 7.ix.49.

21. *CP*, 7.ix.49, p. 1. The figure for the second half of the year is so high in part because the entire year's income tax was collected then.

22. Final figures for 1949 are from *CP*, 16.ii.50, p. 4.

23. *CP*, 28.ii.51, p. 2.

24. *CP*, 7.ix.49, p. 1.

25. According to *CP*, 16.ii.50, p. 4, by the end of 1949, 9,494 of Tientsin's cadres were on the free supply system, which usually applied only to people who had joined the Party before 1949. See Vogel, "Revolutionary to Semi-Bureaucrat."

26. For an excellent analysis of the general problem of integrating the pre-liberation revolutionary cadres, see Vogel, "Revolutionary to Semi-Bureaucrat," pp. 36–60.

27. See, e.g., *CP*, 1.viii.49, p. 3; and *TC*, 12.x.50, p. 1, 17.x.50, p. 1.

28. *CP*, 30.ix.52, p. 2; *TC*, 5.xi.52, p. 2.

29. On the Southbound Work Team in Canton, see Vogel, *Canton*, pp. 51–52, 94.

30. See *CP*, 7.ix.49, pp. 1, 4. No available information indicates how many of these students were assigned to positions in Tientsin.

31. *CP*, 6.ix.49, p. 1.

32. *TC*, 15.xi.50, p. 1.

33. *TC*, 4.v.50, p. 5.

34. On the rules governing Party organization, see the Party rules adopted on June 11, 1945, in *Chung-kuo kung-ch'an tang*, pp. 3–24, especially 10–22. For the rules governing the organizational structure of the Youth League, see *CP*, 19.iv.49, p. 2. The Youth League structure in a national ministry is described in Barnett, *Cadres*, p. 29. On the development of the Youth League in Tientsin, see *CP*, 8.viii.49, p. 3., 11.viii.49, p. 1, and 25.xi.49, p. 2.

35. *CP*, 7.ix.49, p. 1. Summer floods in Hopei exacerbated this situation.

36. *CP*, 17.i.50, p. 2.

37. Based on figures in *T'ien-chin kung-jen*, pp. 17–18.

38. *CP*, 6.ix.49, p. 2, 7.ix.49, pp. 1, 4; Wei Chin, p. 907.

39. *CP*, 7.ix.49, p. 1, 13.iii.49, pp. 1, 4.

40. *CP*, 3.vii.49, p. 2, 13.iii.49, pp. 1, 4; Liu Shao-ch'i et al., pp. 47–50.

41. *CP*, 24.vi.49, p. 1.

42. *SW*, 4: 365.

43. *Liu Shao-ch'i wen-t'i*, p. 211.

44. *CP*, 30.iv.49, p. 3.

45. *Liu Shao-ch'i wen-t'i*, pp. 218–19.

46. *Ibid.*, pp. 206–7.

47. *Ibid.*, p. 211.

48. *Ibid.*, pp. 208–10, 213–15, 217.

49. *CP*, 8.v.49, p. 3.

50. *Liu Shao-ch'i wen-t'i*, p. 201.

51. *CP*, 8.v.49, p. 3.

52. *Liu Shao-ch'i wen-t'i*, pp. 208, 211; *CP*, 17.v.49, p. 3, 7.ix.49, p. 2.

53. *CP*, 7.ix.49, pp. 1–2. These provisions are contained in a draft of a set of regulations for handling labor-capital relations that Liu originally presented to the Tientsin MCC during his April–May visit.

54. *Liu Shao-ch'i wen-t'i*, p. 209; *CP*, 7.ix.49, p. 2.

55. *TKP*, 28.ii.48, p. 5.

56. *CP*, 13.vi.49, p. 2; *Liu Shao-ch'i wen-t'i*, p. 218.

57. *CP*, 1.v.49, pp. 2–3.

58. For the capitalists' reaction, see *CP*, 8.v.49, p. 3, and 1.vi.50, p. 5.

59. *Liu Shao-ch'i wen-t'i*, p. 200.

Chapter Four

1. The complete text of this decree is in *Cheng-ts'e fa-ling hui-pien*, pp. 3–4.

2. See *ibid.*, pp. 11, 13–20, for the texts of these documents.

3. On the relationship between organization and effective action, see Li Chu-ch'en, p. 1; *Liu Shao-ch'i wen-t'i*, pp. 206–7; and *Kung-yun hui-chi*, p. 1, quoting from an article that originally appeared in *TC*, 26.iv.49.

4. On Marx, see Tucker, pp. 3–32; and Avineri. On Lenin, see Meyer, pp. 19–105. On Mao vs. Lenin, see Schram, pp. 15–144; and Schwartz, chap. 1.

5. Groth, pp. 272–78.

6. *CP*, 7.ix.49, p. 2.

7. See Eastman for one of the few available articles on the Blue Shirts.

8. *T'ien–chin shih hsien-k'uang*, p. 3.

9. *CP*, 7.ix.49, p. 2.

10. *CP*, 6.ix.49, p. 2, 7.ix.49, p. 2, 17.i.50, p. 2.

11. *TC*, 28.ii.51. 12. *PKKKTT*, p. 16.
13. An Li-fu, pp. 5–6. 14. *Ibid.*, p. 6.
15. *JM*, 11.v.50, p. 2.
16. *JM*, 25.iii.50, p. 2; *PKKKTT*, p. 57.
17. An Li-fu, p. 7. 18. *PKKKTT*, pp. 48–51.
19. *Ibid.*, pp. 58–63. 20. An Li-fu, pp. 9–10.
21. On the system of "lots," see *ibid.*, p. 3.
22. On the coolie bosses' tactics, see *ibid.*, p. 9; *JM*, 11.v.50, p. 2; and *PKKKTT*, pp. 54–55.
23. The membership figures for the Transport Workers' Trade Union and for its subordinate unions are available in *PKKKTT*, pp. 59, 65, 86, 105.
24. *Ibid.*, p. 66.
25. *Ibid.*, p. 6.
26. *Ibid.*, p. 66.
27. All the information on these two training classes is taken from the detailed reports on each session published in *ibid.*, pp. 93–104.
28. This campaign is discussed in detail in *ibid.*, pp. 105–10.
29. The following analysis of this campaign is from *JM*, 11.v.50, p. 2, and from a case study of the campaign in Tientsin's No. 5 ward in *PKKKTT*, pp. 72–85.
30. Taken from *PKKKTT*, pp. 67, 86; and An Li-fu, p. 18.
31. An Li-fu, p. 15.
32. See *PKKKTT*, p. 2; *JM*, 25.iii.50, p. 2, 11.v.50, p. 2; and *Hsin-Hua yüeh-pao* 2(5): 65–66 (15.v.50).
33. *CP*, 20.vi.50, p. 2.
34. *Ibid.*, *CP*, 24.vi.50, p. 2.
35. *CP*, 24.vi.50, p. 2, 25.vi.50, p. 2.
36. *CP*, 22.vi.50, p. 3.
37. *CP*, 7.vii.50, p. 2.
38. *CP*, 6.ix.49.
39. *CP*, 24.vi.50, p. 2, 7.vii.50, p. 2.
40. *CP*, 31.iii.51; *TC*, 13.vii.51.

Chapter Five
1. China Association, Doc. no. 49/E/15 (1.xi.49).
2. *CP*, 1.ii.51, p. 4. The types and amount of taxes collected directly by the Center changed over time. See, e.g., Chao Kuo-chün, 1:224–29.
3. In 1950 the MPG sold 7.4 million bonds. *CP*, 1.ii.51, p. 4. In June 1951 the population was called upon to make large contributions to the Korean War effort. The government received pledges of over 80 billion *yuan* during the remainder of the year for this cause. *CP*, 29.xii.51, p. 4; *T'ien-chin kung-shang*, 2(6): 7 (20.x.51).
4. Chao Kuo-chün, 1: 202–13; *CB*, 12: 10–11.
5. *CP*, 1.ii.51, p. 4.
6. *TC*, 17.iii.50, pp. 1, 3; *CP*, 11.v.50, p. 1, 21.i.51, p. 2, 1.ii.51, p. 4.
7. The readjustment, like the initial measures to unify finances, was a national program, albeit with significant flexibility at the local level.

This program was discussed by both Mao Tse-tung and Ch'en Yun in June 1950. *CB Supplement,* 1: 1–6, 2: 1–13.

8. *CP,* 11.v.50, p. 1, 25.vii.50, p. 1.

9. *CP,* 11.i.50, p. 3; *Chung-kuo kung-jen,* 70 (15.vi.50); *TC,* 9.i.51, p. 1; *CP,* 21.i.51, p. 2. Most of this growth probably occurred in the late spring and early summer.

10. Fong, *Cotton,* 1: 319. See also Fong, *Industrial Organization,* p. 7. For a brief account of the "contract system," see Chesneaux, p. 59. The labor contract system was widely used only in the construction industry in Tientsin.

11. See, e.g., Schurmann, pp. 228–31; and Lang, pp. 181–84.

12. *Chung-kuo kung-jen,* 4: 32, 40–41 (15.v.50).

13. *JM,* 24.v.50; "T'ien-chin shih lao-tzu"; *TC,* 4.iii.51, p. 1.

14. *TC,* editorial, 24.vii.50, reprinted in *Chung-kuo kung-jen,* 8 (15.ix.50).

15. One hundred nineteen of these were in factories and stores, and three more were for entire trades. *TC,* 9.i.51, p. 1.

16. *CP,* 25.vii.50, p. 1; *TC,* editorial, 24.vii.50, 1.i.51.

17. *CP,* 9.ix.50, p. 4.   18. *Ibid.,* p. 2.

19. *CP,* 21.i.52, p. 3.   20. *CP,* 9.ix.50, p. 4.

21. *CP,* 29.i.51, p. 2.

22. Teams were far smaller than workshops and tended to be functionally more specific. See Schurmann, p. 249; and *CP,* 9.ix.50, p. 2. By 1950 the team was the basic unit both of production and of trade union organization. Its size in Tientsin, as computed from figures on trade union membership and trade union team development, averaged around twelve people per team in private enterprises and close to twenty people per team in public enterprises. *TC,* 9.i.51, p. 1, 29.ix.51, pp. 1,3.

23. On production competitions in 1950, see *TC,* 4.iv.50, p. 3, and editorial, 24.vii.50; and *CP* as follows: 9.vi.50, p. 2, 19.vi.50, p. 2, 26.vii.50, p. 2, 9.ix.50, p. 4, 21.ix.50, p. 2.

24. For a history of the relationship between production competitions and management reform in the Hengyuan mill, see Feng Ch'üan, "I ko shih-li ti ch'i-shih." On management reforms more generally in the private sector, see Feng Ch'üan, "Tsai lun ssu-ying."

25. *CP,* 1.ii.51, p. 4.

26. *People's China,* 1(12): 26 (16.vi.50).

27. *CP,* 1.ii.51, p. 4.

28. See Kao Ch'eng-chih's article in *T'ien-chin kung-shang,* 10(5): 2 (28.ii.51).

29. *People's China,* 1(12): 24 (16.vi.50).

30. See, e.g., Fong, *Industrial Organization,* pp. 1–4, 7–8; and Fong *Carpet,* p. 76.

31. *CP,* 1.ii.51, p. 4.

32. *CP,* 20.vi.50, p. 2.

33. *CP,* 20.vi.50, p. 2, 23.xi.51, p. 1. For the application of these measures in the Tientsin machine industry, see "T'ien-chin shih chi-ch'i

kung-yeh." On joint borrowing, see *T'ien-chin kung-shang,* 1(12): 14–16 (15.vi.51).

34. *CP,* 1.ii.51, p. 4.

35. *Ibid.*

36. The 1951 MPG Finance and Economic Work Report gives a complete listing of these 1951 trade conferences in *CP,* 29.xii.51, p. 4.

37. *Ibid.; CP,* 1.i.52, p. 5.

38. *CP,* 15.vi.51, p. 3.

39. *CP,* 29.xii.51, p. 4.

40. Text in *Chung-kuo kung-jen,* 5: 44–45(15.vi.50).

41. *TC,* 14.vi.50, p. 1.   42. *CP,* 28.ii.51, p. 2.

43. *TC,* editorial, 28.xi.52.   44. *CP,* 2.iii.50, p. 2.

45. For additional information on the expansion of functions at the ward level in various municipalities in mid-1950, see *Jen-min chou-pao,* editorial, No. 7, 1950; *JM,* editorial, 16.v.50; *TKP,* 8.vii.50; and *Ch'ing-tao jih-pao,* 14.ix.50.

46. CP, 24.vii.50, p. 1.

47. *CP,* 25.viii.50, p. 1. This was followed several months later in other wards. See, e.g., *CP,* 12.x.50, p. 2 (No. 5 ward), 20.x.50, p. 2 (T'ang-ta District), and 25.xii.50, p. 2 (Nos. 2, 4, and 10 wards). The No. 9 ward played a leading role in local-level political construction work during 1951–52.

48. *CP,* 18.viii.50, p. 2.

49. *T'ien-chin kung-shang,* 1 (4): 8–9 (25.ii.51).

50. *Ibid.,* 1(12): 14–16 (15.vi.51).

51. *Ibid.*

Chapter Six

1. Details concerning the beginning of this war are still in dispute. See, e.g., the contributions by Robert Simmons, Chong-sik Lee, and W. E. Skillend to the *China Quarterly,* 54: 354–68 (April–June 1973).

2. Whiting.

3. Calculated from the figures presented in the Annual Report of the British Chamber of Commerce, Tientsin, 23.ii.49, p. 17.

4. Indeed, beginning in June a number of Shanghai import and export firms opened offices in Tientsin. *Hsin-wan jih-pao,* 23–24.viii.49; *Wen-hui pao,* 17.vii.49.

5. Associated Press dispatch from Shanghai of 11.viii.49.

6. China Association, Doc. no. 49/G/186.

7. China Association, documents for 1949–50.

8. The Chinese asserted that the United States had artifically lowered the prices on these goods in order to undermine the Chinese economy. *CP,* 1.ii.51, p. 4.

9. *Ibid.*

10. *CP,* 29.xii.51, p. 4.

11. China Association, Doc. no. 51/G/4, 12.i.51.

12. *CP,* 29.xii.51, p. 4.

13. *Ibid.; CP,* 30.ix.52, p. 2.

14. For a complete list, see *CP,* 29.xii.51, p. 4. Percentages are rounded off to the nearest integer.

15. *TC,* 7.i.51, p. 3.

16. For a review of this central directive and a detailed statement of the Tientsin plan, see the two feature articles and the editorial on this subject in *TC,* 18.ii.51.

17. This technique has characterized the CCP's approach to devising and implementing major new policies. Bennett, chap. 2.

18. *TC,* editorial, 15.ix.51, p. 1. Also, these wards were later cited as the main innovators in types of propaganda organization. *TC,* 7.i.52, p. 2.

19. See, e.g., *TC,* 22.vi.51, p. 1, 16.vii.51, p. 1, and editorial, 15.ix.51. p. 1.

20. *CP,* 3.xii.51, p. 4. The number of workers engaged in one or another form of spare-time study climbed from 71,754 in 1950 to 118,130 in 1951. While these schools had emphasized practical skills that would best serve production in 1950, they all added political classes during 1951. *Chung-kuo kung-jen,* 5: 44–45 (15.vi.50); *CP,* 1.ii.51, p. 4, 21.i.51, p. 4, 30.xii.51, p. 4.

21. *CP,* 10.ix.51, p. 2.

22. *T'ien-chin kung-shang,* 2(6): 7 (20.x.51).

23. A translation of this directive, which was issued on July 23, 1950, is available in *CB,* 101: 4–5.

24. Shen Chün-ju's article in *JM,* 15.iii.51, which refers to events in Oct. 1950; article on "boundless magnanimity" in *JM,* 28.xii.50, tr. in *CB,* 101: 6–8.

25. *TC,* 28.ii.51. The CCP subsequently referred to the First Session of the Third Municipal ACPRC (1–3.ii.51) as the beginning of the Suppression of Counterrevolutionaries campaign in Tientsin. In fact, although this meeting emphasized the need to carry out security work because of the Korean War, it gave no indication that a mass campaign would soon be launched as an integral part of this work. For data on this meeting, see *CP,* 2.ii.51, and 4.ii.51. See especially Huang Ching's report to this conference in his capacity as mayor in *CP,* 2.ii.51, pp. 1–2.

26. Nineteen people were arrested, most of whom were priests, *SCMP,* 83: 3–4.

27. *TC,* 9.iv.51.   28. *CP,* 21.iii.51, p. 1.

29. *SCMP,* 93: 28.   30. *CP,* 28.iii.51, p. 1.

31. *CP,* 29.iii.51, p. 1, 30.iii.51, p. 1.

32. *CP,* 31.iii.51; *Ching-Chin jen-min,* pp. 83–91. See also *SCMP,* 90: 15–18.

33. On Shanghai, see Loh, pp. 65–70; and on Canton, see Vogel, *Canton,* pp. 63–64.

34. Loh, pp. 67–68.

35. Executions took place as follows (all 1951): 12 on March 2 (*TC,* 3.iii.51); 1 on March 13 (*TC,* 15.iii.51); 193 on March 31 (*CP,* 31.iii.51); 9 on April 29 (*TC,* 30.iv.51); and 277 on July 11 (*TC,* 13.vii.51).

36. This MPG meeting was also attended by the consultative com-

mittee of the ACPRC, 28 of the MPG's bureau and division heads, and the chairmen and vice-chairmen of the ward ACPRCs. *CP,* 7.iv.51, p. 1.

37. See, e.g., Belden, pp. 222–25.

38. *CP,* 15.xii.49, p. 2.

39. *TC,* 6.vii.51, p. 1.

40. Solomon, especially pp. 76–90.

41. *JM,* 12.xii.50.

42. *CP,* 17.i.50, p. 2.

43. *CP,* 17.i.50.

44. *CP,* 1.ii.51, pp. 4–6, contains a review of the Communists' campaign against the IKT during 1950. An attach on the IKT in the rural areas of North China was launched during 1950. See, e.g., the report on this effort in Shansi. *TKP,* 8.xii.50.

45. Mao anticipated this attack on the IKT and other quasi-religious societies in Tientsin and elsewhere as early as Jan. 24, 1951. *Mao Tse-tung ssu-hsiang,* p. 7.

46. *TC,* 6.vii.51, p. 1.

47. The latter two responses were analogous to the "speak bitterness" meetings and the struggle and settlement meetings previously used with startling effectiveness for mobilizing the peasantry to participate in land reform. See Belden, pp. 163–64, 174–89; and Hinton, *Fanshen,* Parts 2, 3, and 4.

48. *TC,* 8.iv.51, p. 3.

49. *TC,* 6.vii.51, p. 1.

50. *Ibid.*

51. There are marked parallels between this scenario and that of similar meetings conducted during the land reform of 1946–48, as described by Hinton, *Fanshen,* pp. 134–36 and *passim;* and Belden, pp. 164–203.

52. *TC,* 17.iv.51, p. 1. See *TC,* 13.v.51, p. 2, for several good examples of this process.

53. This was 1.5% of the more than 112,600 people who had withdrawn from the IKT by that date. *TC,* 8.vi.51, p. 1. A later report on the "recover-cheated-property meetings" is carried in *TC,* 19.v.51, p. 1.

54. *TC,* 10.v.51, p. 2. Not all, but certainly most of these 270 workers were members of the IKT. This factory was a relatively ideal case because of its very large size, well-developed trade union organization, and history of having been singled out repeatedly as a model factory. For instance, the denunciation mentioned here is one of only 2,269 received by the government during the entire suppression of counter-revolutionaries campaign, only a fraction of which were relevant to the *t'ui-tao* campaign. *CP,* 28.xii.51, p. 4. Articles on other aspects of the Hengyuan Cotton Mill can be found in *CP,* 25.vii.50, p. 1, 18.x.50, p. 1, 1.xii.51, p. 1; *TC,* 19.i.51, p. 1, 11.iii.51, p. 3, 12.iii.51, p. 2; and Feng Ch'üan, pp. 23–25.

55. *TC,* 6.vii.51.

56. *TC,* 17.iv.51. This figure includes some people who did not belong to the IKT.

57. *TC,* 18.iv.51.

58. *TC,* 8.v.51.

59. *TC,* 6.vii.51.

60. The authorities stated that the *t'ui-tao* campaign had been "basically" concluded on June 10, and they issued a summary report on the campaign on July 6. This analysis, therefore, takes July 6 as the date of the actual conclusion of the *t'ui-tao* campaign in Tientsin. *TC,* 6.vii.51, p. 1.

61. *CP,* 28.xii.51, p. 4.

62. *TC,* 6.vii.51, p. 1.

63. *TC,* 7.iv.51, p. 1.

64. *CP,* 31.iii.51, p. 1. These and later public executions were definitely meant to have a demonstration effect. For example, *TC,* 19.iv.51, p. 1, clamied that 1,700 counterrevolutionaries had turned themselves in "since the most recent execution."

65. *TC,* 17.iv.51, p. 1.

66. By May 4, a total of 1,835 IKT clergy had registered with the police. *TC,* 8.v.51, p. 1.

67. In addition, the execution of a group (number not specified) of counterrevolutionaries was announced in *TC,* 14.v.51, p. 2. The authorities released a substantial number of IKT leaders during May 10–20. *TC,* 6.vii.51, p. 1.

68. The May 8th decree spelled out all of these. *TC,* 8.v.51, p. 1.

69. *TC,* 19.v.51, p. 1. This high rate probably continued through May 20; all together, 4,211 middle- and low-ranking quasi-religious society leaders had registered by May 16.

70. *TC,* 6.vii.51, p. 1.   71. *TC,* editorial, 7.vii.51.

72. *TC,* 13.vii.51, p. 1.   73. Solomon, pp. 96–98.

74. *CP,* 28.xii.51, p. 4.

75. *CP,* 1.ii.51, p. 5, 30.xii.51, p. 4.

76. By December 1951, the ratio of propagandists in all private industries and residential areas to the overall population was 1 : 1000. This ratio would undoubtedly be a more unfavorable one if the residential areas were considered alone. *CP,* 7.i.52, p. 2.

77. *TC,* 23.iv.51, p. 2.   78. *Ibid.*

79. *Ibid.*   80. *TC,* 22.iv.51, p. 2.

81. Barnett, *Communist China,* p. 137, gives some information about this campaign in Manchuria.

82. *CP,* 30.xii.51, p. 4.

Chapter Seven

1. This was evidently a widespread feeling during the Five Anti. See, e.g., *TC,* 20.ii.52.

2. *TC,* 24.vii.51, p. 1.   3. *TC,* 1.x.51, p. 6.

4. *CP,* 2.vi.51, p. 2.   5. *TC,* editorial, 24.vii.51, p. 1.

6. *TC,* 24.iii.52, p. 2; Chesneaux, pp. 57–62, 80–81.

7. Chesneaux, pp. 57–62, 80–81.

8. *TC,* 24.vii.51, p. 1, 2.viii.51, p. 2, 1.x.51, p. 6; *CP,* 2.vi.51, p. 2.

9. *TC*, 2.viii.51, p. 2.   10. *TC*, 24,vii.51, p. 2.
11. *TC*, 1.x.51, p. 6.   12. *TC*, 24.vii.51, p. 2.
13. *CP*, 2.vi.51, p. 2.   14. *CP*, 18.iv.52, p. 2.
15. *TC*, 24.vii.51, p. 2, 1.x.51, p. 6.
16. *Chung-kuo kung-jen*, 12: 38 (i.51).
17. *TC*, 26.iii.52, p. 1.
18. *TC*, 24.iii.52, p. 2.
19. *TC*, 4.i.52, p. 2.
20. This campaign was kicked off in the construction industry by a large mobilization meeting on Jan. 10. *TC*, 11.i.52, p. 1.
21. For a review of the first month of the Tientsin construction workers' participation in the Five Anti struggle, see *JM*, 11.ii.52.
22. *TC*, 24.iii.52, p. 2.
23. The full text of these regulations, along with an explanatory article and short editorial, is in *TC*, 26.iii.52, p. 1.
24. *CP*, 18.iv.52, p. 2.   25. *Ibid.*
26. *Ibid.*   27. *Ibid.*

Chapter Eight

1. On liberalism among Chinese intellectuals, see Pepper, pp. 161–218.
2. With respect to the rural areas, see Bernstein.
3. Mao's analysis is contained in his report to the second session of the Seventh Central Committee in March 1949. *SW*, 4: 361–75.
4. *SCMP*, 230: 4–5.
5. Barnett, *Communist China*, p. 131.
6. *SCMP*, 214: 25–26.
7. The institutions that set up branch committees in Tientsin were the universities of Nankai, Tientsin, and Tsin Ku; Chung-yang Music Institute; China Mining Institute; Hopei Normal School; Hopei Medical Institute; and Hopei Aquatic Products School. *CP*, 1.xi.51, pp. 1–2.
8. *SCMP*, 225: 5.   9. *Ibid.*
10. *Ibid.*, 230: 4–5.   11. *CP*, 17.iii.52, p. 1.
12. *CP*, 26.viii.52, p. 2. For a general review of the Thought Reform campaign in Peking and Tientsin, see Barnett, *Communist China*, pp. 125–34.
13. *CP*, 19.v.52, p. 1.
14. For the general development of the Three Anti and Five Anti campaigns, see Barnett, *Communist China*, pp. 135–71; and Montell, pp. 136–96.
15. On capitalists, see the article on Tientsin in *JM*, 2.x.51; and the case of Jen Hai-ch'i in *TC*, 15.xi.51, p. 1. On cadres, see *TC*, 21.xi.51.
16. *TC*, 16.xi.51, p. 1. There are no available figures on the number of capitalists who actually participated in these classes.
17. *CP*, 15.xii.51.
18. *CP*, 16.xii.51, p. 1, published an extensive story on this meeting, and *CP*, 26.xii.51, p. 1, carried the full text of Huang's address to the

meeting. This meeting was attended by over 10,000 cadres. A Dec. 15 report made it clear that in some selected areas, including at least the Railroad Bureau and the No. 9 ward, the Three Anti had been under way at least since November. Although this report did not speak of these as experiments to gain experience, there seems little question that this was in fact their function. See *TC*, 15.xii.51.

19. *CP*, 19.xii.51, p. 1. The subordinate organs were established within the next few days. See e.g., the announcement of the establishment of the AIC branch committees in the Nos. 2, 3, 4, 6, 7, and 9 wards. *CP*, 23.xii.51.

20. Comprised of high-level staff, activists, and trade union cadres who were organized by trade to carry out very extensive attacks on key firms within each trade. Formally under both the relevant secondary trade union and the appropriate ward AIC branch committee. An elite attack and investigation unit. *TC*, 10.ii.52.

21. Set up by a decision of the third session of the Third Municipal ACPRC on 19.xii.51, to promote closer coordination between the municipal and various ward ACPRCs during the following months. *CP*, 20.xii.51, p. 1. The ward subsequently proved to be the key level for implementing the Five Anti campaign in Tientsin.

22. The investigatory unit organized by the ward AIC branch committee to carry out necessary intensive investigations of individual firms within the ward. *TC*, 10.ii.52.

23. Established on Jan. 25, 1952, beneath the municipal AIC to evaluate the seriousness of specific crimes and determine how to dispose of the cases. *CP*, 26.i.52, p. 1.

24. A hierarchy of organs established under the AICs on March 26, 1952, to supply technical information to the People's Tribunals and to resolve disputes over the proper "summary" of a case—i.e., over the proper level of fines, etc. *JM*, 31.iii.52.

25. Set up in late Dec. 1951 in every ward, usually in the ward Party committee or ward office (*kung-so*), to receive oral and written denunciations. *CP*, 29.xii.51, p. 2.

26. Organized groups to tour the city and collect denunciations. The "mayor's" visiting group toured the city for the week of Feb. 21–28 and collected 40,706 denunciations. *TC*, 1.iii.52.

27. Established on March 26, 1952, to handle serious cases of Five Anti offenders. *JM*, 3.iv.52.

28. *CP*, 29.xii.51, p. 2.

29. *SCMP*, 250: 6–8.

30. Po's attack came in his report on Jan. 9, 1952, to a conference of Central, North China, Peking, and Tientsin cadres. *JM*, 10.i.52.

31. *CP*, 29.xii.51, p. 2, recounts these mobilization efforts.

32. *TC*, 12.i.52.

33. *JM*, 13.i.52.

34. *TC*, 10.i.52.

35. For information on the Three and Five Anti in other areas, see

Teiwes, chap. 5; Barnett, *Communist China,* pp. 135–72 (includes a case study of Shanghai); Montell, pp. 136–96; Hua Ming; Gardner, pp. 477–540; and Loh, pp. 82–103.

36. *CP,* 15.i.52, p. 1.

37. *JM,* 18.i.52.

38. *CP,* 15.i.52, p. 1, contains the full text of these principles.

39. *TC,* 10.ii.52.

40. *CP,* 26.i.52, p. 1.

41. *CP,* 29.iii.52, p. 1.

42. See, e.g., the announcement of the dissolution of the Building Trade Association for obstructing the Five Anti campaign, in *TC,* 2.ii.52.

43. The order to reorganize trade associations was issued on March 27, 1952. *CP,* 29.iii.52, p. 1. For the announcements of actual reorganizations, see, e.g., *CP,* 10.iv.52, p. 1. (which also features an article on why the trade associations had to be reorganized), 23.iv.52, p. 3, and 25.iv.52, p. 2. These three articles cover a total of 14 trade associations.

44. For a review of the history of the trade associations in 1949–52, see *CP,* 17.xii.52, p. 3. Barnett implies that the trade associations in Shanghai were able to play the role assigned to them during the Five Anti. *Communist China,* p. 167.

45. The CCP used the same symbolism in the Party rectification campaign in 1948. Hinton, *Fanshen,* pp. 319–66.

46. *CP,* 29.iii.52, p. 1; *TC,* 1.iii.52. The latter is an excellent review of this process in the metal-working industry in the No. 11 ward. The actual implementation of this procedure varied somewhat among different trades and wards.

47. See, e.g., *CP,* 20.ii.52.

48. *Chieh-fang jih-pao,* 1.iii.52.

49. The Chinese text of the Three Anti regulations is in *Chung-yang jen-min cheng-fu,* pp. 10–14. An explanatory editorial appears in *JM,* 12.iii.52. These and the Five Anti regulations are translated in *CB,* no. 168.

50. The text for this order is in *Chung-yang jen-min cheng-fu,* pp. 18–19.

51. *Ibid.,* pp. 20–21.

52. On the March 26, 1952 meeting, see *CP,* 29.iii.52, p. 1. The establishment of the municipal and ward People's Tribunals was announced on April 4, 1952. The occupations of those appointed to serve on these bodies indicate their political rather than judicial character; most of the "judges" were trade union cadres, Party members, and other non-judicial personnel. *CP,* 4.iv.52, p. 1, announces the establishment of these tribunals and names the people serving on them. On the Three Anti People's Tribunals, see *TC,* 29.iii.52, p. 1. On the Arbitration Committees in Tientsin, see *JM,* 31.iii.52.

53. See, e.g., the review of this procedure in the No. 7 ward in *TC,* 29.iii.52, p. 2.

54. *CP,* 29.iii.52, p. 1.
55. *TC,* 29.iii.52, p. 1. While the basic "unit" for the Five Anti was the firm, that for the Three Anti could be a factory, second-level trade union, government bureau, etc. Consequently, the statistics on the number of Three Anti "units" that reached a given stage are of uncertain significance.
56. *TC,* 29.iii.52, p. 1.
57. *JM,* 31.iii.52.
58. *CP,* 30.ix.52, p. 2.
59. *CP,* 7.iv.52, p. 1. For similar announcements of other wards, see *CP,* 6.iv.52, p. 1. (No. 11 ward), and 2.iv.52, p. 3.(No. 2 ward). The lopsided distribution of firms in favor of the "law-abiding" category in the No. 10 ward is probably because this was primarily a residential area, where most of the firms were either small-scale industries or handicrafts. Consequently, very few of these firms would have been wealthy enough to have committed serious Five Anti crimes.
60. *TC,* 9.vi.52, p. 1.
61. The Tientsin government claimed that "according to as yet incomplete statistics," private firms in the city had stolen over two trillion *yuan* worth of state wealth. *CP.,* 29.iii.52, p. 1. Because firms did not necessarily have to pay back all they had "stolen," however, it is impossible to estimate how much the state netted from the private sector as a result of this campaign. For estimates on the national level, see Barnett, *Communist China,* p. 159.
62. *TC,* 29.iii.52, p. 1; *CP,* 1.x.52, p. 6.
63. *TC,* 9.vi.52, p. 1.
64. *CP,* 1.x.52, p. 6.
65. *People's China,* 23: 38 (1.xii.53).
66. See the articles regarding the new processing contract standards for the dyeing, weaving, and cotton manufacturing industries in *CP,* 16.vi.52, p. 1.
67. *CP,* 30.ix.52, p. 2.   68. *CP,* 29.xii.51, p. 4.
69. *TC,* 9.vi.52, p. 1.   70. *JM,* 31.iii.52.
71. In the construction industry, the average amount cheated was 50 percent . *CP,* 29.iii.52, p. 1.
72. *TC,* 9.vi.52, p. 1.
73. For a review of these meetings during January, see *JM,* 25.i.52.
74. For a review of the establishment of these teams in the Nos. 7 and 11 wards, see *Chieh-fang jih-pao,* 12.i.52. The summary figures in this paragraph are from *CP,* 28.iv.52, p. 2.
75. See, e.g., *JM,* 25.i.52, on a Jan. 6 meeting of over 300 shop personnel, which produced 460 denunciations.
76. This occurred after Jan. 20.
77. *TC.,* 18.ii.52, 24.ii.52.
78. *Ch'ang-chiang jih-pao,* 1.iii.52.
79. *CP,* 29.iii.52, p. 1.   80. *CP,* 28.iv.52, p. 2.
81. *CP,* 6.iv.52, p. 1.   82. *Ibid.*

83. *CP,* 28.iv.52, p. 2.   84. *TC,* 20.xii.52, p. 2.

85. See, e.g., *TC,* 30.iii.52, p. 1.   86. *TC,* 9.vi.52, p. 1.

87. *Kung-jen jih-pao,* 10.iii.52, trans. in *SCMP,* 309: 31–33; *TC,* 9,vi.52, p. 1.

88. The roots of such behavior go far back in China. See, e.g., Morse's description of the system of "squeeze," *Trade,* pp. 50–118. See also the assumptions concerning the propriety of bribing government officials in the classical novel *The Dream of the Red Chamber.* In both instances, payment of bribes was viewed as the normal type of relationship between people within the government bureaucracy and those outside of it.

89. The charge of "wild attacks" is in *JM,* 19.i.52.

90. Chamberlain, "Transition," dissertation, pp. 299, 314.

91. A March 11, 1952, CPG GAC announcement emphasized this business–social reform aspect of the Three Anti Five Anti campaign, stating that the campaign should "lead to the establishment of a new moral code of integrity and thrift." *SCMP,* no. 168.

92. The Thought Reform campaign that had meshed with the Three Anti accomplished the same objective among the intellectuals of Tientsin.

93. *TC,* 7.i.52, p. 2.

94. *TC,* 7.i.53, p. 1.

95. *TC,* 16.vi.52, p. 1. These figures exclude T'angku.

96. See the record of the July 26, 1952, Tientsin ACPRC Consultative Committee meeting convened to discuss this program in *CP,* 28.vii.52, p. 2.

97. For the text of this document, see *Hsin-Hua yüeh-pao,* 8–10 (xi.49).

Chapter Nine

1. Arthur Smith noted the same phenomenon in late 19th century rural China.

2. Bodde, pp. 33–34.

3. For contemporary confirmation of this rule in China, see Falkenheim, p. 23.

4. Vogel, "Friendship," pp. 46–60.

5. Lieberthal interview protocols.

6. Lieberthal, "Tientsin." Traditional ties in China's military also became more important as the Cultural Revolution ravaged the PLA, as demonstrated by Parish.

7. This theme was prevalent in the Chinese media from late 1977 to early 1978. The key points of these articles are summarized by Fox Butterfield in *NYT,* 11.xii.77.

8. Bennett; Lifton; Pfeffer.

9. Hinton, *Hundred Day War,* pp. 161–84; Milton and Milton.

10. Aird; Hua Kuo-feng's report to the Second Session of the Fifth National People's Congress in NCNA, 25.vi.79, trans. in *FBIS/PRC* (Supplement 015), 2.vii.79, p. 18.

11. Mao Tse-tung himself argued that this had to be the case. Bennett, pp. 82–83. A different basis for reaching the same conclusion is provided in Skinner and Winckler.

12. See Hinton, *Hundred Day War*, pp. 275–88; and Agence France Presse (Hong Kong), 1.v.78, trans. in *FBIS/PRC*, 5.v.78, p. E-24.

13. Oksenberg. 14. See, e.g., Moore.

15. Pye. 16. *TC*, 5.i.53, p. 2.

17. Lieberthal, "Tientsin."

18. On this question in relation to Soviet politics, see Cocks, "Rationalization," pp. 153–90.

19. Cocks, "Policy Process," pp. 156–78.

20. See, e.g., Yeh Chien-ying's report to the Fifth National People's Congress in March 1978 in New China News Agency, 7.iii.78, trans. in *FBIS/PRC* (Supplement), 16.iii.78, pp. 40–53.

Bibliography

Bibliography

Aird, John. "Recent Provincial Population Figures," *China Quarterly,* 73: 1–44 (March 1978).

An Li-fu. *T'ien-chin pan-yun kung-jen kung-tso pao-kao* (Work report on Tientsin transport workers). March 1950.

Avineri, Shlomo. *The Social and Political Thought of Karl Marx.* London, 1968.

Barnett, A. Doak. *Cadres, Bureaucracy, and Political Power in Communist China.* New York, 1967.

———. *China on the Eve of the Communist Takeover.* New York, 1966.

———. *Communist China: The Early Years, 1949–1955.* New York, 1966.

———, ed. *Chinese Communist Politics in Action.* Seattle, 1969.

Belden, Jack. *China Shakes the World.* New York, 1970.

Bennett, Gordon. *Yundong.* Berkeley, Calif., 1976.

Bernstein, Thomas. "Problems of Village Leadership After Land Reform," *China Quarterly* 36: 1–22 (Oct.–Dec. 1968).

Bodde, Derk. *Peking Diary.* New York, 1967.

British Chamber of Commerce, Tientsin. Minutes of meetings for 1946–52.

Burgess, John Stewart. *The Guilds of Peking.* New York, 1928.

Campbell, Colin D., and Gordon C. Tullock. "Hyperinflation in China," *The Journal of Political Economy,* 62 (3): 236–45 (June 1954).

Chamberlain, Heath B. "Transition and Consolidation in Urban China: A Study of Leaders and Organization in Three Cities, 1949–53," Ph. D. dissertation, Stanford University, 1971.

———. "Transition and Consolidation in Urban China: A Study of Leaders and Organization in Three Cities, 1949–53," in Scalapino, ed., listed below.

Chang, Betty. "We Had Red Soldiers in Our House," *China Digest,* 6(9): 8–9, 17 (Aug. 10, 1949).

Chang Kia-ngau. *The Inflationary Spiral: The Experience in China: 1939–50.* Cambridge, Mass., 1958.

Ch'ang-chiang jih-pao (Yangtze daily). Hankow.

Chao Kuo-chün. *Economic Planning and Organization in Mainland China.* 2 vols. Cambridge, Mass., 1963.

Chassin, Lionel Max. *The Communist Conquest of China: A History of the Civil War, 1945–1949,* tr. Timothy Osato and Louis Gelas. Cambridge, Mass., 1965.

Ch'en I. "Shang-hai shih chün-kuan hui ho jen-min cheng-fu ti kung-tso pao-kao" (Work report of the Shanghai Military Affairs Control Commission and People's Government), in Lai Chih-yen, ed., listed below.

Ch'en Pao-yü. "Chien-t'ao chih-kung yun-tung chung ti tso-ch'ing mao-hsien-chu-i" (Critically review the Left adventurism of the staff and workers movement), in Ch'en Po-ta et al., listed below.

Ch'en Po-ta. "Fa-chan kung-shang-yeh ti lao-tung cheng-ts'e yü shui-shou cheng-ts'e" (The labor policy and tax policy for the developmetn of industry), in Ch'en Po-ta et al., listed below.

Ch'en Po-ta et al. *Kuan-yü kung-shang-yeh ti cheng-ts'e* (On industrial and commercial policy). Hong Kong, Oct. 1949.

Cheng-ts'e fa-ling hui-pien (Collection of policies, laws, and decrees [in Tientsin]). Tientsin Military Affairs Control Commission Secretarial Office, Tientsin.

Chesneaux, Jean. *The Chinese Labor Movement, 1919–1927,* tr. H. M. Wright. Stanford, Calif., 1968.

Chesneaux, Jean, Feiling Davis, and Nguyen Nguyet Ho, eds. *Mouvements populaires et sociétés secrétes en Chine aux XIXe et XXe siècles.* Paris, 1970.

Chieh-fang hou ti T'ien-chin kung-yeh (Post-liberation Tientsin industry). Nov. 1949.

Chieh-fang jih-pao (Liberation daily). Shanghai.

"Chih-hsing ch'eng-shih cheng-ts'e chi-lu ching-yen" (Experience in implementing urban policy and discipline), in Mao Tse-tung et al., listed below.

"Chin-Ch'a-Chi pien-fu pao-hu kung-shang-yeh chih-shih" (Directive from the Shansi-Chahar-Hopei border region government on safeguarding industry and commerce), in Ch'en Po-ta et al., listed above.

Chin-pu jih-pao (Progressive daily). Tientsin.

China Association Archives. London.

China Digest.

China Weekly Review. Shanghai.

Ching-Chin jen-min ta-chang-ch'i-ku chen-ya fan-ko-ming (Peking and Tientsin people suppress counterrevolution with fanfare). N.p., n.d.

Ch'ing-tao jih-pao (Tsingtao daily). Hong Kong.

Chung-hua jen-min kung-ho kuo k'ai-kuo wen-hsien (Documents on the founding of the Chinese People's Republic). Hong Kong, 1949.

Chung-hua nien-chien (China yearbook). 2 vols. Nanking, 1948.

Chung-kuo jen-min chieh-fang chün ju ch'eng cheng-ts'e (The policy of the People's Liberation Army for entering the cities). N.p., Aug. 1949.

Chung-kuo kung-ch'an-tang tang-chang (Party rules of the Chinese Communist Party). Oct. 1949.

Chung-kuo kung-jen (China's workers). Peking.

Chung-kuo lao-tung nien-chien (China labor yearbook). Peking, 1932.

Chung-kuo pang-hui shih (History of Chinese secret societies). Hong Kong, 1970.

Chung-yang jen-min cheng-fu fa-ling hui-pien (Collection of laws and decrees of the Central People's Government). Peking, 1952.

Cocks, Paul. "Policy Process and Bureaucratic Politics," in Cocks et al., eds., *The Dynamics of Soviet Politics*. Cambridge, Mass., 1976.

———. "The Rationalization of Party Control," in Chalmers Johnson, ed., *Change in Communist Systems*. Stanford, Calif., 1970.

Current Background. U.S. Consulate General, Hong Kong.

Davis, Feiling. "Le Rôle économique et social des sociétés secrètes," in Chesneaux et al., listed above.

Delioussine, Lev. "La Société Yiguandao et sa suppression par les autorités de Chine Populaire," in Chesneaux et al., eds., listed above.

Eastman, Lloyd E. "Fascism in Kuomintang China: The Blue Shirts," *China Quarterly* 49: 1-31 (Jan.–March 1972).

Falkenheim, Victor. "Political Participation in China," *Problems of Communism*, May–June 1978.

Fang Fu-an. *Chinese Labour: An Economic and Statistical Survey of the Labour Conditions and Labour Movements in China*. Shanghai, 1931.

Far Eastern Economic Review.

Fei T'ung (pseud. Fei Hsiao-t'ung). *Hsiang-t'u Chung-kuo* (Rural China). Taipei, 1967.

Feng Chüan. "I-ko shih-li ti ch'i-shih" (An actual experience), *T'ien-chin kung-shang* 1(12): 23–25 (June 15, 1951).

———. "Tsai lun ssu-ying ch'i-yeh kai-chin ching-ying kuan-li wen-t'i" (Another discussion of the problems of improving management in the privately run enterprises), *T'ien-chin kung-shang* 1(10): 6–7 (May 15, 1951).

Fong, H. D. *Cotton Industry and Trade in China*. Nankai Institute of Economics Industry Series, 4. 2 vols. Tientsin, 1932.

———. *Grain Trade and Milling in Tientsin*. Nankai Institute of Economics, Industry Series, 6. Peiping, 1934.

———. *Hosiery Knitting in Tientsin*. Nankai University, Committee on Social and Economic Research, Industry Series, 3. Tientsin, 1930.

———. *Industrial Organization in China*. Nankai Institute of Economics, Industry Series, 10. Tientsin, 1937.

————. *Tientsin Carpet Industry.* Nankai University, Committee on Social and Economic Research, Industry Series, 1. Tientsin, 1929.

Fong, H. D., and Y. T. Ku. "Shoemaking in North China Port," *Chinese Social and Political Science Review,* 18(4): 505–38 (1934).

Foreign Broadcast Information Service/People's Republic of China Daily Report. Springfield, Va.

Fried, Morton. *Fabric of Chinese Society: A Study of the Social Life of a Chinese County Seat.* New York, 1969.

Gardner, John. "The Wu-fan Campaign in Shanghai," in Barnett, ed., *Chinese Communist Politics,* listed above.

Gerstenzang, Leon. "Liberated Tientsin," *China Digest,* 5(8): 15 (Feb. 8, 1949).

Grootaers, William A. "Une Société secrète moderne: I Kuan Tao," *Folklore Studies, 5: 324–43 (1946).*

Groth, Alexander. "The Soviet Union: The Elite-Isolated Revolution of the Left," in Welch and Taintor, eds., listed below.

Harper, Paul. "Trade Union Cultivation of Workers for Leadership," in Lewis, ed., listed below.

Harrison, James. *The Long March to Power.* New York, 1972.

Hinton, William. *Fanshen.* New York, 1968.

————. *Hundred Day War.* New York, 1972.

Ho, Franklin, and H. D. Fong. "Extent and Effects of Industrialization in China." Paper submitted to the biennial conference of the Institute of Pacific Relations. Oct. 1929.

Hsin Hua yüeh-pao (New China monthly).

Hsin wan jih-pao (New evening daily). Shanghai.

Hsu Ti-hsin. *Kung-shang-yeh-chia ti ch'u-lu* (The way out for industrialists and merchants). Hong Kong, March 1949.

Hua Ming. *San-fan wu-fan ti p'ou-shih* (Analysis of the Three-Anti Five-Anti). Kowloon, 1952.

Hung-ch'i ch'a-shang T'ien-chin ch'eng-yuan (The red flag is placed on the Tientsin city wall). Tientsin, March 1949.

Huntington, Samuel. "Political Development and Political Decay," *World Politics,* 15: 386–430 (April 1965).

————. *Political Order in Changing Societies.* New Haven, Conn., 1968.

I-chiu-ssu-ch'i nien i-lai Chung-kuo kung-ch'an-tang chung-yao wen chien-chi (Collection of important documents of the Chinese Communist Party since 1947). Hong Kong, June 1949.

Isaacs, Harold. *Tragedy of the Chinese Revolution.* 2d rev. ed. New York, 1966.

————, ed. *Five Years of Kuomintang Reaction.* Reprint from the special May edition of the *China Forum.* Shanghai, 1932.

"Jen-min chieh-fang chan-cheng liang-chou-nien ti tsung-chieh ho ti-san-nien ti jen-wu" (Summary of two years of the people's war of liberation and the tasks of the third year), in *I-chiu-ssu-ch'i nien i-lai Chung-kuo kung-ch'an-tang chung-yao wen chien-chi,* listed above.

Jen-min chou-pao (People's weekly).

Jen-min jih-pao (People's daily).

Jen Pi-shih. "Kung-shang-yeh cheng-ts'e" (Industrial and commercial policy), in *Chung-kuo jen-min,* listed above.

Johnson, Chalmers. *Peasant Nationalism and Communist Power.* Stanford, Calif., 1962.

———. *Revolutionary Change.* Boston, 1966.

Jones, F. C. *Shanghai and Tientsin, with Special Reference to Foreign Interests.* London, 1940.

Kau Ying-mao. "The Urban Bureaucratic Elite in Communist China: A Case Study of Wuhan, 1949–65," in Barnett, ed., *Chinese Communist Politics,* listed above.

Keng Yun, ed. *Hsin min-chu shou-ts'e* (New democratic handbook). Shanghai, 1947.

Kim, Ilpyong. "Mass Mobilization Policies and Techniques Developed in the Period of the Chinese Soviet Republic," in Barnett, ed., *Chinese Communist Politics,* listed above.

Klein, Donald, and Anne B. Clark. *Biographic Dictionary of Chinese Communism.* 2 vols. Cambridge, Mass., 1971.

Kung-jen jih-pao (Workers' daily). Peking.

Kung-yun hui-chi (Collection on the workers' movement). Preparatory Committee of the Tientsin Municipal Staff and Workers' Trade Union, Tientsin, June 1949.

Lai Chih-yen, ed. *Chieh-kuan ch'eng-shih ti kung-tso ching-yen* (Work experiences in taking over the cities). N.p., n.d.

Lang, Olga. *Chinese Family and Society.* New Haven, Conn., 1946.

Lewis, John, ed. *The City in Communist China.* Stanford, Calif., 1971.

Li Chu-ch'en. "Kung-shang-yeh che tui mu-ch'ien t'ung-yeh kung-hui kai-hsuan kung-tso ying-yu ti jen-shih" (The awareness that the industrialists and merchants should have concerning the current trade association reelection work), *T'ien-chin kung-shang,* 1(6): 1–2 (March 15, 1951).

Li Pu-lung. *The Brick Industry in Tientsin and the Problems of Its Modernization.* Tientsin, 1940.

Lieberthal, Kenneth. "Mao Versus Liu? Policy Towards Industry and Commerce: 1946–1949," *China Quarterly,* 47: 494–520 (July–Sept. 1971).

———. "Reconstruction and Revolution in a Chinese City: The Case of Tientsin, 1949–1953," Ph.D. dissertation, Columbia University, 1972.

———. "Tientsin," in Edwin Winckler, ed., *Provincial Handbook for the People's Republic of China.* Stanford, Calif., forthcoming.

Lifton, Robert Jay. *Revolutionary Immortality.* New York, 1968.

Liu, F. F. *A Military History of Modern China.* Princeton, N.J., 1956.

Liu, Grace D. "Behind U.S.-Made 'Bamboo Curtain,' " *China Digest*, 6(5): 5–7, 19 (June 14, 1949).

Liu Lien-k'o. *Chung-kuo pang-hui san-pai-nien ko-ming shih* (The three-hundred year revolutionary history of the Chinese secret societies). Macao, Aug. 1941.

Liu Ning-i. "Chieh-fang-ch'ü ti kung-yeh cheng-ts'e" (Industrial policy of the liberated areas), in Ch'en Po-ta et al., listed above.

Liu Shao-ch'i. *Lun ch'un-chung lu-hsien* (On the mass line). Hong Kong, 1949.

Liu Shao-ch'i et al., *Hsin min-chu-chu-i ch'eng-shih cheng-ts'e* (New democratic city policy). Hong Kong, Aug. 1949.

Liu Shao-ch'i wen-t'i tzu-liao chuan-chi (A special collection of materials on Liu Shao-ch'i). Taipei, Dec. 1970.

Loh, Robert. *Escape from Red China.* New York, 1962.

Lowe, Chuan-hua. *Facing Labor Issues in China.* Shanghai, 1934.

Mao Tse-tung et al. *Hsin min-chu-chu-i kung-shang cheng-ts'e* (New democratic industrial and commercial policy). Hong Kong, Jan. 1949.

Mao Tse-tung ssu-hsiang wan-sui (Long live the thought of Mao Tse-tung). Aug. 1969.

Meyer, Alfred G. *Leninism.* New York, 1963.

Milton, David, and Nancy Milton. *The Wind Will Not Subside.* New York, 1976.

Min-kuo jih-pao (Republican daily). Tientsin.

Montell, Sherwin. "The San-fan Wu-fan Movement in China," in *Papers on China*, VIII. Cambridge, Mass., Feb. 1954.

Moore, Barrington. *The Social Origins of Dictatorship and Democracy.* Boston, 1967.

Morse, H. B. *The Trade and Administration of the Chinese Empire.* Taipei, 1966.

Murphey, Rhoads. *The Treaty Ports and China's Modernization: What Went Wrong?* Michigan Papers in Chinese Studies 7. Ann Arbor, Mich., 1970.

"Nan-ching chieh-kuan kung-tso ching-yen" (Work experiences in taking over Nanking), in Lai Chih-yen, ed., listed above.

Nathan, Andrew. *Peking Politics, 1918–23.* Berkeley, Calif., 1976.

Nei-cheng nien-chien (Internal administration yearbook). 4 vols. Shanghai, 1936.

Nikitin, N., and I. Feodorov. *Tyan'tzin.* Moscow, 1953.

Oksenberg, Michel. "The Institutionalization of the Chinese Communist Revolution," *China Quarterly*, 36: 61–92 (Oct.–Dec. 1968).

Pan-yun kung-jen kung-hui kung-tso ts'an-k'ao tzu-liao (Reference materials on the Transport Workers' Trade Union work). All China Federation of Trade Unions, Peking, Jan. 1950.

Pao Chiao-ming and Ho Tz'u-ch'iang. *Tientsin.* Moscow, 1960. Tr. Joint Publications Research Service, CSO: 7140-N, No. 14466.

Parish, William. "Factions in Chinese Military Politics," *China Quarterly,* 56: 66–99 (Oct.–Dec. 1973).

"Pen-hui chin-jung wei-yuan-hui kung-tso tsung-chieh" (Summary of the work of the Financial Committee of the [Federation of Industry and Commerce]), *T'ien-chin kung-shang,* 1(2): 14–16 (June 15, 1951).

People's China.

Pepper, Suzanne. "Socialism, Democracy, and Chinese Communism: A Problem of Choice for the Intelligentsia, 1945–1949." in Chalmers Johnson, ed., *Ideology and Politics in Contemporary China.* Seattle, 1973.

Pfeffer, Richard. "The Pursuit of Purity: Mao's Cultural Revolution," *Problems of Communism,* Nov.–Dec. 1969, pp. 12–25.

P'ing-chin chan-i hui-i lu (Record of reminiscences of the Peiping-Tientsin campaign). Peking, 1961.

Prentice, Margaret May. *Unwelcome at the Northeast Gate.* Intercollegiate Press (U.S.A.), 1966.

Pye, Lucian, *The Spirit of Chinese Politics.* Cambridge, Mass., 1968.

Rasmussen, O. D. *Tientsin: An Illustrated Outline History.* Tientsin, 1921.

Richman, Barry. *Industrial Society in Communist China.* New York, 1969.

Scalapino, Robert, ed. *Elites in the People's Republic of China.* Seattle, 1972.

Schiffrin, Harold Z. *Sun Yat-sen and the Origins of the Chinese Revolution.* Berkeley, Calif., 1968.

Schram, Stuart R. *Political Thought of Mao Tse-tung.* Rev. and enlarged ed. London, 1969.

Schurmann, H. Franz. *Ideology and Organization in Communist China.* Rev. and enlarged ed. Berkeley, Calif., 1971.

Schwartz, Benjamin. *Communism in China: Ideology in Flux.* Cambridge, Mass., 1968.

Selden, Mark. *The Yenan Way.* Cambridge, Mass., 1972.

Selected Works of Mao Tse-tung. 4 vols. Peking, 1961–65.

Sharmon, Lyon. *Sun Yat-sen: His Life and Its Meaning.* Stanford, Calif., 1968.

Skinner, G. W., and E. Winckler, "Compliance Succession in Rural Communist China: A Cyclical Theory," in Amitai Etzioni, ed., *A Sociological Reader on Complex Organizations.* 2d ed. New York, 1969.

Smedley, Agnes. *The Great Road: The Life and Times of Chu Teh.* New York, 1972.

Smith, Arthur. *Chinese Characteristics.* New York, 1894.

Snow, Edgar. *Red Star Over China.* New York, 1961.

Solomon, Richard. "On Activism and Activists: Maoist Conceptions of Motivation and Political Role Linking State to Society," *China Quarterly,* 39: 76–114 (July–Sept. 1969).

Survey of China Mainland Press. United States Consulate General, Hong Kong.

Ta-kung-pao (Impartial news). Tientsin and Hong Kong.

Tang-p'ai tiao-ch'a chou-pao (Weekly investigation reports on parties and cliques). Tientsin, 1946.

Teiwes, Frederick. "Recification Campaigns and Purges in Communist China, 1950–1961," Ph.D. dissertation, Columbia University, 1971.

T'ien-chin cheng-fu kung-pao (Tientsin government gazette). Tientsin, 1930–36.

T'ien-chin chih-lueh (Tientsin gazette). Tientsin, 1928.

T'ien-chin jih-pao (Tientsin daily).

T'ien-chin kung-jen sheng-huo fei chih-shu (Cost-of-living index of Tientsin workers). Nankai University Institute for Economic Research, *Nan-k'ai chih-shu chuan-k'an* (Nankai index periodical), 2 (Feb. 1950).

T'ien-chin kung-shang (Tientsin industry and commerce).

"T'ien-chin shih chi-ch'i kung-yeh ch'ing-k'uang" (Conditions in the Tientsin machine industry), *T'ien-chin kung-shang,* 1(3): 30–31 (Jan. 31, 1951).

T'ien-chin shih chou-k'an (Tientsin weekly).

T'ien-chin shih chu-yao t'ung-chi tzu-liao shou-ts'e (Handbook of major statistical materials on Tientsin). Tientsin, 1948.

T'ien-chin shih hsien-k'uang tiao-ch'a chi kuang-fu ch'ung-chien kang-ling (Investigation of the current situation in Tientsin and an outline of the glorious reconstruction). Taipei, 1961.

"T'ien-chin shih kung-shang-yeh lien-ho-hui i-nien lai kung-tso chi-yao" (Summary of the work of the Tientsin Municipal Federation of Industry and Commerce over the past year), *T'ien-chin kung-shang,* 1(12): 10–14 (June 15, 1951).

"T'ien-chin shih lao-tzu hsieh-shang hui-i ti ch'eng-chiu ho mu-ch'ien ts'un-tsai ti wen-t'i" (Accomplishments and current problems in Tientsin's labor-capital consultative conferences), *Chung-kuo kung-jen,* 6: 48–49 (July 15, 1950).

T'ien-chin t'e-pieh shih kung-shang lien-ho-hui hui-wu chi-yao (Summary of the affairs of the Tientsin Special Municipality Federation of Industry and Commerce). Tientsin, 1943.

T'ien-chin T'ien-chu chiao ko-hsin yun-tung ti ch'eng-chiu (Accomplishments of the Tientsin Catholic reform movement). Peking, 1951.

Tientsin, North China. Rotary Club, Tientsin, 1943.

Tucker, Robert. *The Marxian Revolutionary Idea.* New York, 1969.

Tung-pei jih-pao (Northeast daily).

Ueda Toshio. "Legal Status of the British Concession in Tientsin," *Contemporary Japan,* 9: 167–72 (Feb. 1940).

Van Slyke, Lyman. *Enemies and Friends: The United Front in Chinese Communist History.* Stanford, Calif., 1967.

Vogel, Ezra. *Canton Under Communism.* Cambridge, Mass., 1969.

———. "From Friendship to Comradeship," *China Quarterly,* 21: 46–60 (Jan.–March 1965).

———. "From Revolutionary to Semi-Bureaucrat: The 'Regularisation' of Cadres," *China Quarterly,* 29: 36–60 (Jan.–March 1967).

Wales, Nym. *The Chinese Labor Movement.* New York, 1945.

Wang, Y. C. "Tu Yueh-sheng (1888–1951): A Tentative Political Biography," *Journal of Asian Studies,* 26(3): 433–56 (May 1967).

Wei Chin. "I-chiu-ssu-chiu nien ti T'ien-chin kung-yeh" (Tientsin industry in 1949), *Hsin-Hua yueh-pao,* 907–908 (Feb. 7, 1950).

Welch, Claude E., Jr., and Mavis B. Taintor, eds. *Revolution and Political Change.* Belmont, Calif., 1972.

Wen-hui pao (Literary news). Shanghai.

Whiting, Allen. *China Crosses the Yalu.* New York, 1960.

Whitson, William. "The Field Army in Chinese Communist Military Politics," *China Quarterly* 37: 1–30 (Jan.–March 1969).

Wilson, Dick. *Anatomy of China: An Introduction to One-Quarter of Mankind.* New York, 1969.

Yang, C. K. *Chinese Communist Society: The Family and the Village.* Cambridge, Mass., 1965.

Yang Yen, "Jen-min cheng-fu tsen-yang chieh-kuan ch'eng-shih" (How the People's Government takes over cities), in Lai Chih-yen, ed., listed above.

Yeh Chien-ying, "Pei-p'ing shih pan-nien lai chieh-kuan yü shih-cheng kung-tso" (Takeover and administrative work in Peiping over the past half year), in Lai Chih-yen, ed., listed above.

Index